Rhetoric

Theory and History of Literature
Edited by Wlad Godzich and Jochen Schulte-Sasse

For other books in the series, see p. 165

Rhetoric

Renato Barilli

Translation by Giuliana Menozzi

Theory and History of Literature, Volume 63

University of Minnesota Press, Minneapolis

Originally published as *La retorica*,
copyright © 1983 by Arnoldo Mondadori
Editore, Milan.

Published by the University of Minnesota Press
2037 University Avenue Southeast, Minneapolis, MN 55414.

Printed in the United States of America.

Library of Congress Cataloging-in-Publication Data

Barilli, Renato.
    [Retorica. English]
    Rhetoric / Renata Barilli : translation by Giuliana Menozzi.
        p.   cm. — (Theory and history of literature ; v. 63)
    Translation of: La retorica.
    Bibliography: p.
    ISBN 0-8166-1728-7
    ISBN 0-8166-1729-5 (pbk.)
    1. Rhetoric—History. I. Title. II. Series.
PN183.B313 1989
808'.009—dc19   88-38516
                                                                  CIP

Contents

Introduction

From a linguistic analysis of the term "rhetoric" we can isolate some features or at least pinpoint issues that rhetoric raised and is still raising in its long existence of over two millennia. A lexical marker, the root *rhe*, can be identified, as well as some morphological markers contained in the group "toric." The Greek root *rhe* means "to say," to use discourse, *logos*. To this must immediately be added an intensive connotation, a connotation of fullness: rhetoric is a comprehensive, total way of using discourse. This means that the physical aspects of speech are not sacrificed to the intellectual dimension. The physical aspects include the sounds of a linguistic message, together with the modes of delivery, pronunciation, facial expressions, and gestures. Obviously all of these aspects intervene only in an oral situation, when rhetorical communication takes place in the presence and mutual involvement of a speaker and an audience, so that the latter can judge, appreciate, and enjoy the physicality of speech. Indeed, this is the hot issue that through the ages has fed the controversy between supporters and disparagers of rhetoric: is it fair to allure an audience with sounds and gestures, or should speech rely only on the noetic powers of communication? Some would say that our senses deceive us and corrupt the best part of human nature; for others human nature is a complex combination of senses and intellect, where the former cannot be given without the latter. The devaluation of the physical components of speech was not always, or not only, due to philosophical, ethical reasons. Very often it stemmed from the material impossibility of preserving the sounds and the presence that characterize an oral communication. Before the technological inventions introduced by electronics, which allow the transmission of acoustic and visual events (radio and television) in space, and their recording on tape, it was materially impossible to provide a thorough account of the components involved in speech.

Rhetoric reveals a vocation for fullness and totality also with regard to meaning. Etymologically, rhetoric means "the art of discourse." It claims to produce discourses on a wide range of matters, in essence, on all the areas that concern ordinary human beings and that no one can ever renounce, for example, state or government activity, the administration of justice, and the setting of ethical values to be followed in private and public life, thus also laying the foundation for standards of judgment: praising or stigmatizing others on the grounds of their behavior. These are some of the spheres that concern all the members of a community and that in most cases do not belong to specific disciplines. Of course politics, morality, the law, economics, social psychology, and sociology will deal with single issues falling under their respective competences: these are the once so-called moral sciences, which today we prefer to call the human sciences. But in all these areas there emerges a thrust crossways, so to speak, that leads each of them to raid domains whose boundaries are more clearly defined in order to borrow what is needed there and then, after which a broader perspective can be regained. For example, it is extremely hard to define what belongs and what does not belong to politics. Under different circumstances it may deal with medical, climatic, geographic, food-related problems, and so on, but it will always have a duty to interrelate and insert specific data in a broad perspective. In fact, herein lies the difference between the role of the politician and that of the expert, whose opinion has become so influential today. Indeed, over the course of time, one of the strongest objections raised against rhetoric has turned precisely on this point. It has been denied that there may be a political role distinct from the technical, or at least it is maintained that if such is the case then politics is only a confusing dilution of the precise data provided by science. According to this view, power should go to the experts, so as to avoid encouraging dilettantism and ignorance. In contrast, the supporters of the need for a unifying moment hold that technical data in and of themselves are too narrow, and must be seen in a larger, motivated perspective.

Rhetoric is concerned with ordinary matters, and ordinary also is the public it addresses, precisely because it deals with issues that interest all the members of a given community. Everybody has a right to take part in debates, discussions, and so on, to understand them, to master the terminology used, to enjoy them if possible, and finally to judge, to approve or disapprove of the speaker's words. This view is very democratic, even on epistemological grounds, since it suggests that the community, the *demos*, ultimately determines whether a rhetorical speech is credible, probable, and whether it can be accepted. In a rhetorical universe the notion of "truth" does not obtain, since it would imply external foundations, to be sought in the nature of things, or in discourses themselves, or in some transcendent entity. This does not mean that all issues will matter in the same way: on the contrary, some will be more important than others; but the final right to assess the degree of closeness to the true belongs to the *demos*, that is, the people, a community, an assembly of politicians, judges, the participants in a discussion, in a debate, and so on.

It is ordinary people, people "just like us," who take part in public and social life, endowed with intellectual faculties, feelings, drives; therefore it will be appropriate to intervene in this endowment with a global and comprehensive set of tools. This is why rhetorical discourse must simultaneously pursue and bring together three different goals: *docere*, teaching on an intellectual level; *movere*, touching the feelings, the emotional "experience" of the audience; finally, *delectare*, keeping their interest alive, soliciting their attention so that they will follow the threads of one's thoughts, without becoming bored, indifferent, distracted. Rhetorical communication does not address superior minds or pure spirits, but rather beings of flesh and blood subject to feeling tired, bored, or bewildered, if arguments are too hard to follow and "narrow." This happens whenever the imagination is left no space, whenever the pressure and the intellectual effort are so unrelenting that no outlet is given to release tension or to bring about its immediate effect: humor.

Against the comprehensive and totalizing features of this form of discourse stands an opposite model, born almost together with it: it is a dense and specialized discourse that privileges the intellectual moment of the signified over the sensual pleasure of the signifier. It tends to focus on well-defined areas, avoiding distracting "discursiveness." It makes the moral and epistemological claim of searching for the "truth" (it may be the truth of facts or a formal-linguistic type of truth or statistical probability). Therefore, it takes the right to judge from the hands of the *demos* and gives it over to the experts. It is a formal, specialized discourse, suitable for application to particular sectors or disciplines. The first historical consideration it received was from Aristotle, who labeled it analytic discourse. It sets itself up at the opposite pole of rhetoric. The vicissitudes of these two poles may be traced back to antiquity and continue, in a process of alternate phases that registers the prevalence of one or the other or their peaceful coexistence in a *modus vivendi*, or also the emergence of intermediate kinds of discourses (such as dialectics).

Retaining an intentionally naive attitude, a layperson's kind of approach, we may observe other interesting features in the term "rhetoric" by looking at the morphological markers, particularly those contained in the suffix "ic" or "ical": these forms may occur in nouns that represent a substantive use of adjectives. Generally, the noun that was implied is *techne*, art, as, for example, in analytics, dialectic, poetics, rhetoric, politics. This poses a series of questions that have long been debated in various moments of the history of rhetoric. We have just seen that rhetoric is a "technique": therefore, rhetoricians are also technicians notwithstanding the fact that, as we mentioned, their task is to intervene in "political" occasions, that is, situations of broad and multifaceted confrontations where one necessarily overcomes the particularity of sectorial data. However, precisely because rhetoric embraces all human concerns, it will never be as "technical" and specialized as analytics, its opposite mode. Thus the issue that has arisen over and over again: Can one become an orator by learning or is one so by nature? In other words, can rhetoric be taught, and to what extent? In fact, even the supporters of the technical view are ready to admit that it will be a fluid technique, "open," so to speak, and not formal the way analytics is. In the context of rhetoric, the technical will always be side by side with the nontechnical, the inside with the outside; and some natural quality, or *ingenium*, will be necessary, if for no other reason than for the physical aspects of a speech performance, such as pronunciation and delivery.

One more remark: the implied noun is *techne* and not *mathesis*. On this point a unity may be established between rhetorical, analytic, and dialectical discourses: their common characteristic is that they stress not content but rather form. They are general discursive modes, and as such they can be applied to the most different subjects. We find here a historical classification that lasted several centuries: the trivium consists of grammar, rhetoric, dialectic — the formal sciences; to the quadrivium belong arithmetic, geometry, astronomy, and music — the sciences of content. As a matter of fact, rhetoric escapes such a rigid classification, and we must recognize that once again it is consistent with the noun from which the adjective will be formed. The notion of *techne* does not at all legitimize the division between form and content, theory and practice, words and things. From this perspective rhetoric is *techne* in the fullest sense: the activity it performs is not only cognitive but transformative and practical as well. It does not limit itself to conveying neutral, sterilized facts (this would be *docere*), but its aim is to carry away the audience; to produce an effect on them; to mold them; to leave them different as a result of its impact. Actually, we have already observed that *docere*, which is a typical theoretic activity, is combined with *movere* and *delectare*, which belong to the sphere of the practical, since they reach our emotions and leave an effect on "experience." Thus, even following this direction, we have returned to that quality of full and total intervention already contained in the lexical marker of the term "rhetoric." Of course competing, rival arts, with analytics at the head, will aim their objections and reservations at this point, too. Can a technique move within such vast boundaries, or does this imply a demobilization and the final recognition that rhetoric is "without art nor part," that is, *atechnon?* At best it would be a pseudo- or impure art, which in practice could not be taught because of its complexity, the lack of a clear definition, and the tendency to expand in too many directions.

After all, these charges end up by converging with the views of a group of supporters of rhetoric, who, to safeguard its full organic character, see it as the child of nature and not of art, and thus irreducible to narrow or rigid rules.

These are some of the issues rhetoric has raised in its long history. We will examine them in detail, following the chronological thread of history and the major cultural periods.

Rhetoric

Chapter 1
The Greeks

Beginnings: The Sophists

Rhetoric is usually seen as originating in Greek culture at the beginning of the fifth century B.C. It first developed in Syracuse, in Magna Graecia, after the fall of the tyrant Trasibulus. This event was followed by many legal suits to return to their rightful owners the lands confiscated during the tyranny. Thus from the very beginning forensic is in the forefront as one of the typical domains of rhetoric. It would be difficult, though, to push this chronological precedence too far, let alone draw from it ideological consequences, as Roland Barthes tried to do in his study of the development of ancient rhetoric. Certainly in a world like the Greek, where the *polis* was the dominant form of social organization, the practice of deliberative rhetoric could not have emerged late. The genre that may have developed with a certain delay with respect to the previous two is the epideictic, also called laudatory or demonstrative, which undertakes to praise or attack prominent figures. This genre is less functional and immediate than the previous ones; it is almost superfluous and will flourish primarily with the Sophists.

Although we only have scanty information about the pre-Socratics, what we have is enough to show that they were on the right track. After the legendary start attributed to Tisias and Corax, we have some records of Empedocles and his tendency to link rhetoric with magic stressing emotional factors. The Pythagoreans introduced the basic notion of probability (*ta eicóta*), and to Parmenides we owe the notion of *doxa* (opinion).

Without a doubt the Sophists constitute the first big event in the history of

rhetoric. They produced a sort of atemporal model, a configuration of epistemological and ethical elements that were extraordinarily favorable to the development of rhetoric. As I have said, rhetoric finds fertile ground only in a situation
in which one doubts that truth may exist as a given outside the interaction of
human beings, their exchange and comparison of opinions that necessarily occur
through language. Protagoras (born c. 486 b.c.) takes a decisive step in this direction when he makes the proverbial statement "Man is the measure of all
things," of which there are at least two versions. The more explicit is to be found
in Plato's *Cratylus*: "Things are to me as they appear to me, and . . . they are to
you as they appear to you."[1] The concept of truth is dissolved by this declaration
of radical phenomenality according to which truth coincides with what is likely
or probable. Also, it clearly puts forward the right of every individual to hold on
to his or her experience, at least in Plato's version. Slightly different is the later
version of Sextus Empiricus, in which the subject's ultimate decision is still af-
firmed; but what is stressed is not so much the relativity of individual experience
as the right of everyone to give an opinion about the existence of things: "Of all
things the measure is man, of things that are that they are, and of things that are
not that they are not."[2]

In any case there is little doubt about the dissolution of the idea of truth, or at
least about its inflationary extension. A phenomenon has a truth of its own, even
if it is temporary and unstable because it may encounter a different truth that
appears later on to the same individual or that may be used by an opponent. Thus
the emphasis on rhetoric as a technique of "speaking against," of antilogiae, at
which Protagoras excels to a degree that today we would call professional. From
the events of his tumultuous life, which are stressed by philosophers and histo-
rians, what emerges and provokes a scandal is that he was the first to require a fee
for the professional service of logography (i.e., the drafting of a speech on behalf
of somebody else). Another dramatic occurrence that biographers report is the
raiding and burning of his library by the Athenians after he dared apply his radical phenomenology beyond the human to the divine, "suspending" judgment
about the existence of the gods (*Peri theón*): "I am unable to say whether they
exist."[3]

Perhaps his most significant maxim, certainly the most pertinent to the exercise of rhetoric, since it best defines its tasks and goals, is summed up as:
"making the weaker argument stronger" (ibid., p. 13). Obviously the detractors
of rhetoric will denounce here the worst "sophistic" iniquity, taking sophistry
in its pejorative sense: this amounts to concealing truth, using unfair practical
weapons on behalf of a position that is logically inferior, so that it may rise up
and impose itself in spite of its weakness. Things look very different if we start
from the presupposition that, at least in the world of human affairs, no stable and
unique "truth" may triumph and there are only more or less convincing arguments. Therefore anybody who is convinced of the soundness of his or her po-

sition has the right and the duty to "better" it by making it more competitive and accepted. An illustration of the complete honesty of Protagoras's statement comes from the Sophists' most ruthless enemy, Plato, who in *Theaetetus* exemplifies it by appealing to the difference of opinion between a sick individual and a healthy one. It is out of the question that there may be a principle of necessity to "convince" the sick individual that he or she is so; on the contrary, one will have to educate and persuade that person in order to "better" his or her opinions.[4] The description of the Sophists' noble undertaking can be found in Protagoras's defense of himself and his method in the Platonic dialogue that bears his name. Plato has the honesty to let him carry out the argument.

Rather more captious are the arguments of Gorgias (born c. 483 B.C. — died c. 374), the other dominant figure on the Sophists' front. In his *On Not-Being; Or, On Nature*, which can be compared with Protagoras's *Peri theón* for the same *ante litteram* metaphysical themes, Gorgias does not limit himself to a cautious "suspension of judgment" as his predecessor did. Rather, he puts forward a series of negative assertions that are as final as the positive theses of the most dogmatic thinker: "Nothing exists; . . . even if it exists it is inapprehensible; . . . even if it is apprehensible, still it is without a doubt incapable of being expressed or explained."[5] Ontology, epistemology, logic: one by one they are dismantled by the same nihilistic thrust. However, the essay is clearly an exercise in sophistry where the method of the antilogiae has become an end in itself. Captious in the same way is the *Encomium for Helen*, which does not belong to laudatory rhetoric, as one may have presumed from its title, but rather situates itself within the forsenic genre, since it is a harangue in defense of the fateful mythological character. Unlike Protagoras, Gorgias shows also in this work a total lack of caution: the argumentation is all on the side and in favor of the emotional and irrational power of words. At stake is no longer the belief in the phenomenality of things that gives the opportunity of measuring arguments one against the other, while trying to make one's own better. For Gorgias, "Speech is a powerful lord [that] can stop fear and banish grief and create joy and nurture pity."[6] Later on, Gorgias compares words to a *farmacon*, almost a drug. The individual who falls under their charm is not guilty because it is impossible to resist their strong fascination, and the moral responsibility lies entirely with the user of such a powerful narcotic. Therefore Helen must be acquitted for "incapacity," one would say in legal terminology, for yielding to Paris's invitation. All the more so since, besides the charm of words that penetrates through the ear, there is the charm of statues and beautiful bodies that passes through the eyes. The emotional and passional power of the verbal "signifier" is so accentuated by Gorgias that it will be easy for Plato to mount a very strong offensive against him. But Gorgias's position remains extreme because even though rhetoric values the physical aspect of speaking, its task is not to separate it from the intellectual level: *movere* must be balanced with *docere*. Given all this, we must keep in mind that *Encomium for*

Helen is an exercise, an *exemplum fictum*, almost a literary *topos*, and as such it has been used later on also by people who are very far from espousing Gorgias's extreme views.

Isocrates (436–338 B.C.) is a case in point. He too produced a defense of Helen that comes to conclusions not that different from those of Gorgias. And yet, the great Athenian orator is perhaps the first to outline a critique of the Sophists (in the oration bearing the same title). He denounces their excessive technicality and their professionalism as an end in itself. He denies the claim that one can construct an intrinsically valid speech in the same way as one forms words by ordering the letters of the alphabet in fixed and mechanical succession. On the contrary, a speech is judged positively if it is fit for the occasion, if it adheres to its subject and shows a certain originality of treatment.[7] Moreover, to the technical rules that make for a good internal structure, one must add elements from other domains, such as morality. A good orator must also take care to keep up a good reputation, must enjoy prestige among fellow citizens (this anticipates the attention Aristotle will devote to the orator's "personality"); and should be equipped with a wide range of notions, not only formal and literary, but philosophical and cultural in a broad sense. Isocrates had many reservations about the physical and mathematical sciences, which he considered idle thoughts: "Such curiosities of thought are on a par with jugglers' tricks which, though they do not profit anyone, yet attract great crowds of the empty-minded."[8] At best they could be useful as mental exercises. Such contempt for the physical and mathematical sciences, which Cicero will deal with and justify in depth, is due to the state of backwardness of these sciences: they were anything but "scientific" during most phases of antiquity and the Middle Ages. It also rests on the fact that rhetoric by its very nature deals primarily with the human sciences. Notwithstanding his stress on ethics and philosophy as components of oratory, Isocrates is known first of all as a great and elegant stylist, so much so that Aristotle, influenced by this competitor's success, in the third book of his *Rhetoric* gave a lot of attention to *lexis*, and thus enriched the frame of a work that in its first two parts followed a strong logical model.

Plato: *episteme* versus *doxa*

The second important moment in the history of rhetoric occurs with Plato (428–348 B.C.). But it is a negative moment that coincides with the heaviest attack and reduction rhetoric ever faced. Ever since then, when a negative attitude periodically returns, at its bottom one can find traces of Platonism.

If the Sophists do away with truth in favor of appearance, Plato does the opposite: he gives unmitigated preeminence to *episteme* over *doxa*. Above all he defends the solitary, silent nature of the search for *episteme*-truth: a search that leads one away from the crowd and the multitude. Plato's aim is to take away from the "majority" the right to judge, choose, and decide. Whence an antide-mocratic connotation, if one takes the word in its literal sense of power to the majority, and even more so if one situates the term on epistemological ground, where common sense is invested with the right to judge on questions concerning the community itself. This antisocial disposition reveals itself also in exterior at-titudes: in not caring about being liked by others or in disregarding one's clothes and behavior. It is almost "rudeness," and it manifests itself even in clumsy movements. In fact, Plato made famous the anecdote of Thales, the first of the pre-Socratic philosophers, who, being absorbed in the contemplation of the sky, fell into a ditch. For Plato, Thales is the symbol of the philosophers searching for *episteme* against all the allures of *doxa*.

This does not entail a complete overriding of *logos* in favor of direct commu-nication, unmediated by speech. On the contrary, it is well known that Plato pre-sented himself as the champion of a particular mode of *logos*: dialectic, which he always opposed to rhetoric. Dialectic is an encounter of souls and should be as immediate as possible: thus it is entrusted to brief interventions, concise state-ments consisting of subject and predicate, with no digressions or intrusions of unrelated elements (brachylogy). On the contrary, rhetoric is understood as a mundane art whose aim is to entertain, distract, or please the crowd: to this end it employs macrology, that is, lengthy discourse, richly articulated, within which one easily gets lost.

One remark seems necessary here. Platonic dialectic is the prototype of what will become analytic *logos* in Aristotle, which in my introduction I proposed con-sidering as the polar opposite met by rhetoric over and over again in the course of time. Dialectic, on which Plato insists so much, is above all an analytic endeavor to break down discourses in order to find their primary elements, and to identify within them a few essential categories. Discontinuity and discreteness are set against rhetoric's roundness and complexity. The contempt for the materiality of language is also part of the analytic attitude: nouns are images, copies of things. Therefore it is proper that they be as transparent as possible; they have the purely instrumental role of a reminder, like traces that are useful but have no autonomy of their own. This means the divorce between words and things, where the latter are considerably privileged. For this reason Cicero will harshly reprove Socrates, whose philosophy to a great extent is filtered and reconstituted in Plato's dia-logues.

However, it is also true that the dialogue, as a game between two parties and an exchange of short questions and answers, has an irreplaceable role of its own within the economy of Platonic dialectic. It is not even conceivable to substitute literal symbols for the living subjects and their expressions, as in fact will happen in Aristotelian analytics. In more general terms, Socratic dialectic is a form of analytics that can never end in a rigorous symbolic logic. One reason for this is Plato's contempt for the materiality of words: not only sounds but above all writing, to the point that toward the end of the *Phaedrus* he includes the famous myth of King Thamus who turns down the offer of writing from the god Theuth exactly for the reason that writing would interfere with the impact of direct communication: it would turn the latter into something external and heavily burdened, and would foster mental laziness by inducing people to rely on an extraorganic memory.

Plato deals with rhetoric, or macrology, particularly in the *Gorgias* dialogue, but *Protagoras* also is useful in understanding his stance on the subject. Plato's fairness must be recognized since the definition of rhetoric the two Sophists give is not at all partial, but clear and correct. In essence, the difficult knot we are grappling with is the relationship between the political and the technical moments, as we noted in the introduction. Gorgias rightly remarks that the political "mediates" the contributions of single disciplines and that its task is to compare these contributions, adopt them at the right time and the right place, taking care to put them into practice too. The walls of Athens are due to the advice of Pericles:[9] therefore, to the political and rhetorical moment goes the credit for reconciling technical data and economic interests, and for persuading the citizens to sustain their considerable effort to realize the work. To Plato's objection that Pericles was not able to hand down to his children his rhetorical ability, which therefore was not a technique, Protagoras adroitly responds that this is only fair: virtues, such as a sense of justice or respect, which are the civic values underpinning rhetoric, are equally distributed among human beings. All alike, human beings have their share, or at least should have it.[10] This is a fundamentally democratic attitude: faced with certain choices or responsibilities, human beings are alike, or should be considered as such.

Although Plato lets his adversaries expound their theories with clarity, he of course cannot be persuaded. His priority is the quest for *episteme* and this leaves no space for surrogates. The scope of *doxa* can be neither that of a science nor that of a technique. At best it will be *empeiría*, that is, a "mundane" practice in the service of the majority. Therefore it is given to cheating and seduction, and ruins everything worthy of the wise. Human beings are made of body and soul. For each of these parts there are suitable arts that provide what is best for them. But there are other arts that, prone to pleasure and gratification, lapse into flattery (*colachéia*). For the body, medicine and gymnastics are the proper arts; cookery and fashion are bad, however, because sensual pleasure insinuates itself into them. For the soul, Plato indicates politics, with legislation and the administration of justice as positive moments, whereas sophistry and rhetoric represent the fall into flattery.[11]

In *Gorgias*, the denunciation of rhetoric becomes the ground for founding a sort of moral eidetics (eidetics of the true and the beautiful are dealt with elsewhere but of course in the Platonic dialogues these different moments converge). In essence, it is the same motif of the contempt for the ways and weaknesses of the majority, such as looking for pleasure, avoiding pain, preferring to be unfair rather than being treated unfairly. Plato opposes to all this the divine rights of precedence that justness has over the pleasant. To the wise individual, authentic pleasure comes from following truth and goodness, while waiting for the reward that will come in the next world, when in Tartarus the just will be separated from the others and chosen for a life of beatitude and contemplation. One can understand how, in the framework of a vertical dialogue between the human and the divine, and of disdain for the majority, rhetoric can only appear as a vile tool of corruption.

All the more so if the adversary is not a Sophist of Gorgias's stature, as happens in the *Euthydemus*, where sophistry degenerates into eristic, the pure technique of fighting with words, the ability to argue for or against a point of view irrespective of its truth. It is pure mental exercise, or, following Isocrates' simile, a combinatory play of letters that does not take into account the context in which the disputation occurs.

In the *Phaedrus* rhetoric holds a slightly better position. There is here a more positive evaluation of its role. This does not mean that there are radical changes or substantial differences in the theoretical framework within which it is set. *Episteme* still has priority over *doxa*; those who try to lead astray with false appearances are condemned (for example, to make believe that a donkey is a horse). Also condemned are those who overlook the aim of certain arts (for example, to know how to induce warmth or coolness in a body without knowing which patients should be given such treatment).[12] Also the relation between the arts of the soul (politics and psychology) and rhetoric is the same. The only difference is that now rhetoric can find a positive function if it works in their service, if it takes a psychagogic role and carries it out according to their goals. It must know the various human types but should not yield to them; rather it will try to improve their value system. It is understood that the individual who wants to master the art of speech "should exert [it] not for the sake of speaking to and dealing with his fellow men, but that he may be able to speak what is pleasing to the gods, and in all his dealings to do their pleasure to the best of his ability" (ibid., p. 519). Indeed, this dialogue is written in the key of organic unity (we could say today a sort of gestalt configuration): we mean that all that strengthens a proper connection of the parts with the whole is praised, whereas detached parts are avoided. Rhetoric would be a case of eristic technicality and would correspond, following Isocrates, to the letters of the alphabet that do not merge into a discourse. It is not by chance that the *Phaedrus* ends with the myth of Theuth, Thamus, and the rejection of writing that would cool off, fragment, and externalize the impetus of direct communication between human beings and the divine (the transcendent nature of truth is considered divine too). But we must point out the cautious reevaluation of psychagogy, if only to confirm that Platonic dialectic hinges on a psychological tissue and does not tolerate formalization.

Aristotle's Rhetoric between Form and Content

Aristotle (384–322 B.C.) reconciles and systematizes in a complex theoretical framework the antithetical pairs over which the Sophists and Plato had disputed: truth and probability, *episteme* and *doxa*, the general and the particular. As I have mentioned, he separates the two cores that were present in Platonic dialectic by identifying an analytic moment and a properly dialectical one, but he also makes clear that both moments avail themselves of brachylogy, and thus constitute a sphere reserved for "the few," the wise, from which the majority are excluded. The technique of analytics is "the assumption of one member of a pair of contradictory statements."[13] Therefore there is no dialogical exchange, no questioning, no psychological contact with the other party. A technique of this kind follows a very solitary path; it is so highly formal, almost inhuman one could say, that it could function without words by employing symbols, such as the letters of the alphabet. It already anticipates the "calculus" of contemporary logic. It starts out from true unquestionable premises (axioms) and then proceeds by deduction through syllogisms. Its aim is to arrive at a demonstration. We already said that from this time on, analytics will be the great rival and opponent of rhetoric.

However, Aristotle is ready to admit that one cannot always start from "true" premises. In many cases one must be satisfied with "an assumption of what is apparently true and generally accepted" (ibid, p. 201), which is the dialectical premise proper. In *Topica* he clarifies what he means by opinion. "Generally accepted opinions . . . are those which commend themselves to all or to the majority or to the wise — that is, to all of the wise."[14] Thus he supplies a democratic basis and reintroduces that respect for the community that Plato had rejected. Moreoever, the relation between analytics and dialectic is not a pact of mutual nonbelligerence: Aristotle does not hesitate to ask who guarantees the truth of analytic axioms, what lies behind them. The two answers that emerge in the *Analytics* are also the two major directions that on different occasions philosophy will adopt in the course of its development. The first envelops analytics in its own self-sufficiency, since the foundations would be the result of an intuition sending back onto itself (this is the path followed by Descartes). The second possibility is to appeal to dialectic and to entrust it with the decision about the ultimate foundations: "It is impossible to discuss (the ultimate bases of each science) at all on the basis of the principles peculiar to the science in question, since the principles are primary in relation to everything else, and it is necessary to deal with them through the generally accepted opinions on each point."[15] This implies a different solution, an alternative to Descartes, which a contemporary scholar of rhetoric, Chaim Perelman, has assigned to the category of "regressive philosophies," meaning those systems of thought that go back searching for foundations and find them in common sense, in the community of laypeople (others would say in experience, in *Lebenswelt*, or in the collective unconscious). The majority takes its revenge on the few; the turbulent confrontation of opinions wins over the silent calculus almost devoid of psychological or physical opacity. On this path opinion sets its preeminence over truth: the latter is but an agreement about which the "many" must give their opinion.

But within the term "multitude" there are degrees, and the part pertaining to dialectic is very limited. Aristotle remains a good disciple of Plato, inasmuch as he keeps the dialectical exchange of opinion inside the restricted circle of the wise, who are capable of bearing the dry rigor of brachylogy. In short, we have moved from the single individual of Plato to the intermediary stage of the few.

It will not be long, however, before Aristotle takes the next step and opens up the field leaving the few for the many, the wise for ordinary people, the experts for the nonexperts. Without doubt he has some regret about the inevitable degradation that follows when the level of the experts is given up. But there is also the recognition that such a step is inevitable, since in several matters "man is the measure of all things," as Protagoras said: we are all human beings with the same rights. Therefore we have to share and compare our various positions, without anybody being in a position to claim a priority in the name of his or her particular rights, or at most such priority will have to be gained in the open contest of discourse. Basically, the Sophists are right and Plato is wrong: there are areas within which truth does not exist, but there is only likelihood, probability. This is nobody's fault, it is just the way things are. Therefore sophistry does not mean that one fights in the name of a high or low probability. What is morally reprehensible is the rhetorician's intention purposefully to discard the most convincing arguments in order to promote arguments where his vested interest is at stake. Otherwise, if one acts in good faith, the word "sophism" does not apply, since inevitably one will try to make "stronger" the "weaker" argument. Rhetoric's democratic vocation carries some consequences, one of which is the necessity to avoid formal logic, since the majority could not follow it. One must infer from close quarters, that is, the listeners should be spared abstruse logical passages. The audience's patience and attention cannot be overtaxed; one cannot bore them with trite points, or bewilder them with obscure notions.

However, because of its link with dialectic, Aristotle's rhetoric receives a solid logical base, which will be decisive for its future: rhetoric is no longer *empeiría*, an adulatory psychological instrument or captivating magic, but an "art" with its own tools. These tools have been amply dealt with in the *Topica*, and are not very different from those in the *Analytics*, except for their different foundation on probability. Therefore *The "Art" of Rhetoric* should be considered as one of the branches of logic and deserves to be part of the *Organon*.

This is why from the very beginning Aristotle insists that he will not be led astray by irrelevant contingent matters, but will expound on the "technical" means of persuasion. His study deals with what is inherent in persuasion and independent of external circumstances, such as admissions made under torture, or witnesses. The stress is on facts, rather than subject matters. His first task is to show the sources from which arise the arguments fit to persuade. The technique of rhetoric is a complex one, and is very far from pure analytic and formal logic. In fact, Aristotle is immediately forced to give three very different sources. The first is in a logical mode inasmuch as it tries to demonstrate everything through discourse itself; the other two employ psychological and social elements, that is, they appeal to the speaker's personality and the listeners' emotions. Within the field of probability, trusting the speaker is a source of persuasion in its own right, since if we received good advice in the past, it may well be the same in the future. Far from being an irrelevant remark, this is something to take into account when determining the degree of persuasiveness of a speech.

For all these reasons Aristotle is perfectly aware that the status of rhetoric is ambiguous: it is suspended between form and content, art and science, theory and practice. It is a formal discipline, like analytics and dialectic, because its sphere is discourse, linguistic material. On the other hand, it must borrow from psychology, ethics, and politics. It is an art, for its character of general skill independent of single disciplines or techniques. But it is also a science that needs a precise set of rules and factual knowledge. Finally, it is theoretical for its relation with logic, but it is also practical because its objective is to move people into action.

Consistent with this formulation that hangs between form and content, theory and practice, in the first book of the *Rhetoric*, just after the first general definitions, Aristotle feels compelled to give a series of outlines of the human sciences or political sciences in the broad sense. This provides the rhetorician with materials that cannot be ignored, although one must avoid being caught entirely by any one of them, since this would mean becoming an expert, with the consequent loss of the ability to interconnect the various subjects. The particular studies within the wider context of the rhetorical treatise are made necessary by the three branches in which rhetoric is subdivided: the deliberative, the forensic, and the epideictic. These genres may well have been present *ab origine*, but nobody had systematized them with the precision, thoroughness, and attention to content that Aristotle shows. Deliberative rhetoric deals with ways and means of a *polis*: its economy, war and peace (i.e., strategy), and various types of constitutions (i.e., politics in the proper sense). A good orator must master the basic elements of these subjects, and one cannot succeed by displaying mere verbal skills separated from things. The scaffolding of formal logic must blend completely with the actual content. Thus a treatise on rhetoric must deal with the human sciences, even if it must do so summarily.

Similarly, it is not surprising that epideictic rhetoric contains a small treatise on ethics providing definitions of virtue and vice. Virtue comprises justice, courage, temperance, magnificence, magnanimity, generosity, gentleness, prudence, wisdom. Finally, forensic rhetoric is supplied with a kind of psychology manual that illustrates the causes of human action: they are chance, nature, compulsion, habit, reason, passion, desire. There follows a definition of pleasure, understood as one of the major springs to action. Then there is a description of psychological types meant to outline the individuals that may be the subjects or the objects of possible crimes, that is, which human characters are disposed to do wrong, and which to be wronged. There is also a distinction between laws of nature and written law; the latter has a specific historical ground and is contained in written articles. Of course the strategy to confute a law of nature, founded on opinion, will not be the same as the one to deal with a law founded on a written text, which after all is an external element.

The specific contents of these commentaries have only a historical value for us today, and in a contemporary treatise they would have to be completely redone. However, still fully valid is the suggestion that ethical and political elements should not be overlooked, since without them rhetoric does not exist, or, rather, it would be reduced to a mere formal and superficial exercise in "beautiful speech." It would be equally wrong to take the opposite attitude, and stress content while abolishing the rhetorician to the advantage of the expert versed in a single scientific field—as if specific disciplines by their very nature had no need to be investigated by the logic of probability and pro and con arguments, of which only rhetoric and dialectic are the repositories.

The second book of the *Rhetoric* also starts with practical observations. Now it is the turn of the emotions, of passions, whose intrinsic role we have already underlined. We are offered a short analysis of passions: anger, friendship, fear, shame, benevolence, pity, indignation, envy, emulation. After a first general presentation, Aristotle proceeds to relate them to stages of life and various situations: emotions obviously change in relation to youth, maturity, and old age; they also are modified by the subjects' different fortunes: nobility, wealth, power, or their opposites. Here comes to an end the outline of the political and moral sciences, that knowledge of human beings with which a good rhetorician must be equipped.

The Quasi-Logical Aspects of Aristotle's Rhetoric

We now come to the part dealing with arguments of a logical nature. This is a relatively formal section, more concerned with language than with things, although in the context of rhetoric the line separating the two is always hard to trace. Actually, Aristotle had already moved in this direction when he introduced the notion of *topos*, of place, that contains the application of a rhetorical figure: the simile. In fact, a relationship of resemblance links the ideal storehouse of topics and the concrete indication of space contained in the concept of place. From the beginning Aristotle had observed that topics are arranged according to a polar tension. At one end there are particular topics: this is the realm of specificity, where each science has its contents between well-defined boundaries. So, for example, all the topics already dealt with are particular; they belong to politics, ethics, the passions, and so forth. At this level there is no exchange, and each subject has its own space. At the other end of the polarity there are general, not specialized, topics, thus suitable for application to diverse inquiries.

Aristotle also proceeds to adapt to rhetoric the two general methods of logic, deduction and induction. Rhetorical syllogism he calls "enthymeme." It is interesting to see the difference from its kin in analytics and dialectic. It is not enough to say that in rhetoric the major premise is provided by an argument that is not true but simply probable, since dialectical syllogism shares this feature too. Once again the difference has to do with a consideration of *demos*, with the need to respect the audience. Ordinary people cannot stand for long the rigorous but boring constructs of analytics or dialectic, which aim at correctness and therefore make use of whole chains of passages. For the general public it is much better when these steps are skipped, and a conclusion is reached quickly. Of course there is a high risk at stake here: the major premises implied must be shared by the speaker and the audience. If this were not the case, that is, if the audience does not unanimously accept the same premise as the speaker, the enthymeme loses its effectiveness and may actually have negative effects. This is why analytics and dialectic prefer to avoid such a risk and make explicit all the passages, even if they may be obvious and become boring.

We will leave behind the outdated examples of enthymemes given by Aristotle and will give instead a contemporary example: a slogan from an advertisement (commercials are one of the fields in which rhetoric is thriving, as we will see). Some time ago, the publicity for launching a new model of compact Italian car proclaimed that the car would rejuvenate its owner. Actually an apocope was used: the car was said to "juvenate" one, thus producing a pleasant effect of novelty and bizarreness. This is a typical example of enthymeme, in which both the major premise (everything that rejuvenates one is good and desirable) and the conclusion (this car rejuvenates, thus it is good and desirable) are implied. Quickness and the omission of passages that are self-evident or obvious aim pleasantly to surprise the general public whose attention has to be captured. But there is a risk: the desirability of youthful products may not be as widely accepted a *doxa* as one may think. At least those among the audience who follow the opposite *doxa* (people for whom good objects are associated with the good sense and balance that come with maturity and old age) will emotionally reject the enthymeme altogether, since they have no chance to discuss the major premise, as would have happened in an analytic or dialectical context, in which the premise would be made explicit from the beginning and debated before going on.

Moving on to the inductive method, its rhetorical tool is the example, that is, the presentation of concrete facts and full-bodied evidence in order to support a broader assertion. This concreteness may borrow from history (when one uses historical parallels), or it may use invented facts (the so-called *exempla ficta*, which are not true but verisimilar). Aristotle makes it clear that he prefers the deductive method, and therefore the enthymeme, which he considers more persuasive. If one wants to apply examples, one must use many of them, in the same way as induction requires a lot of concrete instances in order to derive generalities.

Returning to general *topoi*, that is, to the area of rhetoric closer to logic, Aristotle provides a long list, specifying that one can derive from it demonstrative enthymemes (to prove a given thesis), or refutative enthymemes (to oppose that thesis). Here are some, with examples of how they are applied. The *topos* of opposites: "If the war is responsible for the present evils, one must repair them with the aid of peace."[16] The *topos* of correlative terms: "If selling is not disgraceful for you, neither is buying disgraceful for us, (ibid., p. 299). The *topos* of more and less: "If not even the gods know everything, hardly can men" (p. 301). In the last example, the *topos* goes from more to less, but there is also the opposite way, from less to more, as when one says, "If you complain, you from whom a finger has been taken, what should I do, I, who have lost an arm?" Then there is the *topos* of definition, that is, finding the definition of a concept to turn it to one's advantage. Very close to this is the *topos* of etymology, which uses the literal meaning of a term. The following is an example: to restore the dignity of the adjective "poetic," which today is in danger of acquiring a kitsch connotation, in the mode of cheap sentimentality, it is useful to remember that according to its Greek root it refers to an individual skilled in producing linguistic constructs. Linked with this is the *topos* of names, for example, the well-known "tu es Petrus et super hanc petram aedificabo ecclesiam meam."

Another *topos* is that of division, which breaks down a question in different parts, and argues for and against each of them, instead of dealing with them altogether. There is also the *topos* of proportional results, of which Aristotle gives us a witty example. He recalls a statement Iphicrates made when they wanted to force his young son into public service because he was already tall: "If you consider tall boys men, you must vote that short men are boys" (p. 313). And there are many more: Aristotle provides a list of twenty-eight *topoi*. In fact, some of them are redundant and encroach on others. But this is not the place to analyze them in detail. It is enough that we have thrown light on an area where rhetoric is equipped with quasi-logical tools. The face remains that none of these procedures is decisive or necessary: each of them can be refuted with the help of the others, or it may even be diverted from the demonstrative mode, in favor of a thesis, to the refutative mode, against the same thesis.

Lexis and the Comical

The first two books of the *Rhetoric* analyze the sources of argumentation: formal, general, political, and emotional *topoi*. Thus Aristotle deals with what is considered one of the most relevant parts of rhetoric: *euresis, inventio*, the identification, listing, and description of *topoi*. Consistent with his background, which had been heavily influenced by logic, he gives substantial primacy to *inventio*. But he cannot overlook other significant parts that until then had not been systematized and that in fact he hands down to us with unprecedented clarity. We see in this consideration an argument in support of our position, namely, that the third book of the *Rhetoric* is an integral and necessary part of the work, against the thesis that it was added later, almost as if Aristotle had changed his mind. On the contrary, it is impossible that he may have thought to close his treatise after dealing only with *inventio*. He had to open up and include other aspects as well. Indeed, there are three more parts: arrangement, style, and delivery. To complete the five sections into which rhetoric will crystallize itself in the following centuries an important practical and psychological part is still missing: mnemonics, which was to become very important in the ancient world. Moreover, the order in which the parts are treated does not follow completely what will become the canon, according to which arrangement should be second, for completing the section dealing with logic. But Aristotle puts this section last. He only briefly touches on delivery (gestures, the right management of the voice, performance) and rightly refers back to the *Poetics*, where he deals with the art of performing. Instead, *lexis* is given considerable attention. Aristotle includes elements, identifies problems, and specifies requirements that will remain in the package of themes that a good manual of rhetoric must include. Among the items analyzed, grammar stands out (one must use the proper idiom and the correct connective words; singular and plural forms must be expressed correctly; zeugma is to be avoided, etc.). We will have to wait until the establishment of the trivium for grammar to stop being the last section of rhetoric, and to become the subject of a course in its own right (in a *schola*) preceding it.

When Aristotle turns his attention to *lexis* proper, he makes clear that for him logic would have more dignity: "For as a matter of right, one should aim at nothing more in speech than how to avoid exciting pain or pleasure. . . . Nevertheless . . . it is of great importance owing to the corruption of the hearer."[17] This the usual warning that accompanies Aristotle's acceptance of the "majority" and its standards, but it remains unquestionable that he adopts this point of view. It does not matter whether he has been led to this stance by the success of Isocrates' school, as some have assumed, or on the contrary by a fair consideration of all the aspects of reality, each understood in its proper place and hierarchy. The fact is that even on this subject his model will be insuperable. *Lexis* runs between two opposite poles: one is the "degree zero," as we would say today, a discourse absolutely obvious, clumsy, pedestrian, and "redundant" according to information theory. The other pole is an "extremely elevated" discourse, "informational" according to the same information theory, where every word is used in a figurative sense, so that it becomes a matter of problematic interpretation, an obstacle to direct and simple comprehension. As one moves toward this pole, one leaves the prose of ordinary language and enters the territory of poetry. In fact, in the *Poetics*, Aristotle returns to these same problems, and the investigation he conducts there can be considered complementary to the one carried out in the *Rhetoric*.

The pleasure that the speaker must arouse in the audience through *elocutio* rests on the observation that "men admire what is remote, and that which excites admiration is pleasant" (ibid., p. 351). This is why one's language cannot be limited to current or common words, but sometimes it is good to employ archaisms or foreign words, and above all figures, whose mainspring is a connection between meanings not normally linked. So we come to the most important of all figures, or tropes: the metaphor. Aristotle does not offer a definition in the *Rhetoric*, but we can find one in the *Poetics*: "Metaphor is the application of a strange term either transferred from the genus and applied to the species or from the species and applied to the genus, or from one species to another or else by analogy."[18] It is worth reporting some of the example, considering the relevance metaphor has in the history of rhetoric. A metaphor of the first type: "Here stands my ship," for riding at anchor is a species of standing. An example of the second type: "Indeed, ten thousand noble things Odysseus did" (instead of the generic "many" the specific "ten thousand"). An example of the third type: "Drawing off his life with the bronze," "Severing with the tireless bronze": "to draw off" and "to sever," Aristotle explains, are species of the generic "to remove," which in the two sentences are used interchangeably. Finally an example of the fourth type: "Old age is to life as evening is to day": thus one can say that old age is the evening of life.

Also in employing metaphors one must find a proper balance. Similarity should not be too obvious, otherwise one falls into commonplace metaphors, such as "the legs of the table": in the same way, "in philosophy it needs sagacity to grasp the similarity in things that are apart."[19] Thus welcome are uncommon and unexpected comparisons, which will also return in the poetics of the baroque, or in the exasperated analogism and unbridled imagination of some contemporary poetics. But Aristotle suggests a corrective for maintaining propriety and good taste: the analogy, the transference, must be between things "close in genus," so that verisimilitude is not too forced and one avoids falling into artificiality or exaggeration. The same warnings are given in connection with the other figures of speech analyzed here, such as the epithet, the simile, the *enárgheia* (which is the evidence, the concreteness of examples).

Beside metaphors that link diverse things, brevity is another great source of pleasure. As we saw, it is the need fulfilled by the enthymeme that eliminates some steps in order to reach a conclusion quickly, so that one avoids boring the audience with self-evident remarks. Unexpected similarities and quick passages are also the best way to produce comic effects; in fact, jokes are one of the elements that Aristotle includes and that will stay with rhetoric forever. Ever since then, a good treatise on the art of speech will include a section on the comical and jokes. Although Aristotle only briefly touches on it, he is able to identify one of the most important techniques of jokes, one that will be recognized and analyzed by Freud, namely, paradoxical effect produced "by jokes that turn on a change of letter; for they are deceptive" (ibid., p. 409). This is one of Aristotle's examples: the expression *thrattei* means "you are troubled," but it is very similar or almost identical in sound with *thrattei se*, which instead means "you are no better than a Thracian slavegirl" (pp. 410–11). Of course Aristotle does not ask himself why this is not a generic case of "surprise," the appeal of the remote, or why it makes one laugh. He lacks the ability to catch the aggressiveness and the impudence of the lower libidinal sphere, on which Freud will ground psychoanalysis many centuries later. Along with homophony, homonymy has an even greater comical effect: for example, the phrase "There is no bearing Baring" is quite funny if an individual by that name is an unbearable person (p. 411).

After dealing with *elocutio*, Aristotle shifts the focus to *dispositio*. Here too he maps out a territory that will be revisited over and over again. This is also the space of "quantitative" or diachronic parts of speech, which follow a precise strategic arrangement, whereas qualitative elements, to which *dispositio* belongs, are synchronic. The order of a standard sequence is as follows: prologue, statement of the case (i.e., the narration where the terms of a problem or a lawsuit are advanced), argument (this comprehends a refutation of one's opponent and what Latin rhetoricians will call *confirmatio*, or development of proofs to support one's position), and epilogue. The epilogue has its own order: first, one may magnify the facts stated; then one may disparage one's adversary; this may be followed by a peroration to the listeners, the *captatio benevolentiae*, and finally a rapid recapitulation to close the speech. Aristotle is perfectly aware that his subject lends itself to innumerable subdivisions. In fact, a crowd of narrowminded rhetoricians will eventually take possession of it, and will develop a body of sterile, oversubtle rules. But Aristotle tries to safeguard rhetoric from this danger and to neutralize the pretensions of excessively rigid and predetermined formulas. Once again his appeal is for a happy mean, for a smooth graduation between extremes capable of regulating itself according to the circumstances. In this context, his simile of the baker suits perfectly: asked if he was to knead bread hard or soft, the baker answered that his aim was to make it just right (p. 445).

Further Developments, the Anonymous *Sublime*

The thoroughness of Aristotle's *Rhetoric* stands unchallenged. Moreover, most of the works written after him have been lost, or only a few fragments remain, or sometimes we just have quotes and free paraphrases cited in different works. To the immediate successor of Aristotle, Theophrastus (c. 372–c. 287 B.C.), is attributed further research in the direction of *lexis*, and, most important, the introduction of three stylistic levels: high, middle, and low. This notion was already implicit, however, in Aristotle's suggestion that style should be appropriate to the dignity of the subject treated. After Theophrastus the Peripatetic school declines and there is no indication of relevant studies on rhetoric. Nor are there significant contributions from the Platonic school, the Academy, although it continued for a considerable length of time and adopted a variety of approaches during its various phases: the Middle Academy, with Arcesilaus (315–c. 241 B.C.), and the New Academy with Carneades (214–129 B.C.). But in relation to the original Platonic model there is a considerable shift of perspective that ends by touching issues that concern rhetoric. In fact, the New Academy attacks the concept of truth and replaces it with *pithanón*: that which can persuade. It is almost a conversion to the side of *doxa*. Also, there are different degrees within *pithanón*, depending on whether persuasion is obtained immediately, or whether it must overcome opposition: in this case its credibility is even strengthened. We will see that Cicero employs this probabilistic mode of the epistemological question and makes it the basis for his *De oratore*.

Instead, Cicero will express aversion, sometimes veining it with irony, for the Stoic school, which arose after the Platonic and the Aristotelian in the fourth century. Its founder, Zeno (c. 335–c. 263), is famous for his visual, concrete definition of the relationship between dialectic and rhetoric: "With a closed fist Zeno used to show the fast, concise character of dialectic; with an open palm and the fingers stretched the amplification and diffuseness of rhetoric."[20] In essence, this is nothing new in terms of the Platonic division between brachylogy and macrology, which Aristotle had not rejected either. But Cicero must have disliked the technical sheen displayed by such a view, which stems from a logical basis that comes down rather hard on the "diffuse" modes of eloquence. On the other hand, the Stoics, besides being interested in a very rigorous and technical logic, were trying to construct a physics that would be as scientific as it was "mute." Those who want to learn how to become dumbfounded should go to the Stoics' school: this was one of Cicero's ironic comments, which he repeated on various occasions in his works. Of course he does not question the scientific validity of their contribution. The problem is to make the Stoics eloquent, to make them accessible, not just to an audience of a few learned individuals, but to the people: one has to translate them from the dialectical mode in which they excelled into the *oratio continua* of rhetoric.

Several technical innovations were introduced by Hermagoras of Temnos, who lived in about the middle of the second century B.C. He is perhaps the only one to introduce significant changes to the framework of Aristotelian rhetoric. To him is attributed the distinction between general themes for debate (theses) and particular themes (hypotheses). But such division was not unknown to Aristotle: it was already contained in the distinction between general and particular topics. Actually Aristotle may have perceived that there was a risk in a radical separation of the two moments. The distinction would inscribe theses in the space of abstract universal formulations while hypotheses would fall into the maze of a banal and fragmented casuistry. Along the same lines, one would arrive at a dangerous separation between the philosopher and the rhetorician, since the former would be removed from the contact with things, with praxis, and the latter would be deprived of any theoretical ground. Consistent with his new technical mode, Hermagoras introduces the notion of "stasis" (issues; Latin rhetoricians will translate it as *status causae*). Perhaps herein lies the most important difference with respect to Aristotle. Hermagoras treats rhetoric no longer according to the objectives of a speech (deliberative, forensic, and epideictic), but according to its mode of presentation. It is a crossways classification, so to speak, in relation to the various branches of rhetoric. It has primarily a technical usefulness, especially in the forensic field. Hermagoras describes the rational "issue," deriving from common sense and natural reason, and the forensic "issue" when one deals with an existing body of laws on a subject. The former is further subdivided into types: the issue of conjecture (did A commit the crime?); the issue of definition (how is one to define a certain action, once it is established that it was performed?); the issue of quality (what were the intentions when it was performed?), and so forth. As for forensic issues, their classification deals with the correspondence between the letter and the spirit of a law; contradictions between different laws, or textual ambiguities in one of them; and finally inferences and applications to a case never before contemplated. As a matter of fact, Hermagoras's doctrine of *status causae* will not be able to supplant the three traditional branches of rhetoric, but, at least in Latin treatises, it will join them as another possible classification: it will be particularly useful in the forensic field, which is the one where Latin rhetoricians were keenest.

The first century B.C. and the beginning of the Christian era is characterized by a dispute between Atticists and Asiatics. The former are the followers of Apollodorus of Pergamum and the latter of Theodorus of Gadara. For the Atticists rhetoric should be concise, and should employ an agile turn of phrase. On the Asiatic front rhetoric grants considerable space to *lexis* and pathos. This debate, which is linked with the events happening in the field of grammar and the law (analogists versus anomalists), is of interest to us for two reasons. The first is that many works and commentaries about it have come down to us. The second is that we can assign to the Asiatic front, or at least to a position very close to it, the author of the *Sublime*, a work that marks the last great moment of Greek rhetoric. After several attempts, philological analysis had made clear that the first attribution to Dionysius Longinus was not correct. One had to split the names with the dubitative conjunction "or," affixed by an unknown amanuensis: Dionysius *or* Longinus. The hypothesis that it could have been the Neoplatonic Longinus, who lived in the third century, was discarded because references to contemporary events in the text do not go beyond the rule of Claudius, that is, the first half of the first century, which is too late. The attribution to Dionysius of Halicarnassus was discarded for the opposite reason: he lived too early. One was left with the hypothesis that the author was a follower of Theodorus; therefore, in a mediated way, the work could be assigned to an eclectic Platonic-Stoic school that was active during the rule of Claudius.

In short, we might say that the author of the *Sublime* has written the only treatise on rhetoric compatible with the teaching of Plato: his notion of rhetoric is one that, contrary to the etymology of the term, marks the victory of silence, the absence of words as a tool of persuasion. Pascal shows himself to be a good follower of this approach when he writes his well-known aphorism "La vraie éloquence se moque de l'éloquence" ("True eloquence scoffs at eloquence"). If we recall the three elements on which Aristotle based the function of rhetoric (*logos, ethos, pathos*), we may say that in this case everything is centered on pathos. First of all the orator must manifest his own pathos, in order to convey it to the audience: "A well-timed flash of sublimity scatters everything before it like a bolt of lightning."[21] To show that one is inspired by strong passions is in itself a persuasive argument. The audience will not doubt the expertise and mastery of the orator, who otherwise could be suspected of employing cold artificiality. In other words, technique is not negative; it can be taught and it can be adopted, but it needs as guarantee a filling of strong feelings. In fact, if the author of the *Sublime* does not exclude technique, and actually lays down a set of rules, he continuously warns us about its limits: *logos* cannot have much space at its disposal. In this way, in line with Pascal's statement, even the absence of *logos* can sometimes be a tool of persuasion: "And so even without being spoken the bare idea often of itself wins admiration" (ibid., p. 145).

After praising silence, the focus shifts to advocate a simple, poor or ordinary, language: these traits sometimes mediate the sublime much better than a lofty style. By so doing, the anonymous author opens the path to the antirhetoric that the church fathers will discover in the Holy Scripture. However, if one wants to employ magniloquence, or figurative language, the warning already given is still valid: there must always be a genuine emotional thrust to support it; figures should not give an impression of cold artificiality, and should not be used to please the audience through the use and abuse of novelties. Also in this direction the unknown author reveals himself to be radically opposed to the Aristotelian line. For Aristotle metaphors are the first instrument of *delectare*, since they perform a horizontal operation that links distant terms, which however are part of the same universe. To the vast horizontal expansion of metaphors is here opposed a vertical vector of intensity, a sort of gradation from shallow to deep, or from low to high. As a consequence, quality is preferable to quantity: it is better to use a few figures at the right time and the right place rather than to display an unrestrained proliferation that would be tedious and would not be matched by a corresponding degree of pathos: "To sound bells in every sentence would be unduly pretentious" (p. 199). The intensive criterion of quality also allows one to justify possible faults and imperfections as long as these are balanced elsewhere by exceptional peaks of sublimity. Better a style that sometimes is not impeccable but that can rise to the heights of pathos than a style displaying a smooth technical mastery but offering only an elegant and cold homogeneity with no soul. One metaphor of Plato or Demosthenes is worth more than all the elegance of Hyperides: in fact, "each of these great men again and again redeems his mistakes by a single touch of sublimity" (p. 227).

So much for tropes, metaphors, and transfers of meaning. With regard to figures of speech related to the internal order of sentences, the anonymous author confirms his preference for concise and direct solutions that do not hinder the flow of emotional intensity. He is hostile to the use and abuse of connecting particles and conjunctions, on which the Attic school relied for the construction of discourses with symmetry, shrewdness, clearness, and agility. On the contrary, "just as you deprive runners of their speed if you tie them together, emotion equally resents being hampered by connecting particles and other such appendages" (p. 193). He prefers solutions that are technically simpler but also more solemn, such as the use of hyperbaton (a transposition of words that alters the syntactical order so as to do violence to its natural sequence, to the "degree zero" of a flat and trivial syntagm), or the use of the plural in place of the singular, and vice versa. These are little infractions that recall the ones on which Freud's psychoanalysis or Spitzer's stylistic analysis will concentrate to find the symptoms of the unconscious (which is a good contemporary heir to the pathos preached by the author of the *Sublime*).

In conclusion, a good technical rule is to break the rules at the right time and the right place. One must be moved by inspiration, by genius, by quality and not by quantity or vile professionalism, even when this will bring along a certain unevenness of effects. Also, the orator who wants to reach sublimity must avoid the baseness of low passions, greed for possessions, sloth—all of which are at the origin of the decadence of rhetoric. In reality the danger that the author is trying to neutralize is that of a rhetoric subject to a stalemate and utter boredom, which has tried to overcome this plight by teasing and by pleasing the audience's curiosity through an immoderate search for the new. These are the terms of the conflict between the ancients and the moderns that will reemerge in a short time in Tacitus's *Dialogus de oratoribus* (A dialogue on oratory). They will also accompany the development of a postclassical, "baroque" literature, if for a moment we are allowed to conceive of an atemporal baroque model characterized precisely by an unbridled linking of diverse things. Against such a model, the approach of the *Sublime*, which remains close to the Platonic line of thinking and to its techniques, will always stand up to voice condemnation and rejection.

Chapter 2
The Romans

Beginnings: *Rhetorica ad Herennium* and *De inventione*

It is mostly through the historical reconstruction that Cicero (106 – 43 B.C.) made in *Brutus* that we know the first centuries of Latin rhetoric. However, this is a biased account since Cicero's aim is to make himself the final objective and synthesis to whom previous rhetoricians had progressively opened the way. Many figures are dealt with, among them: Cato the Elder, Lelius, Galba, Tiberius and Gaius Gracchi, and Rutilius; also Antonius and Crassus, whom Cicero will make the most important interlocutors in his *De oratore*; then Sulpicius and Cotta, and finally Ortensius. The direct evidence we possess goes back only to the beginning of the first century B.C. To this period belong the two treatises *Rhetorica ad Herennium*, and *De inventione*. *Rhetorica ad Herennium* for a long time was attributed to Tully (i.e., Cicero himself), but today it is generally considered the work of a different writer who was close to Cicero; *De inventione* is a youthful work of Cicero's (written perhaps in 87 B.C., when he was nineteen), which he will later strongly criticize and trust to his readers' clemency.

Neither work is particularly original, but both show a good grasp of Greek rhetorical texts, of which they provide good summaries and renderings, including translations of Greek terms into Latin. To be sure, their relevance cannot be overestimated because it is through these two texts that in the Middle Ages, for over one thousand years, Western culture could have access to classical rhetoric. In addition, they helped to preserve the image of Tully or Cicero, since the later and more original works that he produced around the middle of the century remained practically unknown or not so widespread.

Among the elements that stand out in *Rhetorica ad Herennium*, we should mention the awareness that rhetoric addresses particularly in the civic and moral fields: "The task of the public speaker is to discuss capably those matters which law and custom have fixed for the uses of citizenship."[1] There is also a good definition of probability: a discourse is probable "if it answers the requirements of the usual, the expected and the natural" (p. 29); and a good distinction between historical subjects and fictional ones, or *fabulae*: this is almost a bridge between rhetoric and poetics. Moreover, the treatise shows that the fusion between Aristotle's system (the qualitative and the quantitative parts of the oration) and that of Hermagoras (the *status causae*, or *constitutiones*) has occurred. The model that I described in Chapter 1 and that I attributed to Hermagoras in substance has come down to us through *Rhetorica ad Herennium* and also *De inventione* (one more proof of the high degree of similarity between these two works).

The most original contribution of *Rhetorica ad Herennium* is a long analysis of memory that becomes one of the five standard parts of rhetoric, and that, as we saw, Aristotle did not include. Of course its origin cannot but be Greek: and in fact our anonymous author reports the anecdote of Simonides of Ceo who, surviving the falling of a roof by the protection of the gods, helps the relatives of the victims to identify corpses by availing himself of visual memory through which he remembers everybody's place at the banquet before the accident. This is an example of a physical space to which one can assign one's ideas: one locates them as if they were in a storeroom where they could be retrieved at the proper moment. The author invites everybody to choose backgrounds he or she likes, as long as they are familiar and sufficiently well structured (like the rooms in an apartment), to be suitable for storing a lot of information. Along with spatial and topical backgrounds that metaphorically correspond to the process of finding logical arguments, images also come to the aid of memory. For example, suppose we are the prosecutors dealing with a poisoning and that there are witnesses to this act. We can visualize all of this in one very strong and dramatic image: the defendant is at the bedside, holding in his right hand a cup, and on the fourth finger he wears ram's testicules instead of a ring. This is a very striking example of a technique that makes use of symbols, condensation, and displacement (the testicules, or "small testes," in place of the witnesses), where the movement is from one genus to a totally different one, and where the only legitimation is provided by linguistic resemblance, something that recalls the dream work. In the same way, playing with synonyms introduces us to the contiguous area of jokes. And in fact such is the nature of some of the devices suggested, perhaps unconsciously, to remember given sentences. For example, "Iam domitionem reges Atridae parant" (And now their homecoming the kings, the sons of Atreus, are making ready): the first noun is divided into smaller parts (this too is a typical technique of jokes), one of which is *domiti*, which can be remembered if it is linked to some Domitius; in the same way *reges Atridae* can be connected with the two actors that usually interpreted the role of Agamemnon and Menelaus in the famous tragedy of the day. This is the basis of artificial memory, which constitutes a body of mnemonic devices, of connections between the physical and the mental, that will be applied for centuries to come, as Francis Yates has taught us in a work that has become a classic, and that draws from secret esoteric correspondences (gnostic, cabalistic, astrological). In fact, here the ram's testicules could already suggest a link with the sign of Aries, and is not the zodiac the best example of a place where one can store a great number of elements?

Somewhat limited in scope are the two books of Cicero's *De inventione*, although he may have intended to follow up with an analysis of other parts of rhetoric. As we observed, the work is very similar to *Rhetorica ad Herennium*, including a good fusion between the Aristotelian and the Hermagorean models. But Cicero's greatness does not reveal itself here, not even when his originality abruptly erupts in the sections where he confutes the distinction between thesis and hypothesis (this was a ground for debate, as I pointed out before). These parts might well have been added later on, when the mature Cicero may have decided to publish a youthful work, and so had to make it more consistent with his later thought.

Cicero and the Primacy of Rhetoric

It is only after a few decades, in 56 B.C., the Cicero displays all his greatness in his *De oratore*. Cicero's stature is such that it is no exaggeration to see his contribution as marking one of the greatest moments for rhetoric. If the Platonic moment is one of negation, and the Aristotelian one of Olympian acceptance and systematization, Cicero's model marks the triumph of rhetoric, which with him is privileged and raised to the rank of art of the arts. Of course Cicero does not reach this position by working out rules and technical improvements within a theoretical frame that would seal off rhetoric. He sketches a view of the world, a global conception of culture, within which rhetoric finds a centralizing and unifying role. This conception is not peculiar of Cicero alone, however, but belongs to the entire *way of life*[2] of the Roman republic, which was oligarchical and senatorial. It can also be seen as a "worldview" founded on the preeminence of praxis over theory. The *negotium*, that is, the constant engagement in the affairs of the *res publica*, imposes itself on *otium* (leisure). Only in the moments reserved for leisure is the Roman citizen allowed the ease to speculate; only then can he dedicate himself to some theoretical activity, such as the contemplation of the stars, or physical and metaphysical mysteries. But his full-time occupation is to measure his strength in the affairs of the state, which means that he will take on various roles and functions, all of which pertain to the practice of politics in the broad sense of the word. During the well-known *cursus honorum* the *civis romanus* will take on at different times military, economic, administrative, judicial, and last of all, political responsibilities. From all of this take shape the characteristics that we find in Cicero's rhetoric: first of all, the impossibility of becoming too specialized, of being an expert in a small field, since the citizen will go through the different tasks without having the time to take root in any of them (thus the necessity of a vast encyclopedic knowledge in each field); and finally the awareness that in each case one will have to deal with ''the great number'' of the people, that one's task will be to persuade them, lead them, carry them away. In a *res publica*, in fact, the ''majority'' has the last word, but this is not seen as a drawback and there is no aristocratic regret for the rights of a small group of wise men, or for a mute and solitary quest for truth as happened with Plato. However, let us keep in mind that the majority here consists of an oligarchy of peers, of individuals invested with the same responsibilities, worries, and privileges, and therefore worthy of great respect.

Consistent with these premises, Cicero traces a magnificent restructuring of rhetoric in relation to the complex system of Aristotle's *Organon*. He does not add anything new, and consequently he has been accused of lacking originality. But he consistently proceeds to take parts away or he moves them around, so that his originality reveals itself in ''trimming''; it is obtained by simplification and by elimination. The first part to disappear from his arrangement is analytics, since truth, especially the scientific truth of physics and mathematics, was not highly esteemed in Roman culture. What will become the quadrivium is not considered suitable to the *civis romanus* but may be reserved to the Greeks, or can be taken up in the marginal moments of *otium*. It is true, though, that at that time science and technology had not reached a significant development; one's best energies could be diverted from theoretical undertakings to be invested in practical activities, above all the sociopolitical machine. Dialectic is highly thought of, but here too Cicero proceeds to a firm restructuring of the Aristotelian model and arrives at overturning it. In the *Organon*, dialectic ranked higher for the reason that the wise men in their chamber were considered superior to the crowd that gathered in the forum; here the exact opposite is true, and rhetoric is privileged because the forum is much more important than the chamber.

So, although no new elements are introduced, there is a rearrangement of the parts. This too, of course, is a way of being original, and to Cicero certainly goes such merit, provided that the issue is formulated properly. Here the incessant controversy with the Stoics finds its origin: not an insignificant matter, but almost the symptom of an allergy, of a mutual incompatibility. The Stoics are too rigid, too dry, too lean in their way of speaking. They lack redundancy and resonance, and cannot reach the ''great number.'' So much so that in *Paradoxa Stoicorum*, a curious little work of 44 B.C. that some consider part of the Ciceronian rhetorical corpus, the author tries, of course tongue in cheek and as an exercise, to give a befitting style to the dry ethical statements of a Chrysippus or a Cleanthes, such as "only the wise man is happy, free, and rich," which were running the risk of not finding an audience.

We must say that on principle Cicero is not against the content of those paradoxes. His criticism of Epicurean amorality is much stronger than that of the Stoics' rigor, which he sometimes appears to appreciate and even makes his own. But here too Cicero's genius and his extraordinary modernity become apparent in his refusal to privilege content and meaning over modes, signifiers, situations, or contexts within which one operates. He rejects any systematic, dogmatic philosophy, outlined *una tantum*; on the contrary, he is for openness and flexibility, for a philosophy that bears the unmistakable touch of rhetoric rather than of analytics or dialectic. All this helps us understand why Cicero supported the New Academy's probability (Philo of Larissa, Carneades) and eclecticism. The contempt that a certain philosophical tradition used to show for eclecticism came from a choice, whether conscious or not, that favored the theoretical over the pragmatic moment. To be sure, Cicero is one of the most fervent and consistent advocates of praxis of all times. One can see it in the *Academica*, where, engaged in controversy with Lucullus, he defends his concept of probability against the charge that it would fall into skepticism, or that it would be affected by a paralyzing insecurity. That one cannot rigorously demonstrate (*adfirmare*) the so-called *probabilia* is not negative in itself, nor does it mean that they cannot be relied on and followed easily (*sequi facile*). Probability is an excellent building material that can be made into the foundations of one's life. What is more, the probable, unlike the true, has an intrinsic historicity or temporal dimension: what is probable and can be "followed" today, may not be so tomorrow, or vice versa, as situations change. This is admirably expressed in the *Tusculan Disputations*: "in diem vivimus; quodcumque nostros animos probabilitate percussit, id dicimus" (I live from day to day; I say anything that strikes my mind as probable).[3]

As one can see, originality is not lacking in Cicero's thought, even if, as remarked, it is an originality that "trims" and removes; it does not put forward new principles but tones down those of others, and above all it applies them to different practical areas. In any case, one understands how Cicero has been in ages past and for a long time one of the most important writers in Western culture—certainly not inferior to Plato and Aristotle, and often in competition with them.

This general background was necessary to introduce properly the most important rhetorical work of Cicero: the dialogue *De oratore* (The making of an orator). It was written in about 56 B.C., but it is set a few decades earlier in the villa of Tusculum. The participants are Licinius Crassus and M. Antonius: the two most preeminent figures in the forum, in whom Cicero saw some basic traits that he would later inherit and incorporate in himself. There are other participants, among them Q. Mucius Scaevola the Augur and Julius Caesar Strabo Vopiscus. The dialogue has nothing fictional about it but unfolds in the climate of a real debate, in which the for and against of each thesis are examined. The major theme is a rejection of specialization and technicality: rhetoric must be brought back to the complex and rich model I described earlier; rhetoric is the fundamental art that accompanies the Roman citizen in every step of the *cursus honorum*. Consequently, it cannot be considered a mere art of forms, words, signifiers. Words must constantly be conjugated with things, in a strict relationship. This is the thesis the author himself puts forward in the introduction and that Crassus supports in the course of the dialogue (especially in Books I and III). Wisdom must be full and comprehensive and the fullness of content must go together with the intensity of forms. This was well known to the pre-Socratics and also to the great legislators and statesmen of the past, such as Lycurgus, Themistocles, and Pericles. Clearly Cicero insists that theory and practice go side by side; actually they should be fused. Unfortunately Socrates and Plato are responsible for the big gap between *res* and *verba*, since they singled out the latter as an object of contempt for the wise. Ever since then *sapere* and *dicere* have been separated. Also, here finds its origin an unfortunate hierarchy based on the assumption that philosophy and dialectic are superior to rhetoric. Unfortunately the separation has been favored by rhetoricians, who willingly gave up to their competitors the parts related to content (knowledge and science), and the logical-formal parts (*inventio* and *dispositio*), being satisfied to keep for themselves only *elocutio, ornamentum*. The blame for this situation falls on *Graeculi* deprived of practical tasks, of the responsibilities that come with the management of the republic: they have been forced to cultivate a mere formalistic art, cut off from the heat of debates and the rough clashes with opponents, judges, witnesses, and so on, in such a way that their rhetoric has been diverted from the major track only to become the ground for an easy training, for fictitious exercises fit for young students. To overcome this formalistic hollowing, and the consequent pedantry of petty rules, rhetoric must be brought back to the old levels of knowledge. First of all rhetoricians must keep in mind that their duty is to master the contents, the material data of the different types of issues they happen to debate. Thus it is necessary to recover the particular topics, the disciplinary foundations that already Aristotle saw as useful: in fact, in his *Rhetoric* he produced in condensed form treatises on ethics, psychology, and jurisprudence. In short, philosophy must be rhetoric's closest ally, so that one may be able to restore the unity that was broken by Plato and the Stoics.

Immediately after Crassus it is Antonius's turn to speak, and his views will be the exact opposite. The task outlined by Crassus of rejoining eloquence with wisdom, of requiring orators to master the principles of almost all the human sciences, is too heavy. Who will ever have the time to acquire such a vast range of knowledge? And prior to that, who will have the strength to carry it out?

Crassus (that is, Cicero) cannot take himself as an example because only a few individuals would be able to follow him on such a difficult road. Also, the fact that in one person there are different virtues and qualities does not necessarily mean that they will be unified. One must be able to pursue different disciplines and arts while keeping separate the specificity of their features. Rhetoric requires first of all a command of language and eloquence. All the rest pertains to specialists: from them the orator will borrow the elements that are beyond his general culture and that it would be both useless and impossible to acquire. Clearly the notion of rhetoric here advocated by Antonius is quite narrow, even if it is certainly close to and in agreement with the one that many have today. Crassus, disappointed, somewhat ironically remarks that according to such a flat view the rhetorician becomes an *operarium*, that is, a mechanic, a vile practitioner and menial laborer of words.

But Book II opens with a surprise: Antonius withdraws the thesis he had supported the previous day, under the ostensible pretext that he was jealous of the success Crassus enjoyed among their young interlocutors and that he had tried to win them over to his side. In reality, it is in the logic of *De oratore*, which is an excellent example of rhetoric in act, to develop thoroughly also the theses of one's adversary (in the same way as Plato had skillfully expounded the point of view of the Sophists in *Gorgias* and *Protagoras*). Having returned to Cicero's perspective, Antonius's task is to deal with the first two parts of rhetoric: *inventio* and *dispositio*. He does it properly, with an expertise that comes from experience, but also shows at every step a great contempt for rules, for "art," and he makes the point that nature and the orator's *ingenium* and *diligentia* (i.e., attention to the cause and its context) always "pay off" against a cold application of rules from a manual. The great Roman politician, from the vantage point of his experience, wants to show that he is not a slave to the mechanical and dogmatic precepts of the "Greeklings."

For example, dealing with the quantitative parts (introduction, narration, confutation, etc.), it is useless to formulate strict rules for each of them; to establish where one has to linger or on the contrary where one should go fast; where one should move the audience (*movere*), or teach (*docere*) or please (*delectare*) it. The parts of an oration are all equally demanding. The good orator must always work as hard as he can, and his aim must be a synergic *docere-movere-delectare*, in a complex knot that cannot be undone or cut. Shame to the orator who does not feel intimidated at the moment of the introduction, since this means that he has fallen into dull routine. To step onto the tribune should be like starting over again each time, to experience once again the emotions one felt as a beginner.

In this way, always in a disdainful tone and almost *en passant*, Antonius pours out the usual rhetorical manual, but each time adding sharp personalized observations, for example, on the *status causae*, general topics (analogy, difference, opposites, correlatives, discordant terms, more and less, parity), on the importance of the orator's personality, and on his morality (the notion of *vir bonus*).

Antonius ends his intervention by dealing rapidly with *dispositio* and artificial memory, but before he is finished there is a long digression where Caesar Vopiscus discusses wit (*iocus, facetiae, cavillatio, dicacitas*). Once again we must emphasize that, ever since Aristotle, a treatise on rhetoric will inevitably contain a section dedicated to wit and humor: there will be attempts to provide a general definition of this varied and unpredictable phenomenon. Cicero tells us through his spokesman that the comical is provoked when perceiving something unseemly or ugly (*turpitudo et deformitas*). But these qualities should not arouse strong disgust or deep sympathy in the audience; one must restrain oneself and attack one's opponent without offending the audience or the judges, who will determine the result of the debate. As to the techniques of wit, as in Aristotle a significant role is reserved for plays on words, that is, slight variations of letters, that allow a connection between different meanings, one of which, evoked surreptitiously, is enough to hit an unseemly or ugly aspect of one's adversary. This occurs, for example, with a certain Clodius who was lame, and of whom one could say that he wobbled.[4] Another man nicknamed "the Noble" was referred to as "the Mobile." These examples contain another feature of the comical: it must come unexpectedly and must take us by surprise, as long as the surprise sounds spontaneous enough: "art" must not expose itself too openly. Beside cases of *dicacitas* depending on plays on words (paronomasia), there are cases of double entendre, ambivalence of meaning, and finally more complex ones involving the whole turn of a phrase: these are the three general ways of producing figures of speech.

In Book III it is again Crassus who speaks. He should deal with *elocutio* and *actio*, but he reaffirms his rejection of the dangerous separation between words and things. One cannot treat embellishments by separating them from the content. Actually, that grand view of philosophy, dramatically divided between those who unify in one network signifiers and signifieds, and those who split them, finds here its most justified treatment, together with a condemnation of the *homines leviter eruditi*. Today we would call it *midcult*, referring to the crowd of those who break up the unity of knowledge into schemes and forms of convenience to make its understanding easier.

After stressing his point of view, Crassus, in the same way as Antonius, goes on to expound the canonical parts of rhetoric. As Aristotle had done, he distinguishes between proper words, terms used metaphorically (tropes), new coinages (*novatae*), or archaisms (*inusitatae*). Of course it is tropes (*verba tralata*) that are analyzed extensively. First it is the turn of metaphor, which is presented in terms not that different from Aristotle's: "It is a mark of cleverness of a kind to jump over things that are obvious and choose other things that are farfetched."[5] Then the focus is on another primary figure, not treated by Aristotle: metonymy, the use of a specific term (even a proper name) instead of the general one. For example, Mars in the place of war; Bacchus for wine; Ceres for harvests; toga for peace. Other tropes analyzed include synecdoche (to indicate the whole by naming one part); allegory; litotes and its opposite, hyperbole; and rhetorical questions. All these are figures of speech since they involve meaning. There are also figures of thought (schemata), which consist of interventions on the syntagm, on the arrangement of words in the phrase, or of phrases within the sentence: among them are repetition, ascending gradation, starting and ending a clause with the same word, the scale, antithesis, asyndeton. There follows an exposition on the three styles (*sublime, temperatum, humile*) that in fact is connected with the general premises on *elocutio* reported earlier: its requirements are clearness and correctness, which are the distinctive features in relation to poetry; elegance is also necessary to please one's audience. It is exactly here that a space is opened up to metaphors, tropes, and the various pleasant violations to the degree zero of a purely informational communication.

Delivery (*actio*) is the last element analyzed. It consists in the orator's voice and gestures—aspects that intervene to complete his global role. On this totalizing role Antonius had expressed himself very well by stating that what one demands of an orator is "the subtlety of the logician, the thoughts of the philosopher, a diction almost poetic, a lawyer's memory, a tragedian's voice, and the bearing almost of the consummate actor."[6]

Among Cicero's works *De oratore* remains unequaled for the greatness of its theoretical and expository execution. None of his other works rivals its breadth, unity, and thoroughness. Moreover, the work stands alone chronologically, since at that time no other text of rhetoric was produced. Only about ten years later circumstances led Cicero to write other texts, of various sizes and depths, but the general frame of his vision will not change. Details are added, often of a technical nature, while issues that were essential to the economy of *De oratore* are not mentioned or are overshadowed. The only substantial novelty is that the preeminence of rhetoric no longer goes unchallenged as before. But a new generation is arising, influenced by the Atticist school, as against Asianism, or the Rhodian intermediacy of which Cicero was a representative. M. Junius Brutus is the most outstanding representative of the Atticists, who were followers of Lysias and Hyperides and preferred asyndeton and short sentences. Intellectually Cicero felt very close to Brutus, to the point that he dedicated some of his minor treatises to him. Perhaps by means of the *captatio benevolentiae* he was trying to gain the consideration of the younger people who were pressing on him. In fact, *Brutus* is the title of a dialogue of 46 B.C. in which the third interlocutor is Atticus, whose *Liber annalis* had suggested the idea for the work. *Brutus* is a chronological history of Latin rhetoric that follows the course of different generations. To Brutus is dedicated also *Paradoxa Stoicorum*, an exercise typical in its kind in which dialectic is rendered in a rhetorical key. To the same prolific year belongs also the

Orator, a work that gives special attention to rhythm and sound in rhetorical prose. *Partitiones oratoriae*, perhaps written the following year, is a manual, an epitome for the use of his son Marcus who was to leave for Athens to study philosophy. *Topica* was written from memory during a voyage from Velia to Rhegium in 44 B.C.; it had been requested by the judge Trebatius, who had found Aristotle's *Topica* in Cicero's library. This work too is an attempt to render in a rhetorical key (i.e., in a form accessible to nonspecialists) a difficult technical prose conceived in the "rigorous" style of dialectic. Finally we should mention the short and perhaps unfinished *De optimo genere oratorum*.

Dialogus de oratoribus

After Cicero the times change rapidly, at least for a few decades. Contemporaries feel that a rupture with the immediate past has occurred. This is so deep that oratory is evoked only as an art that inevitably belongs to the past; it is perceived as becoming ever more removed and distant from the actual living conditions of Roman citizens. To this dramatic change bears witness the work *Dialogus de oratoribus*, which is portrayed as having taken place in 75 A.D., but in fact may have been written a few years later. Today the work is attributed to the young Tacitus: the great historian would have been about thirty at the time, which would explain the discrepancy in style with respect to his mature works. The text has also been attributed to Quintilian, and in fact he may have been one of the interlocutors: Messalla, for example, whose role is that of praising the oratory of the "ancients," in particular of Cicero, and of analyzing the causes of the present decadence. That rhetoric is in a state of decline is also the author's point of view, and it will be Quintilian's too, not too far down the road. The other two points of view in the dialogue also are very interesting and clearly reflect the attitude that was taking shape at that time. Their two spokesmen are J. Secundus Curatio and M. Aper Maternus. The former, who completely aligns himself with Messalla, concludes with a praise of poetry: since eloquence is in a state of decay, it is better to choose solitude and spiritual meditation. Consequently the woods are exalted above the forum, which was the symbol of civic involvement and public life. This too is a sign of the times: only a century before, in Cicero's age, it would have been unthinkable for a Roman citizen to exalt leisure (*otium*) and theoretical activity in this way.

The dialogue becomes a sort of *querelle des anciens et des modernes*, where Maternus, in turn pleasantly provocative and charming, takes the role of uncompromising advocate of the "moderns." He starts out by questioning the limits of notions like "ancient" and "modern" and remarks that after all Cicero was born but yesterday: someone may still be alive who, when young, may have been so lucky as to have listened in person to the orators of the Augustan age. Therefore the notion of "modernity" is somewhat broader than its detractors would wish.

But even if one limits modernity to a short period of time, the fact remains that the modern public is shrewd and demanding and could not bear the long speeches of the old orators; it especially could not tolerate the "Asian" pomposity of Cicero, for example, that mania of his to decorate each sentence with the tag *esse videatur* (Chapter 23, p. 75). In short, Maternus fully espouses the line of the Atticists, who had already made difficult the last years of Cicero's career and had compelled him to be on the defensive. The bottom line in support of the Atticists is that the pace of the times is quicker and people are not going to listen for long, so that speakers, orators, lawyers, and others must hurry to their conclusions.

Messalla sees as totally negative the change of taste that Maternus tries to analyze from a positive side, or at least with indulgence. Messalla is a consistent *laudator temporis acti* and has sharply perceived the great historical change, that we, with the wisdom of hindsight, know well: it is the passage from the republic to the principate, from the rule of many to the rule of one, which has brought to an end the permanent state of conflict in public life. Rhetoric is no longer the tool indispensable for success, but has become an ornament that is applied on paper to gain a useless and sterile literary fame. The youth, given up to leisure, neglected by their parents, removed from the affairs of the state, are trained by means of fictitious causes and kept away from the real battles.

But Maternus does not give in and insists on his view: the modern condition has its advantages, including practical ones. He agrees that there no longer is a liking for taking risks and challenging others; consequently public life no longer offers the glory of overpowering one's adversaries. But was that freedom, or was it not rather license, which could easily degenerate into quarrelsomeness? One has to choose between "living dangerously," with the possibility of acquiring fame for oneself, or on the contrary, the humble but secure compensation of living in peace, a peace made possible by the rule of one who imposes silence on many, but takes upon himself the responsibility of resolving conflicts. Since modern times offer peace, one should accept this state of affairs and be content, with no regret for the past.

Quintilian's *Institutio oratoria*

The most persuasive and well-grounded answer to Maternus's defense of the "modern" point of view is developed not by Messalla but by Quintilian (c. 35 A.D.– c. 100) in *Institutio oratoria* (The training of an orator). The work stands as a good document of the changed circumstances under which rhetoric could be practiced, and consequently of a nostalgic attitude toward the past. Unlike Cicero, Quintilian is first of all a teacher of rhetoric, a theoretician and a historian of this "art," rather than an orator or a politician who may use it in his own right as a tool to support a cause. Also, Quintilian's intervention does not come unsolicited: he is an intellectual hired by his prince, who has conferred on him the

official task of drafting his *magnum opus*. Praising the past acquires a rather hypo-
critical tone when it is the prince himself who requests the reaffirmation of the
old republican values: evidently it is an attempt to separate the restauration of a
certain type of morality from actual political conditions that had disappeared, but
that nevertheless had been at its origin. For all these reasons, and for being a
planned undertaking, executed on paper, *Institutio oratoria* is unequaled in its
systematicity and breadth. It consists of twelve books that examine in detail
every aspect of rhetoric. It attempts to offer a historical and critical compendium
of all the theses expressed on the subject: it is an encyclopedia, rather than a treatise, since it endeavors to reconcile and include every point of view. It is an enormous retrospective work, and a painstaking and tireless collection of material.

Of course a massive enterprise like *Institutio oratoria* renounces the formulation of an original theory of its own. This could be in line with Cicero's critique
of dogmatism and his support of probability. But Cicero's position, in favor of
"opening up" and of the right to change one's mind, is in itself sustained in a
courageous, original, and very personal way (we saw earlier that his creativity is
best expressed in "trimming," in taking away). Although Quintilian's position is
weak, it displays the necessary methodological caution of a compiler, who is
eager to put in his collection every party and every opinion, and who is willing to
give judgment only in the name of good sense and a happy mean. On the other
hand, the breadth of *Institutio oratoria* is really extraordinary: nothing is left out
that may be useful for the training of the orator, including the very first stages.
For example, the issue addressed in the first book and in part of the second is the
education of the young child, and the subjects dealt with are genuinely pedagogical: Is private education better than public education? How should one go about
choosing the teacher? What reading material and what exercises should be supplied? The analysis is detailed and offers rich psychological insight. A pathetic
note is the dedication to the son Marcus Vitore, the first of the young students,
whose premature death leaves the father bereft when the work is but half
completed.[7]

In Book II, after the pedagogical part, Quintilian tackles the more demanding
problem of a definition of rhetoric. Here the work to some extent reveals its lack
of strength, and also tends to favor a formalist point of view. But actually, Quintilian for his part declares a preference for content: he supports the view that an
orator must have wide-ranging knowledge of all subjects and arts. Thus he shows
himself to be a follower of Cicero and a supporter of the "heroic" Roman line,
for which in any case he has been hired by his prince. And yet, the definition he
chooses after a long examination comes from the Stoic Cleanthes and sounds
somewhat unsatisfactory because too general: rhetoric is the "science of speaking well."[8] This definition does not show the conflicts that rhetoric has been carrying along, for example, the relationship between theory and practice, or between words and things, that anyway is amply analyzed in *Institutio*. In fact, the

text seems to give preeminence to the former (theory and words). Another occasion revealing a certain theoretical shortsightedness emerges right in the middle of a statement Quintilian is compelled to make because of his edifying effort. It concerns the praise of the orator's virtuous character if he wants to be worthy of the name. But how does it come about that even a good orator may sometimes support the false? The most subtle and rigorous answer, which Protagoras had already given, is that rhetoric finds its space exactly where true and false cannot be clearly separated, where there is only probability in one direction or the other, so that each debater can try to steer the argument toward his side, provided good faith and intention are maintained, thus avoiding the trap of sophistry in the vulgar and pejorative sense of the term. On the contrary, Quintilian makes a sophistic blunder without realizing it. He maintains that the good orator, when he happens to substitute falsehood for the truth, is fully aware of it and knows the difference very well. This safeguards rhetoric as theoretical activity as well as the orator's ability to speculate, but it inevitably condemns the orator's virtue and morality, which after all are the qualities Quintilian should feel obliged to defend before anything else.

Apart from these subtleties, which however reveal a quantitative talent rather than a qualitative one, the fact remains that *Institutio oratoria* deals with everything, and in a more extensive way than any other treatise past and future. To give a close account of the work is therefore impossible, and we will have to limit ourselves to a very short overview. Book III deals with Hermagoras's distinction between thesis and hypothesis, and with *status causae* and their complex classification. Book IV analyzes quantitative parts: the exordium, the statement of facts (*narratio*), possible digressions, "propositions," that is, parts recapitulating arguments, which have also been called *confirmatio* and *confutatio*. Here too Quintilian provides a mine of important observations, backed up by flexibility and solid good sense. He shows mastery of his subject, in such a way that he can sum up and compare material from different historical schools. Book V tackles the well-known distinction, already made by Aristotle, between proofs that lie outside the art of speaking, and those that are deduced by the case at hand. Among the latter, Quintilian carefully explores enthymemes, examples, similes, proverbs, sayings. Book VI begins with the announcement of his young son's death,but it soon gets on its way. It also provides an extensive analysis of wit and the comical, offering such a rich classification as never before had been offered in a treatise. It includes *urbanitas; salsum*, that is, that which has the salt of wit; *facetum*, a graceful and polished remark; *iocum*, or playful remark; *dicacitas*, or witticism. Book VII deals with *dispositio*, or arrangement. Book VIII conducts a very energetic examination of stylistic ornament. On this subject it is worth taking up a distinction we have already seen, but one that only Quintilian analyzes to the last detail, to the point that he ends by creating an overwhelming proliferation of possibilities. What happens here and elsewhere is that under the eagerness of an extremely analytic inquiry, every definition, every part, every term undergoes such a multiplication that it is difficult not to feel lost. Then Quintilian has to keep things open, to be conciliatory and avoid rigid distinctions. The point we are interested in is the difference between tropes and figures. A trope is a change, the substitution of one meaning for another. Therefore, it is not strictly tied to signifiers, and could resist being translated from one language to another. A figure, in contrast, is defined *novata forma dicendi*, that is, an "expression to which a new aspect is given by art":[9] it intervenes in the construction of a phrase or a statement by making it "new" and unusual. Figures can be divided into figures of speech and figures of thought. Typical examples of the former are rhetorical questions, irony, hesitation (when one doubts or belittles in order to mean the opposite). Figures of thought play on the position of words, and thus are of a more formal nature. Examples include repetition, *climax*, asyndeton, polysyndeton. But while making all these classifications, Quintilian himself admits that the borders between them are often ambiguous and uncertain.

Book XI deserves special mention because it undertakes a rich description of everything dealing with *pronuntiatio*. It is a treatise on behavioral psychology, proxemics, kinesics, staging devices for the orator. Quintilian's analytic diligence considers every aspect of the body to suggest the attitude it must adopt to obtain the best results from the speech. He does not forget anything: face, hands, brows, hair, even dress. As usual the basic rule is to maintain a good balance without crossing the limits befitting the Roman citizen's nobleness. Book XII is a final roundup and reconsideration of the most important themes dealt with, and in this book a Ciceronian approach is clearly adopted. This is evident in the recommendation to maintain a good relationship between rhetoric and philosophy, knowledge in general and culture in its totality. Caution is expressed with regard to dialectic, in whose subtleties the orator should not indulge, if he does not want to end up like certain animals that, nimble in a a confined space, are easily captured in an open field. Perhaps Quintilian assumes a certain distance from Cicero when he examines the orators of the past and declares that he prefers the Atticist school. Thus he accepts the critique of the "moderns" about the excessive pomposity of Cicero's rhetoric. But immediately afterward his conciliatory side intervenes, and he goes on to say that it is not easy to define the Atticist style in any one simple way. In such an enormous survey as this, an analysis of the three styles could not be missing. They are tied to the three goals of rhetoric: *genus subtile* is suitable for *docere; medium* for *delectare; robustum* for *movere*.

Chapter 3
The Middle Ages

The Church Fathers and Saint Augustine

In the light of the rhetorical models I have presented, the advent of Christianity is characterized by a revival of Platonism. In fact, it will be a super-Platonism: the foundation of truth, so strong as to drive away the shadows of appearances, and the superior convergence of motifs from knowledge and ethics, which Plato tried to ensure with mere human energies, now return with a quite different endorsement, namely, the support of the revelation. The revelation as a material, concrete historical event comes to the aid of reason and brings to it the foundation of an unquestionable authoritative principle. Actually, the relationship is overturned: the works of Socrates and Plato now seem a faint echo of the teaching contained in the Scriptures. A myth takes shape, to which Saint Augustine also will refer, of a voyage to Egypt that Plato may have undertaken to obtain that divine wisdom without which Greek philosophy by itself could not have developed. The Greeks are not to be rejected, but one has to realize their limits. The same applies to the great Roman authors. For example, Cicero and Seneca are of great value when they exhort their audience to endure pain sternly and not to fear death; but the mere probabilistic foundation of their thought deprives them of the power to persuade and carry away, which only the revelation will have.

The thrust of truth in the Scriptures is so powerful that it will have no use for what it considers the technicalities of rhetoric. The church fathers, who represent the first stage of Christian thought, substantially agree with and anticipate Pascal's maxim "La vraie éloquence se moque de l'éloquence." Also, this stage shows an unconscious resumption of the sublime of Pseudo-Longinus, perhaps as a result of a mutual adherence to a model that remains basically Platonic. On the other hand, it must be underlined that the writings of the church fathers belong almost entirely to the judiciary genre, which is a typically rhetorical field, since the first task of the fathers is to lay out a defense of Christianity against the vile accusations made by paganism. Christian literature has never been so eloquent and has never so well applied the rules of rhetoric (if not those of the classical period, at least those of the postclassical one: from the Atticist school to Seneca) as in the apologetics of the fathers. It does not matter that one of their recurring themes is contempt for rhetorical rules and for the privileges offered by an elitist literary education, to which are opposed the merits of a pure and simple soul. On the contrary, after the advent of Scholasticism, when more respect is paid to the precepts of the *artes*, the rhetorical and literary value of Christian literature will suddenly drop because of its clumsy textbook style, which we can call "scholastic" in the pejorative sense of the word.

Tertullian (born c. 160 A.D. — the date of his death is unknown) composed the *Apologeticum* toward the end of the second century. This work is the most thorough and vigorous example of a "judiciary" type of intervention made to defend the Christian religion from absurd charges, such as infanticide, incest, and blood served at banquets. Of course, these were distortions, rumors produced by misinterpretations of the dogmas of the new faith. The text uses all the best devices the defending counsel must follow for the construction of a harangue. It even includes a counterattack in which it is demonstrated that the irrationality and barbarism of which Christians are accused are in fact in the *leges iniquae, stultae*[1] (unjust, silly laws) on which paganism is founded. Actually, the best philosophers have already started to move away from these religious beliefs, rites, and myths, in the attempt to achieve unity and to rationalize the field. But why aren't philosophers persecuted too if for centuries they have said the same things as the Christians? The face is that philosophers speak without much conviction; they suspend judgment; they reconcile an external respect for the old beliefs with an internal, purely theoretical adherence to more rational principles. Thus Tertullian underlines the uncertainty and insufficiency of Greek and Roman philosophical traditions at their best, even if their teaching is not to be totally rejected since it has some elements in common with the Christian faith.

Similar themes return also in the dialogue *Octavianus* by Minucius Felix, which appears to have been written after the *Apologeticum*. From the latter, as well as from many other well-known Latin works, the *Octavianus* takes up and quotes many passages — further proof that at the beginning the church fathers were imbued with classical literature and good rhetoric. Perhaps because of such deep influence, the suspicion against *eloquentiae tumor* (frothy eloquence)[2] becomes very strong and to it is opposed *rerum ipsarum soliditas* (actual solid facts) (ibid.). Minucius Felix even admits being disturbed by the fact that sometimes the clearest *veritas* may be invalidated by the strength of eloquence, and that unfortunately in eloquence can lie *mendacium*, falseness (*Octavius*, 14.4, pp. 350–51), whereas truth may present itself in incredible garments. Blessed are the pure in spirit because they conform to revealed truth, instead of trusting the seductions of probability and the tricks of eloquence.

In short, we are in the orbit of the *credo quia absurdum*, of the scandal of reason attributed to Tertullian, although he did not literally say so. All this goes without having to stress the incompatibility between the absurdity of revealed truth and the road the best human beings have covered by themselves. In fact, Minucius Felix, just like Tertullian, reviews the pre-Christian poets and philosophers, even though they are considered pale announcers, like so many John the Baptists, of revealed truth. The relationship between faith and reason (between truth and verisimilitude) will find a balance at the beginning of the fourth century with Lactantius, whose aim is a conjunction and mutual conversion between religion and knowledge (*Divinae institutiones* I, 1).

All these themes converge and are more powerfully developed in the writings of Saint Augustine (354 – 430). It is worth spending some time on one of his early works, which he composed toward the end of the fourth century near Milan, where he had retired to rest and meditate with a few close friends immediately after his conversion (and after leaving the teaching of rhetoric). I am referring to *Libri tres in Academicos*. Here Augustine has to perform a rather delicate theoretical task: he must confute skepticism once and for all, thus aligning himself with Minucius Felix and the other fathers. However, while doing this he cannot forget that the probability of the New Academy had been the philosophy of Cicero, ''his'' favorite writer, whose dialogue *Hortensius*, as he himself declared, had put him on the right track. Also, isn't Plato at the origin of the Academy, and don't the fathers see in Platonism the moment of utmost closeness between ancient philosophy and Christianty? Nevertheless, adherence to truth, the belief of being illuminated by it, and the hope of attaining it, are values a Christian cannot exchange for the good conscience of the thinkers who believe they have done their best while obtaining assertions that are at least probable. Was Carneades correct in his belief that it is impossible to construct sentences untouched by doubt? Augustine's answer is developed in Chapter XI of Book III, and it is one of the most beautiful and moving defenses of evidence that has ever been written. It bears a strong resemblance to Descartes's *cogito*, and even to Husserl's phenomenology. A wide range of different types of evidence is examined: from the rational and mathematical, (e.g., three times three is nine) to consciousness and psychological experience, to phenomenology and perception: ''I know not how the oleaster leaves may be for flocks and herds; but to me, they are bitter.''[3] Thus certainties do exist, even though they have different degrees. Moreover, it is impossible to undermine them under the suspicion that what appears to us would be only a dream, and not an actual encounter with reality. At least this would become an argument of empty words because one would call "dream" what is usually called "world," without undermining the evidence of phenomena, of what gives itself to an individual here and now. But while logical, rational evidence requires the agreement of all, phenomenological factual evidence may clash against the evidence that others experience. As the Sophists had well understood, it is exactly here that the space for rhetorical debate is opened up. There is no univocal phenomenological truth; there are only degrees and countless variations, which allow everybody to try make "better" and stronger their points of view.

On the other hand, the spiritual affinity with Cicero is confirmed in the rejection of Stoicism. It is better to espouse academic probability than the Stoics' materialistic, physical certainty. But Augustine has a suprise in store at the end of the dialogue: an interpretation in an allegorical key that allows a reconciliation between the Old and the New Academy, between Plato and Cicero. The great orator had established a hierarchy between truth, located in the space beyond the heavens, and worldly probability. His followers, foreseeing that the former would soon be untenable because of the decadence imposed by the materialistic views of the Stoics and other sects, decided to maintain at least the latter, so as not to surrender to the negativity of materialism, a decision that at least had the advantage of keeping open the possibility of recovering Platonic thought in all its strength and originality.

Augustine deals with the rhetoric particularly in Book II of *De doctrina Christiana*. Just like Minucius Felix, he is aware of the risks naked truth may run into when confronted by a likely falsehood. One may use rhetorical devices for false or true arguments, so the faculty in itself cannot be blamed. It is a neutral tool, as Aristotle had observed. But even granted all this, it does not follow that Augustine will find it necessary to provide an analysis of detailed and trite precepts. It is one more sign that he follows Cicero: with him he shares the belief that nature comes before art. It is easier to understand things intuitively, rather than to understand "the intricate and thorny discipline of such rules."[4] On top of it all, the teachers of rhetoric make the mistake of weakening the unity of thought by breaking it down into various parts: "It is just as if a man wishing to give rules for walking should warn you not to lift the hinder foot before you set down the front one. . . . For what he says is true, and one cannot walk in any other way; but men find it easier to walk by executing these movements than to attend to them while they are going through them (ibid., p. 654). Consistent with this "intuitive" or natural line, which marks the triumph of common sense, Augustine remarks that even tropes, which are a typical part of rhetoric, are employed intuitively, in everyday speech, without the need of liberal arts or grammar. In fact, everybody employs the formula *sic floreas* (So may you flourish), which is a metaphor. And everybody applies the term "fish pond" even to places where there are no fish, which is a catachresis.[5]

It does not take long before Augustine moves from a praise of natural *ingenium*, unaltered by art, to a celebration of the Holy Scripture, the locus where truth and divine nature spoke directly. It is here, in reading Scripture, that a good Christian will find the rules for eloquence: an eloquence that, as usual, *se moque de l'éloquence*. Certainly it does not follow the laws of Greeklings, but on the contrary it establishes its own laws. Wicked are the people who, bedazzled by the *rotunditas* of pagan rhetoric and the pleasure it offers, disparage the hidden internal eloquence of the Holy Scripture, where form and content perfectly match, without either of the two prevailing over the other. Although Augustine is not aware of it, we can see how close he is to the author of the *Sublime*, and of course the same idea had already been expressed by the first church fathers. "O eloquentia tanto terribilior, quanto purior, et quanto solidior, tanto vehementior!" (O eloquence, which is the more terrible from its purity, and the more crushing from its solidity!)[6] On the other hand, Augustine likes to make comparisons and subtle textual analyses. The tropes suitable to the Scriptures will be those that stress the parallelism between literal material meaning and spiritual meaning (like allegory, enigma, parable). The figures to be used should include dry and striking connecting devices, for example, asyndeton and climax—Longinus would say those figures that do not stop the flow of the emotions, but on the contrary help to convey it directly. Even *numerus* is not to be discarded, and if it so happens that it is not used in the Scriptures, the reason is that we read them in translation. Of course the *pondus*, that is, the weight of an argument, must prevail over any slack in the form of the expression caused by a search for words. In the same way, of the three traditional aims of rhetoric, the most important is *docere*, teaching. And of the three styles the most suitable is the "grand," because *violentum animi affectibus*: it is sublime, it stirs the hearer with vehemence. But the other styles also are appropriate. Augustine produces a sort of history of the church fathers when he examines some of their texts. For example, he defines the style of Cyprian and Ambrose as moderate, "temperate," but this is not the style that best suits him because of the *vehementia* he wants to convey.

Boethius and Scholasticism

Only about a century separates Boethius (480–524) from Saint Augustine, but the difference between them could not be greater. As much as Augustine was original and complex, so is Boethius a superficial imitator: quantity rather than quality is what characterizes his works, which may properly be called Scholastic. Augustine makes choices, stands up for his beliefs, has likes and dislikes, whereas in Boethius we see the beginning of an eclecticism that finds a place for all the great authors of antiquity, from Plato and Aristotle down to Cicero, but after depriving them of their most original thoughts, so that a reconciliation becomes possible. It is interesting to observe which works of Cicero Boethius analyzes:

certainly not *Hortensius* or other philosophical texts in which Cicero investigates fundamental ethical questions and comes to his tormented, uneasy probability. With regard to rhetoric, the choice does not fall on *De oratore*, a text in which rhetoric comes to center stage. Boethius selects minor and more technical works, such as the *Topica* (*In topica Ciceronis commentaria*), where it is more difficult to find Cicero's originality in relation to Aristotle. We already noted that the other Ciceronian treatise well known to the Middle Ages, together with *Rhetorica ad Herennium*, is the manualistic, inventory-like *De inventione*. Thus the image that takes shape and circulates is that of a Tully, teacher of rules and precepts, quite different from the Cicero, master of meditation and soul-searching that was dear to Augustine. In fact, a reevaluation of technical aspects and rules is the distinctive feature that may be ascribed to Boethius, so much so that in all the treatises and epitomes in which he describes classical thought, the Christian faith and doctrine are never mentioned once. The separation between *scientia* and *fides*, between particular disciplinary interests and religion, would not have been conceivable to Augustine or any of the church fathers. Such a blatant exclusion led some scholars to doubt the veracity of Boethius's conversion and to deny the authenticity of some of his writings on dogmas, or to believe that the conversion had served to break up his career. Today the authenticity of these works is no longer in doubt. At most the contradiction is further proof of the Scholastic separation between the technical scientific moment, in which knowledge is acquired and imparted, and the moment that addresses religious and moral issues, which in turn can be channeled into particular specialized fields.

The only occasion in which Boethius shows complexity and depth is in the well-known *De consolatione philosophiae*. The work also marks one of the most significant stages in the fortune that allegory enjoyed during the Middle Ages: it had already met with the approval of Augustine, who had observed how this trope was often used in the Scriptures. Philosophy in the guise of a woman (another rhetorical trope: prosopopoeia, the personification of an idea) talks to the author about the transience of riches and fortune. Also very important is the alternation between parts in prose and in verse, which Dante will take as a model for his *Convivio*.

It is still the prevalent spirit of specialization that leads Boethius to establish the classification, already present in the works of antiquity, between the formal discursive disciplines, or arts, and the disciplines of content, or sciences—in other words, the trivium and the quadrivium. A powerful encyclopedic thrust brings him to produce epitomes for each of these fields. To illustrate disciplines of content he writes *De arithmetica*, *De musica*, and *Euclidis geometrica*. Astronomy is the only part missing to attain a complete delineation of the quadrivium. Much broader and more thorough is the attention given to the discursive arts, where Boethius's eminently logical approach is manifest. For example, there is no study of grammar, and rhetoric does not fare too well either. Dialectic is far from occupying the whole field of logic but remains tied to the scope and definition Aristotle assigned to it. In essence, Boethius is a faithful epitomizer of the *Organon*. He knows it well and produces commentaries on each of its parts: on the *Prior* and *Posterior Analytics*, on the *Topica*, although for each of them he considers only some books; to these must be added the commentary on *Peri ermeneias* and writings of authors with a subsidiary function (among whom is Cicero's *Topica*). On the whole this corpus constitutes what will be called *Logica vetus*, and for a few centuries it will be the basis of scholastic logic. In any case, also the *Logica nova* will be but a broadening of the previous one, after the rediscovery and the translation of other books belonging to Aristotle's *Analytics* and *Topica*. But the spirit of Scholasticism, deeply informed by a logical thrust and removed from Platonic and Ciceronian humanism, is already entirely manifested in this first encyclopedic endeavor of Boethius's.

As for the matter properly related to our inquiry, Boethius offers a precise summary of the various distinctions we already know: dialectic deals with "theses" (general cases) and rhetoric with "hypotheses" (particular cases). The former is "split," interrupted, since its form is the dialogue. The latter is continuous. There is only one interlocutor in dialectic, and two in rhetoric, since in this case the adversary and the judge are two different individuals, while in a dialectic debate these two roles belong to one person. In the field of logic, there is another Aristotelian distinction between dialectic and analytics, between the probable arguments of the former and the necessary ones of the latter, which also lead to a different degree of specialization in the *invenire* (i.e., finding the topics) and in the *iudicare* (i.e., applying them). If one looks carefully, the *dialecticus* becomes engaged in some kind of match, from which he comes out the star, the winner, because he uses both *probabilia* and *necessaria*; the *philosophus* employs only the latter, the orator only the former, and the Sophist neither of them. What emerges here is the primacy of dialectic, but it is mainly at the nominal level, understood as the predominance of one label over the others to designate the whole logical field. However, one never reaches the point where the distinction between the probable and the true is suppressed, and actually the whole Scholastic tradition will remain very faithful to it. To be sure, between these two giants the space of rhetoric is being progressively eroded. But this will be its fate every time it is placed within a general and comparative perspective that embraces all logical forms, as had already happened in Aristotle's *Organon*.

Beside these dangerous occasions for global, systematic comparisons, rhetoric lives in a wide variety of particular treatises that are handed down through the centuries. Their tendency is to become ever more synthetic and compendious, but the principal characteristics are not lost, and a particularly stable and secure tradition seems to survive the so-called Dark Ages without much damage. The anthology *Rhetores latini minores* edited by Carl Halm allows us to follow the stages of the transmission and to verify its stability. Cassiodorus (490– c. 583), who comes soon after Boethius, shows himself to be well capable of identifying the central feature of the "art" when he finds its field of application in the *civiles quaestiones*, which he defines as those of general interest that concern moral issues, such as welfare and justice, and therefore should be understood by anybody. He gives a detailed enumeration of the *status causae*, in which he follows Tully (it is the technique expounded in *Rhetorica vetus* backed by *De inventione* and *Rhetorica ad Herennium*). If Cassiodorus takes care to transmit the logical and juridical properties of rhetoric, the Venerable Bede (672–735) undertakes an examination of style: he takes up, in a definitely technical key, the analyses already developed by Augustine on the Scriptures, in order to show that they perfectly applied the rules on figures and tropes. Of both Bede provides a precise and exhaustive list, which will be extremely valuable for future treatises on *Poetria* and *colores rhetorici*. The *Disputatio* by Alcuin (730–804) is an excellent example of a didactic epitome on these subjects, whose understanding is made easier by the form of the work: it is presented as a dialogue occurring between Charlemagne and Alcuin. It once again shows that the conceptual network of rhetoric holds well and has no broken links. We may mention also the *Praeexercitamina* of Priscian the Grammarian, who focuses his attention mostly on *narratio*. Priscian tries to define various types of the latter, from the "fictitious" to the historical ones (*fabularis, fictilis, historica, civilis*). This is a useful crossing of the borders into the territory of poetics, at a time when all trace of the Aristotelian treatise was lost.

In short, the transmission of rhetorical tradition through the times of decadence, the Dark Ages (the tenth and eleventh centuries), does not suffer any setback in its network. At most there is an impoverishment, a sort of drying up, meaning that, with this, rhetoric is progressively reduced to a body of rules. Instead of introducing radical innovations, the various "renaissances" that occur will consist of new formulations of the old baggage of notions, now put forward with more eloquence, a deeper thrust and conviction. This is true of the "renaissance"of the twelfth century, whose best representative is John of Salisbury (c. 1110–80), author of the *Metalogicon*. In this work one would search in vain for new concepts or new terms, but at least the transmission of rhetoric is carried out with enthusiasm. There is a defense of this "art" and its rights, against the Augustinian accusations of those who stressed the primacy of natural talent and the uselessness of precepts. John of Salisbury does not deny the need for natural qualities, but he sees in eloquence the faculty of *expedire*, that is, of expressing oneself properly and effectively, and of developing the *naturaliter possibilia*. For this reason the authority of Cicero is called on to sustain the idea that those who cultivate eloquence will be able to lend an air of probability to what is incredible, and will make sound attractive what was at the beginning *horrendum et incultum* (repulsive and rude).[7] This means that rhetoric has the property of changing the cards on the table, something the church fathers, for example, Minucius Felix, considered negative, or at most it convinced them to learn it in order to neutralize possible reprehensible usage from bad-intentioned individuals. As Etienne Gilson observes, the straightforward defense of eloquence by John of Salisbury is without doubt a sign of "renaissance," of flourishing, but in the following century it will be followed by a "freeze," a return to the strictest logic in all its strength. We must add that the *Metalogicon* deals extensively with grammar, and even poetics: John of Salisbury advises the retention of poetics as a part of grammar in order to protect it. In brief, he shows a lively interest in the literary, discursive aspects of the trivium. This does not prevent him, however, from drawing an ascending scale toward dialectic, and he is far from undermining its primacy. In the *Metalogicon* one also finds the various distinctions we met in Boethius: thesis (dialectic) and hypothesis (rhetoric); probability and necessity, with the observation that *ratio demonstrativa*, analytics, " . . . vacillat in naturalibus plerumque (corporalibus et mutabilibus dico)" whereas it is very effective " . . . in mathematicis."[8] Also dealt with are *invenire* and *iudicare, topica*, analytics, and *sophistica*. There is also an invitation to the reader not to criticize one's teachers at all costs, out of a sheer polemical spirit: on the contrary, one should follow their teaching with humility.

Dialectic in the Thirteenth Century

Etienne Gilson observed that there is more difference between the twelfth and thirteenth centuries than between the twelfth century and the preceding ones, or even the following ones, when the Renaissance proper will occur. We know that the thirteenth century marks a rupture due to the spreading influence of Aristotle mediated by Arab thinkers. It is the Aristotle of the *Physics* and the *Metaphysics*, since the *Analytics* and the *Topica* had been stable assets of Scholasticism from at least the time of Boethius on. Now the new big interest in physics leads to an as yet unmatched development of "demonstration," and thus of analytic logic. In the meanwhile the attention to metaphysics leads to an increase of the dialectical spirit. There is also a clearer demarcation between these two discursive practices. Rhetoric is the big loser: it is not explicitly rejected, but indifference and lack of attention are worse than a warm and eloquent criticism of the kind Augustine had expressed in *De doctrina Christiana*.

For example, Thomas Aquinas (1225–74) is always correct when dealing with rhetoric. He follows the already established and stereotypic Aristotelian distinctions: "In the business affairs of men, there is no such thing as demonstrative and infallible proof, and we must be content with a certain conjectural probability, such as that which an orator employs to persuade."[9] However, his main interest is not in the *negotia humana*, so much so that in the entire *Summa theologica*, rhetoric is mentioned only three times: to reaffirm its inferior position in relation to dialectic; to confirm the ambiguity between theory and practice (*prudence*);

and finally in a simile—something can be loved even without knowing it thoroughly, as if somebody were fond of rhetoric only on the basis of its general definition as the art of persuasion.

Thomas Aquinas's attention is all taken up by the demonstration in the physical sciences and the dialectical dispute on theological questions. Already Albertus Magnus, his teacher, had written an *ars opponendi et respondendi*. Even on the didactic level, the *quaestio*—the debate, the split, discontinuous (*intercisus*) discourse, based on questions and answers—takes the place of the *lectio*, the continuous commentary. But it would not be correct to define this state of things as marking the unique triumph of dialectic, since these two important logical branches, analytics and dialectic, proceed together, as the best Aristotelian tradition prescribed. There is only some linguistic instability, as Eugenio Garin has noted, since dialectic sometimes comprises the whole logical field, and sometimes goes back to its proper boundaries within the area of probability. But it receives the following exaggerated praise from Petrus Hispanus (d. 1227) in his *Summulae logicales*: "Dialectica est ars artium, scientia scientiarum, ad omnium methodorum viam habens" (Dialectic is the art of arts, the science of sciences, that holds the way to every method). In the same text, however, he differentiates dialectic from logic, which avails itself of a syllogism based on necessary premises.

The passage from Thomism to the nominalism of William of Ockham (c. 1295– c. 1350), author of a *Summa logicae*, strengthens, if that is possible, the logical attitude of mature Scholasticism. In fact, nominalism, after having bracketed away rhetoric, also invades and assimilates grammar, the first of the arts of the trivium. Grammar loses any "historical" characteristic as embodied in the texts of different authors to become a purely theoretical construction based on abstract concepts (terms, predicates, the differentiation between categorematic parts of discourse—nouns—and syncategorematic ones—prepositions and adverbs). As Garin remarks, "In the logic of language . . . nominalism rediscovered ontology; but at the price of transforming what had arisen as a technique for debate into an 'absolute' science, while the inquiry did not limit itself at all, as it claimed, to *verba* by bracketing away *res*; on the contrary, in the links between *verba* it thought it exhausted the knowledge of *real* relationships without the need for a return to reality."[10]

Perhaps the most interesting example of how deep the spirit of logic ran at that time is the *Compendium totius logicae* by Joannes Buridanus (1300–58), a work whose very title is revealing, and in which the analysis starts from the sound to go back to the *vox* (the term) and *oratio*. The text offers a wide range of notions (for example, proposition, predicate, copula) that will become the foundation of the dreaded sentence analysis, which till not so long ago was basic to the Italian education system in junior high schools, when the teaching of Latin was fundamental. The following are some of the examples given by Buridanus: *homo*

currit, homo potest currere, omnis homo currit. These are elementary propositions, that is, barren expressions of geometrical accuracy, which the humanists
will soon identify as the extreme betrayal of the beauty and richness of language.
It is important to remember, however, that even during an age that had such a
passion for analytics, a broad consideration of dialectical probability is still to be
found. The Middle Ages are faithful to the teachings of Aristotle and do not
know that intense abhorrence of probability that modernity will display with Descartes, and that our time shows in logical positivism. Even enthymemes find a
place in Buridanus's compendium, of course only out of a concern for whole-
ness. In fact, they are cut off from any possibility of rhetorical application and are
reduced to the function of technical syllogisms lacking one of three parts. We
must stress it again: analytics and dialectic always get along well and integrate
each other, whereas rhetoric ends up being totally put aside.

Only in the case of authors who do not aim to reproduce a synthesis of the
whole *Organon*, but concentrate on isolated parts, does rhetoric fare better. For
example, this happens with Brunetto Latini (c. 1220–94) when he translates and
comments on Cicero's *De inventione*. We know that this early work of Cicero's
has always been present in the medieval tradition; therefore the undertaking of
Brunetto should not be seen as an innovation that would announce humanism.
Moreover, this is one of Cicero's most technical works, so it is well suited for
the mechanical outlook of the thirteenth century. Also, as if Brunetto were afraid
to be trapped within too narrow a branch of knowledge, he takes every opportunity to open up and include all the possible arts and disciplines, thus adding
issues and concerns totally unknown to the original text.

The Technical Character of the *artes rhetoricae* in the Late Middle Ages: Dante

Ousted from the *Organon*, rhetoric nonetheless will have some success during
the twelfth and thirteenth centuries as a very specialized and technical art. In
fact, the spirit of the time readily accepts the division and fragmentation to which
Cicero (the great Cicero of *De oratore*) had always been opposed. Thus rhetoric
is quickly deprived of *inventio* to become a mere body of rules on *elocutio* or
even *dispositio*, the latter understood primarily as the stylistic decoration of
phrases and sentences. This is evident in the various treatises written throughout
this period. In chronological order, the most important authors are Matthieu de
Vendôme with *Ars versificatoria*; Geoffroi de Vinsauf with *Poetria nova*; Evrard
l'allemand with *Laborintus*; and Johannes de Garlandia. These works are mainly
concerned with the purely technical aspects of writing verse, or with *dictare*, that
is, drawing up letters, official orations, pleas, and the like. Poetic practice and
civic affairs are joined (the latter particularly developed with notarial art, which

flourished under Guido Faba and others in Bologna). But both moments are conceived as definitely formal and arise from a concern for speaking well (*bene dicere*), which separates *verba* from *res*. We should also note the autonomy reached by *dictare*. The difference between speaking and writing, between orality and prose, was already present in classical treatises; Quintilian, for example, dealt with it. But the moment had not yet come when writing, or letter writing, would be a genre deserving to be treated in its own right, or at least under a specific heading. When this happens, in the late Middle Ages, it means that civic life offers little opportunity for public debate (juridical, political, laudatory). Culture is shifting toward the primacy of the written text, something that will definitely be sanctioned by the Gutenberg revolution. It is also another proof of the practical, technical attitude of the age, which did not share Cicero's view of rhetoric as a global concern. Analysis is opposed to synthesis, but the tendency toward universalism, the *summa*, the encyclopedic knowledge does not hinder, and actually favors, the particular, the exhaustive study of specific sectors.

We will skip over the details of these treatises. In general they all pay a lot of attention to *dispositio*, which, as I have said, is understood not as arrangement of the arguments, but rather of words and sentences. It is the triumph of figures (asyndeton, polysyndeton, zeugma, hypozeuxis, natural or artificial construction, different types of beginnings, etc.). Of course all of these were already present in classical treatises, but there they would never have achieved such a degree of autonomy and would have been held in check. Generally *dispositio* is followed by *descriptio* or *narratio*, which is the part dealing with content and which now becomes ossified into strict precepts for adornment and propriety: rigid and cumbersome rules establish which attributives, epithets, and properties suit the different ages, social statuses, professions, and so forth. Then there usually is a grammatical-stylistic analysis of words. It is very attentive to sounds, so, for example, Matthieu de Vendôme advises against using words ending in "alis," "osus," or "atus." Dante also will be a good heir to this concern. Then it is the turn of tropes, which are listed according to established classical tradition, but now their usage is tied to a series of minute captious rules. This is evident above all in Vinsauf's *Poetria nova* and *Documentum de modo et arte dictandi et versificandi*, where he identifies as many as seven ways to arrive at the *ornata difficultas*, in essense proceeding on the basis of metonymies, synecdoches, an exchange between container and contained or between consequent and antecedent. For "moderate" fields of application there is also *ornata facilitas*, which is less demanding than the previous one but still decorously elaborated. This is not in contradiction to the bareness of nominalistic logic of a William of Ockham; it is rather a complementary effect, an internal variation. One always starts from the assumption that a degree zero is possible, that a sentence can be built in a natural way and according to a universal logic. By degrees, through combinatory rules, substitutions, figures, it will be possible to reach "difficult" elaborations. But the humanists will not agree on this. In spite of the importance they will attach to formal elegance, they will not accept the concept of a degree zero, of the bareness of the logical grammatical forms. At least they do not think such a form can be called "natural," primary, or consentaneous to human beings. On the contrary, it will be regarded as a crude simplification.

These various tendencies toward universalism and encyclopedic knowledge, but also toward the particular, with excessive attention to the technical aspects of each branch, find in Dante (1265–1321) their culmination. Dante is careful not to sacrifice any "art" and science in adherence to a totalizing conception of the individual who "can be called a true philosopher." Surely to be a philosopher it is not enough to deal with rhetoric and music, "to delight in composing odes and in studying them" under the pretense of abandoning other sciences, all of which on the contrary are "members of wisdom."[11] A special place will be reserved for "demonstration" (analytic logic), which according to an ingenious application of allegory taken from the great and pressing example of Boethius, is assimilated to the sense of sight, to the eyes: analytics is a theoretical art founded on *acies oculorum*. On the contrary, to rhetoric, the art of persuasion, belong laughing and sensual delight, and in fact rhetoric is put under the sign of Venus. Without doubt, in Dante's hierarchy of the various arts and disciplines eloquence holds a low position, since it is understood as an intervention on the surface, a cosmetics, a "veil" through which "the inner light of wisdom is revealed."[12] The notion of the veil will soon be taken up by the humanists, who will apply it not only to rhetoric but also, and perhaps more strongly, to poetry. But for them the materiality of the veil will be a plus, something that enhances the thoroughness of rhetoric and poetry as opposed to the bareness of logic. On the contrary, Dante thinks in specialized compartments and separates *delectare* and *docere*: "Adornment is the addition of something suitable."[13] This somehow marks a return of the old Platonic prejudices against what seems to him mere sensual appearance; it is a view basically in agreement with that of Gorgias, who had described eloquence as an irresistible charm for poor Helen of Troy. I have already said that in Dante's view of the world rhetorical persuasion is under the sign of Venus. But in relation to Platonism the *Convivio* takes a different stand since Dante is a good heir to utilitarianism and late medieval specialization, so that he readily finds the right place even for the seductions of Venus, and pays considerable attention to them, as on other occasions he quite readily applies Aristotelian analytics, taking it from some *summula* or manual of logic. For example, in *De monarchia*, when he wants to demonstrate that the monarch is the most effective form of justice, he does not hesitate to employ the syllogism of the second figure, even using letters as symbols: "All B is A; only C is A; therefore C is B."[14]

So much for demonstration. Moving on to rhetorical persuasion, Dante resolutely proceeds to give very detailed distinctions, so minute that their like could never be found in the writings of Petrarch or the other humanists, in spite of the importance the latter attached to elegance, and in much the same way as they would never accept the bare and crude propositions of syllogisms. On the contrary Dante applies the same analytic attitude to the search for the truth as well as to the search for the beautiful, and considers the latter as the end result of the joined contributions of grammar (construction), rhetoric (discursive order), and finally music, a science of the quadrivium. This for adornment, for the garment. As for the content of discourse, it is to be found in the theoretical power of demonstration, since "its worth lies in its meaning," whereas beauty resides only in the "adornment of words."[15]

Everything must be in its place, and there it must be properly cultivated. For example, music is so important that there is no piece of poetry that can be "transferred from its tongue into another, without shattering all its sweetness and harmony."[16] With regard to grammar and rhetoric, Dante perfectly applies the extremely precise rules of the previous century. He insists on the various degrees for constructing sentences, starting from the degree zero of logic, which is seen, however, as colorless in terms of aesthetic and persuasive fruition. An example would be, "Peter is much in love with Mistress Bertha."[17] Dante's analysis continues with the description of a rich scale of tones that go from the flavorful to the graceful and the grand: these effects depend mainly on the choice of the linguistic material. One can use terms that are puerile, feminine, virile, rustic, or urbane. Basically this corresponds to the three styles, but Dante rearranges and imaginatively diversifies his material. Once again he displays his taste for the analytic, the captious, which the more synthetic humanists will abandon. He also proposes another detailed sorting of good and bad terms, according to the different interactions between grammatical and rhetorical rules, with the contribution of music; dialectic, however, has no place here. "And I call well-groomed those [words] — either trisyllables or very close to trisyllabicity, without aspiration, without acute or circumflex accent, without the double *z* and *x*, without liquids in succession."[18] Some examples are *amore, donna, disio, virtute, donare*. Dissonant terms will be called lubricious, shaggy, harsh.

Chapter 4
Humanism and the Renaissance

Motifs of Early Humanism: The Circle and the Center

On the wave of the Arab Aristotelians, the "spirit of the thirteenth century" had favored a great revival of the studies of physics and metaphysics and had over-emphasized analytic and dialectical logic. Starting with Petrarch (1304–74) and Boccaccio (1313–75), the humanists will attack these two strongholds and will harshly criticize them with all the weapons at their disposal, including irony and contempt. Petrarch's pamphlet *De sui ipsius et multorum ignorantia* is the best critique of the pedantic encyclopedism of a physics founded exclusively on the authority of Aristotle's *ipse dixit*. Here Petrarch has a bone to pick with four "friends" who are good representatives of the type of pseudoscientist who is a strict follower of Aristotle: full of *levitas* and *iactatio* (superficiality and conceit), the pseudoscientist is intent on collecting naturalistic oddities and asks idle questions; for example, how many hairs does a lion have on its head; how many feathers are there on a vulture's tail; with how many tentacles does an octopus attack somebody who has been shipwrecked?[1] Finding an answer to such questions is just a waste of time and causes one to overlook basic questions, such as *unde et quo pergimus?* (whence do we come and whither are we going?). Adequate answers are certainly not to be found in mechanical rules, in the overelaborate but shallow system of Aristotle and his followers. For Petrarch, one must go back to Plato, whom he reads using the interpretation of the church fathers. For them Plato was the philosopher who came the closest to the revelation and who would have been a Christian if the times had allowed him. The same applies to Cicero:

Petrarch attributes his respect for the old pagan gods to a sense of prudence and regard for state institutions, but obviously these feelings were not really so deep as to penetrate the depth of Cicero's soul, who would have been a devout Christian if only he had lived a few decades longer.

But the cult of Cicero is nourished not only by the master of spirituality and reflection on the human condition who had inspired Saint Augustine. In Cicero Petrarch finds also the full fusion of *res* and *verba* on the theoretical as well as on the practical level. Meaning and a fine form are welded together: this is the property Petrarch and all the other humanists will particularly admire. A charge against Aristotle is that, in addition to placing all emphasis on cumbersome subjects, he writes rather poorly and clumsily, or perhaps this is how his works sound in the Latin translation—to the point that for Petrarch it would almost be preferable to render Aristotle's ideas in our own words, providing them with some formal dignity. Latin authors on the other hand, and Cicero first of all, use the power of eloquence so effectively that it is as if they were plunging their arrowheads into our hearts.[2] What we see emerging here is the dyad, which the humanists try to bring to the closest synthesis, of the reasons of the heart (the return to spirituality, questioning the human condition) on the one hand, and of formal dignity, propriety, vigor in the language on the other. This concern was already in the writings of the church fathers, in Augustine for example, who in this atmosphere enjoys a strong revival, but it was also in his predecessors, such as Ambrose and Jerome. To a great extent humanism appears to be a return to the church fathers, and one reason for this is that through their mediation Latin *elocutio*, which as we saw the fathers had inherited, can return in all its splendor. The break, the change over to a poor uncouth Scholastic language starts only with Boethius and reaches its climax in the barbarism of the thirteenth century, all absorbed in dialectical disputes, *quaestiones*, terminal logic. In this light it seems incorrect to ascribe a loss of religiosity to humanism, since in fact the level of religiosity increases. Rather, humanism launches the idea of a direct relationship of the soul with God, following Augustine's model.

Certainly the intimacy of one's conscience with God does not result in a short-circuiting of silence and mute intuition; on the contrary, it postulates a linguistic expression in which poetry has precedence over the rhetorical moment. Poetry comes first, and its significance is not seen as lay, profane; on the contrary poetry finds validation in the Scriptures, then in the great Latin authors, or at least in the eloquent, religious spiritual works of Cicero. What takes shape in the first place is a defense of poetics, the art that had not even been given a fixed status in the trivium, and that had to carve a difficult space for itself within grammar and rhetoric, with some incursions into music. Above all, poetics had to rest satisfied with performing the technical duties of versification, of external embellishment. Now it is relaunched as the privileged mode of expression, with priority over any other art. The series of passionate defenses of the merits of poetry is opened by

Boccaccio. In *Genealogia deorum gentilium* he claims that the *fabula* is totally legitimate and useful on the ground that it can be found in the Scriptures as well as in the best classical authors. It is also a "full," sophisticated, and complex means of expression when compared with the means pertaining to philosophers, who are compelled to move *apertissime* and by way of schematic syllogisms. On the contrary the poet, free of the cumbersome mechanics of syllogisms, is allowed to mask the true in artificial forms and under the veil of fiction. If the language of philosophy is prosaic and without embellishments, that of poetry stands out for its excellence and propriety. In this same passage Boccaccio comes to an important conclusion: he opposes the place appointed for philosophy, the gymnasium, to the place that seems proper for poetry, which to him is solitude. Evidently here are overtaken both the Ciceronian ideal, exclusively directed to defending the rights of practice, and the ideal of the fathers, who would never have accepted the use of eloquence for such a private end. What emerges is rather the line we met in Tacitus's *Dialogus de oratoribus*, where instead of attending public places, an activity now seen as useless and tiresome, it was proposed that one withdraw to the solitude of *otium* (leisure) and the woods.

The praise of solitude is a theme that may be better applied to Petrarch than to Boccaccio, however. Especially in the *Decameron*, Boccaccio strikes a balance that is properly rhetorical: to the austere bareness of the gymnasium, the space for philosophical debates, he opposes gardens, places of amusement, where a group of ordinary people will meet. Although well educated, these individuals are certainly not expected to speak according to the rigorous rules of dialectic, all the more so since there are several women in the group. The author's task is to tell *fabulae* where pleasure and instruction go together, facing the moral issues stemming from the human condition, and also trying to express the silent emotions that crowd the mind of the young women, who are without rhetorical skills. Boccaccio comes to the women's aid as a careful speech writer who gives voice to their thoughts, worries, and emotions, which otherwise would not be revealed. More generally, the *Decameron* may be considered a huge rhetorical enterprise in progress, where the author "rewrites" old *fabulae* with the same richness of details a good lawyer must offer in the *narratio* when, for example, the scene of a crime is reconstructed, or when incisive character analysis is used to defend or to accuse the parties involved in the case at hand, or finally, with the ability to confute the opponent's theses and to defend one's own, which is in fact the ability a lawyer must constantly display.

Later on the defense of poetry is proposed by Coluccio Salutati: the occasion is a controversy he engages in with Fra Giovanni da S. Miniato. His interlocutor believes that poetry represents a negative factor, a dangerous weakening of the naked truth that theology studies through analytic and dialectical tools. The undue obscuring of the truth lies in the superficial pleasure poetry offers. In contrast, Salutati vigorously defends poetry, following in the steps of Petrarch and

Boccaccio; actually his defense is carried out in even more resolute terms. For him poetry is a "plus," in the sense that it is a totality of which theology and philosophy themselves are only a part. This part is necessary as a constitutive element of poetry: thus the latter is superior, if it is true that the whole must be considered superior to its parts.[3] Returning to the same subject in *De laboribus Herculis*, Salutati makes the radical claim that poetry is the most important human activity, because it comprehends in itself the arts of both the trivium and the quadrivium. Paradoxically the fact that it has been excluded from that traditional division turns to its advantage. Not having had a territory of its own to cultivate means that it makes itself available to a transversal intervention on the entire spectrum of disciplines. The bad luck encountered in the Middle Ages now becomes a springboard for an incredibly lofty destination. It is worth remembering that rhetoric had enjoyed a similar position in Cicero's *De oratore*, where in much the same way it was regarded as an art not limited by territorial boundaries, but free to comprehend within itself all the realms of knowledge. It is typical of humanism to transfer the primacy of rhetoric onto poetics. Salutati's position will return during the mature stage of the Renaissance, in Fracastoro and many others; in fact, it will be one of the basic reasons for the prevailing of Ciceronianism.

On the other hand, this shift of prerogatives carries certain risks: after opposing the aridity of Scholastic logicism and scientism, the humanists do not stop at a healthy rediscovery of the practical moment in the human sciences. They quickly end up by affirming the primacy of poetry, and therefore of the moment of *otium*, whose space, as Boccaccio had recognized, was the solitude of the woods. We can detect here the possibility of an involution — what Vasile Florescu has called the "literaturization" of rhetoric, which consists in too fast a transfer of its rights to the close but more private field of poetics. However, we cannot but recognize the appeal, almost in absolute terms, of an atemporal model that is periodically reproposed and that tends to isolate a locus or a moment that can comprehend and merge within itself all possible human concerns: practical, theoretical, emotional, and doctrinal. A very good image for this conception of poetry is proposed at that time and in the climate of those debates by one of the detractors, Friar Giovanni da Mantova, the author of *Epistula Mussato poetae paduano invehens contra poeticam* and an advocate of the primacy of theology. His starting point is the fact that poets receive a laurel wreath as sign of honor. For him the wreath is a symbol of the art: he identifies in it a circle within which every point is equidistant from the center, which manifests the nature of poetry as being above all an art of variety and considerably removed from the center of truth. But Albertino Mussato answers, saying essentially that after all the circle contains the center in itself; variety does not exclude truth but constitutes a richer, enjoyable, and fascinating presentation of it.[4]

In other words, truth has to marry the science of letters, as in the writings of the fathers, and not only Augustine or Jerome but Lactantius and Firmianus as well. This is also the theme of Leonardo Bruni's *De studiis et litteris liber*. In this work Bruni offers a very effective simile to emphasize the importance of the physical-perceptual aspect of communication: those who care for their stomach don't swallow just any food. Also the outward garment is basic to the health of the body and the mind. The knowledge of facts must be closely wedded to literary skill. As usual, the best example is Cicero, whose oratorical skills Bruni extolls with conviction and sincerity, as will many other humanists: "What a man, immortal God! What fluency! What wealth of language! What perfect style! What thoroughness from every point of view!"[5]

The obligatory start from Cicero is also stressed by Aeneas Silvius Piccolomini in his *Tractatus de liberorum educatione*, which is perhaps the widest and most systematic pedagogical work of humanism. One finds here the usual praise of the fathers, which in this case is directed to Jerome, in whom Piccolomini perceives "the fragrance of Cicero's eloquence."[6] Moreover, in a burst of generosity and broad reevaluation of the origins, Piccolomini reinstates even Boethius. Of course his interest goes to the allegorical individual to whom Lady Philosophy speaks in verse and who appreciates the increase of value produced by *fabula*. The strongest condemnation — actually an utter rejection — is directed against a Germany with very vague features: a land of barbarians where theologians are revered and poets despised. In fact, this territory, more a creation of the mind than an actual geographic space, should include also Paris with its dialectical pomp as well as the Oxford of Ockhamist logic. Along with linguistic barbarisms, the Germans, and the Viennese in particular, are accused of inconclusiveness in their "sophistical and captious" logical exercises, which never come to useful results. Here Ciceronianism is motivated not only by admiration for stylistic skills but also by the fact that Cicero maintained the primacy of praxis over theory, of *negotium* over *otium*. On this occasion the humanists are reconsidering their target. They do not rush to eulogize solitude in the woods, but more effectively rediscover the dignity of the forum, of engagement in the affairs of the state and the community.

Lorenzo Valla's Conception of Rhetoric and Dialectic

All of the foregoing themes return, more powerfully expounded and well systematized, in the works of Lorenzo Valla (1407–57), the best representative of early humanism. In *Elegantiarum libri* he states unconditionally that "we have to read eloquent books or not read at all."[7] Valla also confirms the *topos* of homage to the fathers, which in him is charged with a precise rhetorical connotation: their importance, and the reason they are worthy of praise, lies in the fact that they adorned the language of the Scriptures with "gold, silver, and gems" (p. 120), which is the "plus," the contextual-organic enrichment on which all of the humanists heavily insist. This theme is further developed in the opposition between the notion of public and private. By private is meant the particular use of a single science that may be satisfied with poor humble language, "house clothes" so to speak; whereas by public is understood (following Cicero) that which concerns the interest and welfare of all. Thus the first place is assigned to religion and theology (here of course Valla distances himself from the pagan Cicero and follows Augustine and the fathers). From this view there stems the necessity to speak of divine things with a magnificent language; in other words, one has to embellish the language as is proper for public occasions, and to exert a psychagogic effect on the crowd of believers; the eyes and the senses in general also want their share. Otherwise, if God's mansion is left plain or poor, one could be tempted to disparage it instead of admiring its majesty. This is one reason why the Schoolmen are to be blamed: starting with Boethius they adopted a "barbaric" language (Avicenna and Averroës, Valla observes, were real and not just metaphorical barbarians). They are guilty of impropriety, as one would be who goes to a public ceremony wearing shabby clothes, thus debasing God's word through a degree of modesty that does not adequately manifest due respect. The same idea is repeated with a very incisive simile: the fathers were like bees that synthesized and reelaborated the nectar gathered to reoffer it enriched in sweetness and attractiveness. The Schoolmen, in contrast, were like ants hiding and storing up their little grains, not allowing others to enjoy them.

Valla also challenged the "barbarians" on their own ground with a treatise on dialectic that begins with a harsh critique of Aristotle, the very founder of the "art." To the rejection of the authority principle we already saw in Petrarch (Aristotle is a human being like everybody else, so he may have been wrong) and an invective against the "superstitious, mad, and pusillanimous race of those who deprive themselves of the faculty to seek the truth,"[8] Valla adds a more significant theme. Aristotle is guilty of excessive abstract theorizing devoid of any practical application. It is the Ciceronian claim of the primacy of practice over the speculative moment, something on which Piccolomini also had commented. Aristotle in fact in the *Organon*, "did not dedicate his research to those concerns by which are identified superior individuals, and that consist in participating in public assemblies, administering provinces, leading armies, debating causes, practicing medicine, practicing law, writing stories or poems," and so on.[9] With Valla, humanism avoids the risk of falling into literaturization, that is, of privileging literary solitude. Rather, through his works runs a strong practical thrust, balanced by the need to keep it matched with literary elegance. Actually, Valla goes so far as to claim that the study of letters goes together with another area of activity where praxis is strongly enhanced: the skill of using arms. Cicero's age is a good example of the integration of the importance of eloquence and success in military enterprises. The same idea returns when Valla proudly compares the *orator* to the *rector*, the *dux populi*. On the contrary a logician must be satisfied with a "private" end: his proper space is the gymnasium, not the forum or the drill field. Rendered in one of Valla's so effective similes, our logician behaves like a small vessel that prefers the security of the coast and dares not sail offshore. Valla goes so far as to give a sexual connotation to his unfailing conviction about the primacy of rhetoric over dialectic: the latter seems to him like a modest and chaste virgin that must live in seclusion.

Eventually, provided it accepts its limitations, dialectic has a role of its own. To recognize these limitations means to be aware that its function is that of a simple, direct technique aimed at particular interventions, as when a syllogism may stand in its bareness and there is no need to sway a vast audience with grand style. Unfortunately, the "barbarians" (that is, Aristotle's followers) have made it into something enormously complicated and captious. Valla sees his task as one of clearing a forest that has become monstrously overgrown. His intervention, of course, addresses two fronts: form and content. As to form, Valla gives the usual warning of the humanists not to use an abstruse, incomprehensible language with neologisms that do not belong to tradition and that lack propriety. One should follow the beaten path, and employ common language or the language already used by the learned. As to content, which has a properly philosophical relevance, Valla "clears" the forest of Aristotelian categories and its consequent proliferation of universal *realia*. His opinion is that the only real universal category is that suggested by common sense and that corresponds to the *res*. As a reaction against the proliferation of official Aristotelianism, he opts for Ockham's nominalism, although he certainly would not totally accept the extremely technical jargon of Ockham's *Summa logicae*, which probably would not have escaped the charge of barbarism. Almost a century later, Nizolio, another fanatical admirer of Cicero's, will adhere to the same view. In any case, for Valla philosophical content must always be backed up by philology. As a matter of fact, the dismantling of one Aristotelian category had already occurred in *Elegantiarum libri*, where he had severely criticized Boethius for the barbaric use, not supported by any linguistic tradition, of the word *substantia*. Valla has no doubt that Scholasticism starts with Boethius, that first commentator on the *Organon* who cannot be considered in the same line with the fathers. To the fathers Valla pays an extremely brave homage. Asked to give a speech to celebrate Saint Thomas Aquinas, he does not hesitate to begin with Saint Augustine and maintains that Aquinas took from Augustine much of his doctrine (*Encomion S. Thomae* [In Praise of Saint Thomas Aquinas]).

From a Return to Platonism to the Triumph of Ciceronianism

In any case, humanism is not a closely knit, monolithic movement, in much the same way as Scholasticism contained in itself a variety of currents and attitudes. For example, in the last decades of the fifteenth century in the Florence of the Medici a content-oriented reaction takes shape: It finds its center around Marsilio

Ficino (1433–99), who relaunches Plato and Plotinus and becomes an indefatigable translator of their works. This Neoplatonic burst has been tied to the sociopolitical conditions of the time (the fall of the independent city and the rise to power of the Medici family), but it is hard to say how much such a deterministic view corresponds to the facts. Certainly this return to Platonism moves away from praxis; it abandons Valla's aggressive ideal of the orator as *dux populi* in favor of a theoretical orientation, which nevertheless is centered on the notion of humankind as the *copula mundi*, as the bridge between beasts and pure spirits: human beings are the only ones to share both conditions. As in the thirteenth century, there is a revival of the contemplative interest in theology. The model is no longer provided by Thomas Aquinas's Aristotelianism, however, but rather by Plato and Plotinus. There is a also a return to the church fathers, but for reasons the humanists of the previous generation could not share, since stress is now laid on technical and systematic aspects, which are removed from that immediacy of contact dear to Augustine and Petrarch. Indeed, the tutelary figure for this return to theology is certainly not the Petrarach of *Secretum* or *Rime*, but rather the encyclopedic and theologically oriented Dante, who is reanalyzed by Cristoforo Landino, a philologist of that circle (Sandro Botticelli, who is very close to Ficino's position, dedicates very beautiful illustrations to the *Paradise*).

Toward rhetoric the Neoplatonists can have only a negative attitude. The official spokesman on the matter is the second prominent figure in the circle: Giovanni Pico della Mirandola (1463–94). Pico has a famous epistolary debate with Ermolao Barbaro, a humanist from Padua, who in his turn was engaged in fighting the Aristotelians who were still strong in the University of Padua. Pico overturns all the arguments of the humanists and against them fervently propounds the ideas of those who, a century before, had defended the primacy of theology. "Bare" style once again is regarded as more worthy than a refined linguistic expression, since the embellishments the latter introduces are unnecessary, or worse, "histrionic trickery." The fruit is better than the flower, and content strictly depends on how one expresses it. Appearances are negligible and unworthy of philosophers: could one be angry at Socrates because, "while he discusses moral issues, his shoes are undone, his dress is untidy, or his nails not trimmed"?[10] Of course if Valla had been alive, he would have defended the idea that one must wear clothes matching the importance of the arguments discussed. Pico rejects also what had been first Augustine's and then Petrarch's attempt to punctuate the elegant style of the Scriptures. His opinion is that the Scriptures make manifest the strength of bareness. A point shared by the early humanists and the Platonists could be the importance attached to the *fabula*, the enigma or allegory; for the former, however, this is an enrichment, something that as usual adds to the unity of the context, while for the latter it works as a kind of obstacle that must keep away the profane crowd and thus prevents access to hidden truths:

"If you look at its outside you see a monster, if you look inside you recognize a god" (p. 813).

Another controversy, this time on imitation, once again sees the two parties opposed. The spokesman for Ficino's followers is Pico's nephew, Giovanni Francesco: he claims the right to draw inspiration and employ elements from a variety of authors, so that the originality of a writer may emerge through the choices made. On the other front the spokesman is Pietro Bembo (1470–1547), the best representative of the early and more classical stage of the Renaissance, who is not himself free of Platonism, as his *Asolani* shows. However, it is true that in this work Neoplatonic themes lose theoretical and theological rigor only to become a *topos* for the refined literary society of the time. As for imitation, Bembo fully restores the tenets of Ciceronianism, and states the necessity to draw inspiration from the "best" source, rigorously and without eclecticism.

Rather than in the classical texts of the early Renaissance (e.g., Castiglione's *Cortegiano* [Book of the courtier] or Della Casa's *Galateo* [Galateo: a treatise on manners and behaviors]), our inquiry will find fertile ground in the many treatises on poetics that were produced in the first part of the century. At that time a sort of neohumanism was taking shape: themes and ideas were resumed that had been developed by Coluccio Salutati over a century before, but that had been left interrupted because of the theoretical, content-oriented interval of Ficino and his circle: it is almost as if recurrence, or bounds and rebounds, were one of the laws of history. In the treatises on poetics of Bernardino Daniello, Bernardo Tasso, and above all of Gerolamo Fracastoro (1478–1553), the model of Aristotle's poetics appears extremely removed, in spite of the superficial homage paid to it. But it is more from hearsay than from actual knowledge of a text that still scarcely circulated in our culture. The prevailing idea is that of the totalizing function of poetics, which is able to give unity and synthesize within itself the whole spectrum of disciplines. A poetic work says more and says it better: this would be the slogan summing up the views of those first Renaissance treatises. Actually, Fracastoro points out in his *Naugerius*, if the other arts aim at a *bene dicere* closely related to a particular end, only poetry aims at an absolute *bene dicere* that employs and reconciles all possible ornaments and that treats an argument in all of its aspects. He offers an effective example by comparing the description of a wood made by a geographer (only data relative to the location and the climate are offered), and the "absolute" wood in a passage of Virgil's *Georgics*, where the wood is the locus of all possible qualities and pleasures, according to a conception of discursive contextual unity that almost seems to anticipate some contemporary aesthetic theories.

Our brief consideration of these poetics has not led us astray, because these authors have undoubtedly arrived at such a totalizing and comprehensive conception by transferring to poetry the properties Cicero had attributed to rhetoric. In Cicero's vision, however, the organicity of rhetoric was a function of active engagement in political life. The displacement to poetics runs the risk of literaturization that we saw in Coluccio Salutati, in whose steps Fracastoro clearly follows, although his position is more elaborate and self-assured.

Apropos of recurrence, nobody can equal Marcio Nizolio (1498–1576), who reproposes with indefatigable fanaticism and tenacity the ideas Valla had expressed a century before. With Nizolio, Ciceronianism reaches an insuperable climax, and in fact somehow after that moment Cicero's relentless decline begins. Nizolio's intervention is prompted by the stand taken by Maioragio, who in *Ciceromastigen* had challenged the primacy of Cicero and of rhetoric, as well as by the position taken by Calcagnini, who saw some passages in *De officiis* as dependent on the Stoics—as if we did not know the deep hostility that ran between Cicero and the Stoics. Nizolio's considerations are contained above all in *De veris principiis et vera ratione philosophandi contra pseudophilosophos libri IV*. This work marks one of the most climactic moments for rhetoric ever, since it faithfully restores its primacy in the terms of *De oratore*. In analyzing the trivium, Nizolio deprives dialectic of any right, and the same treatment is reserved for analytics: both are guilty of dealing with matters "useless, unnecessary, impertinent." Also, they "screech and chatter, annoying human ears in the way of magpies or crows,"[11] while grammar and rhetoric, especially when founded on a knowledge of Greek and Latin, use words "correctly, according to usage and in a way appropriate to an ordinary mind." Also, Nizolio does not believe that the trivium is part of "rational" philosophy, as the Schoolmen and Boethius maintained, following Aristotle. Does not *ratio* intervene also when one tackles philosophical subjects? In the term "rational" Nicolio perceives the presence of an abstract, vague entity, so that he prefers to call grammar and rhetoric discursive arts to make manifest their verbal nature. *Verba* and *res* are, in fact, the two pillars of his system. But what is "real"? Certainly not metaphysics, which is the monstrous construction of dialectical philosophers and of Aristotle in the first place. Real universals do not exist; only *res* exists, that is, the being in its unity, as it appears either in our mind as *verbum*, or in single concrete objects. There is nothing else between these two. Also, Nizolio declares his firm adherence to Ockham's nominalism, which, however, requires further simplification, in the same way as Valla's dialectic needs it, since Valla did choose the right track, but did not uproot all the weeds. At this point the entire system of knowledge can be simplified in such a way that there remain only two big branches: philosophy, which deals with *res* (both physical and political; the distinction between theory and practice no longer makes sense since both are at the same time "rational" and "real"), and oratory, which takes care of *verba*, with the elegance and the good sense of classical tradition.

Of course Nizolio does not realize that he falls into the aporias of every nominalistic position, which is forced to find some substitute for the abstraction or the eidetic intuition, that is, for the processes through which one rises from the particular to the universal. He too in fact resorts to an act tht he calls *simul comprehendere*,[12] through which he explains how it is possible to maintain the unity and uniqueness of being while finding its presence in a number of actual things. Moreover, he fails to realize that if the need to simplify the number of arts and sciences is surely Ciceronian, this is no longer the case when he advances a rigid separation of words and things; this is something Cicero blamed on the unfortunate change brought about by Socrates and Plato. For his part, Cicero would never have adhered to the strictness of nominalism, almost Stoic in its foundations, and certainly far from his views on probability. However, it is with remarkable consistency with respect to his background and formation that Nizolio finds faults with Aristotle's *Organon* and dismantles one part after the other. Thus his position is diametrically opposed to the one Boethius took in his time.

The Humanist's Rehabilitation of Dialectic: Ramism

However, not all Renaissance treatises are so hostile to dialectic or convinced of the preeminence of rhetoric. After all, Valla himself produced a commentary on dialectic, and this had been enough for Nizolio to reproach Valla for lack of radicalism. There is a trend, cultivated by German or French rather than by Italian humanists, that insists precisely on dialectic, although giving it in a reformed version. The work at the head of this current, which is more inclined to maintain the continuity with the Middle Ages rather than to break all ties abruptly, is *De inventione dialectica* by Rudolphus Agricola (1443–85). Agricola too criticizes Aristotle for his obscurity, lack of common sense, and fallibility, since like all human beings, Aristotle was liable to make mistakes. Agricola fights on two fronts: against the obscurity of Aristotelian Scholastic logic, as well as against the literaturization for which he held responsible the Italian humanists. For him *docere* is by far more important than *movere* and *delectare*: thus it needs to be defended against the "usurpations of rhetoricians"[13] who are suspected of hedonistic tendencies. Agricola even reproposes the classical opposition between continuous oration and "contrast," that is, dialectical disputation. The former is certainly "more beautiful" because it is able to feign the "color of truth," but the latter is decisively "more diligent" (p. 155). And anyway, he goes on to say, rhetoricians cannot claim an autonomy of their own, since the *topoi* of invention, that is, the logical parts of a discourse, are totally dependent on dialectic. Thus Agricola's position already anticipates the "reform" that Ramus will carry out almost a century later.

Also in the first part of the sixteenth century, while in Italy Ciceronianism is the dominant trend, dissenting voices arise in other countries. For example, in his *Ciceronianus* Erasmus openly and polemically takes sides against the *simiae Ciceronis*, but he admits that it is necessary to find a balance between them and the revival of Scholasticism brought about by the followers of Duns Scotus. Erasmus asks himself what may replace the allures of eloquence, which are not even valid from a social point of view, because he thinks that there no longer is a public ready to listen to lengthy and pedantic discourses. Erasmus relies on content-centered elements: first, one must have a thorough knowledge of one's subject, and second, one should be moved by sincere feelings.

The Spanish Jesuit Juan Luis Vives (1492–1540) is closer to the position of Italian humanism, and closer also to the Roman Catholic church (whereas in Erasmus there is already the scent of the Reformation). On the one hand Vives makes considerations we already found in the *homines novi* of the early fifteenth century; on the other hand he anticipates what Nizolio will say shortly. However, Vives's views appear much more balanced; he is reluctant to conclude with an absolute exaltation of rhetoric. He thunders *adversus pseudodialecticos*, that is, against those who had corrupted what in his mind was the good and proper dialectic. But he does not preach its total suppression the way Nizolio will. Certainly the assault on the Sorbonne and its Scholasticism is ruthless, even out of proportion considering that the prime of this adversary belonged totally to the past. For Vives in Paris one cultivated only the study of "idiotic and frivolous frothings";[14] or one would pay attention to "the riddles which children and gossiping women put to each other for their own amusement" (p. 80). Of course the attack goes back to the origins, to Aristotle himself, against whom Vives repeats the charges already made by Valla; above all the Stagirite lacked good sense and had no notion of practical application. At the same time Vives severely criticizes the "necessity" of logic, a criterion that he believes is difficult enough to reach even in the apodeictic and natural sciences. He prefers to take sides with Cicero's probability, which, however, he entrusts to dialectic and not to rhetoric, and is not aware that in doing so he is applying the orthodox teaching of Aristotle. However, Cicero's misgivings about apodeixis were legitimate in a cultural context that was completely stagnant with regard to scientific research. Whereas Vives's reservations occur at a time of ferment, and although the "new science" is still far from emerging, his remarks have a curbing effect that well serves the Catholic church and its rising fear of scientific research. Florescu is right when he observes that there is a change of roles between the trivium and the quadrivium: the trivium is progressive when scientific research in physics and mathematics is weak and wrapped in superstition, and it becomes restraining when content-oriented sciences give signs of moving again.

Vives's dominant theme, which is also the theme of any humanist of the early or later stages, is of course the grammatical-linguistic reform of the trivium. Vives wishes to take it away from the "barbarians" who defiled it by using Gothic or Vandal languages, and wants to return it to Latin. He has sarcastic comments for Peter of Spain and for all those who thought that his strange jargon was the same language as that of Cicero, Quintilian, or at least Boethius and Martianus Capella. It must be emphasized, however, that the return to a more elegant, literary language is sought not only for superficial, cosmetic reasons, but also for reasons of clarity and naturalness: only the use of a clear, effective language will allow common people to understand, and it is the people who hold "the customs and conventions"[15] of language.

The line in favor of reforming logic for the needs of the Renaissance individual reaches its climax in the prolific output of Pierre de la Ramée, or Peter Ramus (1515–72), who already belongs to the middle of the sixteenth century. Ramus too focuses on the arts of the trivium in their traditional formulation as grammar, rhetoric, and dialectic. He does not want to give up any of them and so he is very careful not to merge them, nor does he let one absorb the others, as had happened with the scholars who had been tempted to apply Cicero's model. Actually, his *Scholae in tres primas liberales artes* insists on a rigid separation of the competence of each one in its own field. He advocates a rigorous control on the borders, even if he admits that in the process of application there can be exchanges and positive cooperation between the different arts. Following this rigid division, rhetoric surrenders *inventio* and *dispositio*, the parts that are more related to logic; and it undergoes that unhappy breakup against which Cicero had thundered in *De Oratore*. Rhetoric reserves to itself only *elocutio*, which opens it up to the risk of literaturization. Curiously enough, Ramus, not satisfied with bringing about this painful separation, which will be disastrous for the future of rhetoric, wants to persuade of the legitimacy of such a surgical operation Cicero himself — the one who had always been opposed to it. It is in the course of an imaginary conversation with the great Latin orator that Ramus argues in favor of his radical solution. This is a sign of the times, an indication of the conflict between the belief in the authority principle, and the free questioning of nature on the part of reason or common sense, with the claim that the answers of these autonomous agencies will be validated by the *auctoritas* of the texts one cherishes. It is also the ultimate proof of the immense influence exerted by Cicero even on scholars who, like Ramus, clearly belonged to a different blood type, so to speak. Cicero is also the banner used to fight Aristotle, who as usual is the *bête noire* throughout the humanistic and Renaissance traditions.

Against the literary aspects of humanism Ramus strengthens the position of logic, of reason even in its direct bare form; nevertheless his rejection of analytics confirms that he remains a humanist. He is not attracted to apodeixis, to necessary demonstration. After all, he holds a difficult position of compromise between the old and the new, between adherence to the old structures of logic that go back to Aristotle's *Organon*, more than he is aware of, and a foresight about the Cartesian revolution to come. Of this revolution, he anticipates the need to unify the field (*inventio* and *dispositio*, the latter also called "method," intervene on any human or natural subject), and to submit it to the control of a *naturel usage*, or a *vray practique de raison*, as he says in his *Dialectique*, which he wrote in French. But this form of enlightenment, natural and rational at the same time, is not sought in mathematical apodeixis. Rather, it is filtered through the discursive arts, although these are "reformed," deprived of ornamentation and taken back to their essential frame. The proof of this lies in the examples Ramus gives of his method: he takes them from classical and contemporary poets (Pléiade poets such as Ronsard and Du Bellay). The method, which he defines as "disposition par laquelle entre plusieurs choses la première de notice est disposée au premier lieu, la deuziesme au deuziesme" (disposition by which out of many things the most important is placed first, the second is placed second),[16] is not constructed *more geometrico*, but it is taken by force from the linguistic structures employed by poets and orators. Ramus makes the attempt to rationalize the field of the *humanae litterae*. The aim of his generous undertaking is to keep together two cultures, in the attempt to prevent the formation of a gulf between them. But the result is actually a cross-breeding, a cross-exchange of prerogatives between analytics and rhetoric. Dialectic tries to mediate between them so as to avoid a clash or the necessity of having to choose between one or the other.

First Signs of Modernity and the Decline of Rhetoric

Toward the middle of the sixteenth century Ciceronianism is losing ground in Italy too, and so is the importance of rhetoric. This can be verified in the big change that takes place in relation to poetics. Poetics ceases to be considered a discursive art that may be added to the trivium, or better, an art that comprehends the other arts within itself. Now it is interpreted in the light of Aristotle's *Poetics*, which in the meantime was circulating in Latin translations, then in vernacular translations and "expositions" even in Italian. At a time when Aristotle's reputation is still very low (at least in the most prominent philosophical milieus), he enjoys a revival, albeit one that is limited to his *Poetics*. In fact, with his excellent ability to offer a thorough overview matched by a well-articulated arrangement, Aristotle had identified different aspects of the *poién: inventio* and *dispositio* in long poetical works (epic, tragedy, and comedy), corresponding to the structural needs of the *fabula*, of the plot; and along with them, the aspects of *elocutio*, or even grammar, which in part he developed in the *Poetics* but which to a great extent refer back to the *Rhetoric*. At this time Italian scholars discover an interest in and an openness to the first type of question that bring about several changes. Poetics is displaced from the group of discursive (rational) arts to the group of "real" arts, which deal with representation (i.e., with the imitation of the real). Thus it is linked to the arts that aim at portraying social usage and custom, in other words, what we today would call psychology and morality. The first duty of a good poet is to adhere to verisimilitude, that is, to know and to respect the data of the practical moral order. Thus poetics no longer appears as some kind of doubling of the rhetorical needs for elegance. Its purpose is no longer an absolute *bene dicere*; on the contrary, it has become instrumental and subject to the task of portraying characters with verisimilitude. In short, it undergoes a restructuring, which involves rhetoric as well.

This process of change emerges clearly in the writings of Ludovico Castelvetro (1505–71), the foremost Italian commentator on Aristotle's *Poetics*, and a scholar who will achieve considerable fame also among the French classicists of the seventeenth century. One instance will suffice to verify the inexorable decline of rhetoric among the followers of Aristotle's *Poetics*. Castelvetro severely criticizes Boccaccio for the speech that Ghismonda gives in a novella of the *Decameron* (IV,1). Before commiting suicide, the young noblewoman denounces her father's prejudices: he had her lover, guilty only of belonging to a lower social class, killed. As we know, Boccaccio specialized in expressing the mute agitation of young women who could not reveal their feelings because of timidity or lack of linguistic skills. He had no doubt that the poet-orator should render with the utmost eloquence the emotional storm felt by his characters. For Castelvetro it is a question of psychological verisimilitude, and for this reason he unconsciously shares the position of the anonymous author of the *Sublime*: when pathos presses, it is mute and should be left mute. Rhetoric has to retire in good order, or, as Manzoni will say, it must become subtle and discreet, instead of openly revealing its presence.

Castelvetro dealt directly with rhetoric in *Esaminazione sopra la ritorica a Caio Erennio*. His choice of the text to analyze is revealing in itself, since *Ad Herennium* was a work dearer to the Middle Ages than to the humanists and the Renaissance. His comments, which he inserts in his explanatory notes and which often have nothing to do with the text itself, are very harsh and scornful, and are completely aligned with the "modern" rational pre-Cartesian spirit that we saw in Ramus's logic. "If [rhetoricians] are to explain what 'to adorn' means, certainly they only answer that it means to provide something unnecessary. And if they are to tell what it means to put something in front of one's eyes, well, it is nothing else but the full meaning."[17] The stress on visual simile should not go unnoticed (to put something in front of somebody's eyes). The principle of evidence present in Ramus makes its appearance here too. This is radically different from rhetorical procedures, which rely on the benevolent ears of listeners. What is taking place here is a clash between two modes of knowledge: on one side is the belief in the presence of truth, something everybody can reach "through their eyes" and through intuition. The other side is marked by the absence of an absolute truth, which is replaced by arguments with varying degrees of probability, about which one must talk and to which one must listen: the stress is on the mouth-ears circuit. The spread of printing, already a century old at the time, provides crucial help, in terms of the technological structure it offers, to the success of the first model, as McLuhan has convincingly shown (we will come back to this point later). For the same reason Castelvetro declares a preference for "absolute'' words, by which he means words that aim at a direct relationship, preferably mathematical, with things, rather than ''comparative,'' metaphoric words that circle the object and weave a periphrasis around it. Is it better to encircle things, or to hit their center? As one may recall, these two alternatives were present at the start of humanism in the debate between theology and poetry. Castelvetro's view is the following: ''No comparison can signify as clearly as the words that I call absolute: in this way two oaks signify less clearly in relation to Pandarus and Bizia than absolute language does, that is, the numerical measure of sixty arms'' (p. 127). In stressing denotation over connotation, the work of our ''commentator'' from Modena precedes by a century the grammar of Port Royal and the statute of the English Royal Society.

Francesco Patrizi (1529–97), another complex and versatile scholar, arrives at similar results but by means of a different path. He is a good representative of the second Italian Renaissance within which his position is marked by a ''return'' to Platonism and Neoplatonism. He will almost pass this over from the Florentine circle to Giordano Bruno, who will add a variety of his own motifs, producing a very energetic doctrine. If Castelvetro is a forerunner of Cartesian rationalism and classicism, which constitutes a fundamental mode of modern thinking, Patrizi represents the alternative mode: emotionalism and the revival of the sublime. The two modes are quite different but sometimes they converge; for example, they share a mutual rejection of rhetoric. Rhetoric is barely tolerated by the rationalists, as long as it is restructured and accepts its role as a secondary discipline, while it is openly turned down by the others. In fact, Patrizi produced a short work on rhetoric in which he utterly destroyed it. He progressively took away from it all of its traditional parts: *inventio* and *dispositio* are too important to be left in the hands of rhetoricians; what science can be left without them or has no need to be grounded on proper *topoi*? As to *elocutio*, it is the scandalous occasion where ''figurative'' meaning deprives us of a clear and precise description of things. Obviously Patrizi shares Castelvetro's liking for ''absolute words.'' But from the start, Patrizi, being a convinced Platonist, affirms the primacy of mathematics and apodeixis. For him, it is useless to argue about the properties of the triangle, or of a concave and convex mirror, since the principle of evidence is the proper way to handle these subjects. If one argues that in some social contexts rhetoric has a space of its own (e.g., justice or the government), Patrizi's aristocratic views spring up: he holds in low esteem democratic regimes, assemblies, popular juries. For him power should belong to the few, who must be wise and versed in philosophy, rather than to the loud populace that is subject to the evils of public opinion.

The ground shared by these two scholars does not go beyond a mutual preference for denotation over connotation; their divergence over other issues is, above all, a divorce between two very different philosophical approaches. Rationalism leads Castelvetro to reject the notion of Platonic furor: the poet is a skillful

individual, with a talent for inventing stories, and it is only out of people's ignorance that these abilities are worshipped as divine. Patrizi's views are the opposite: it is exactly this divine agitation, this emotional outburst that constitutes the
poet's distinctive feature and that opens up a mode of action, if not a space for
poetry, since, if we run through the various disciplines, there is not a single one
that exclusively belongs to it. Thus a poet can intervene in any subject whatsoever: human or natural, common or learned, practical or theoretical, provided it
is brought to life with the force of passion, which is technically revealed in versification. Versification is like a fever with the power to confer poetic quality on
whatever it touches, whereas for Castelvetro, orthodox Aristotelian also on this
issue, versification is simply accidental and superficial. What distinguishes the
poet is the ability to make a structural intervention in which is offered a representation, mimetic and cast in a *fabula*, of a subject taken from psychology or
morality.

As I have mentioned, the content-oriented views of Ficion's circle find their
climax in the *Dialoghi* of Giordano Bruno (1548—1600), a work that marks one
of the moments of deepest depression for rhetoric. In a sense, it is a time of widespread crisis for the discursive arts and for the disciplines that stress form. To
them is preferred the pregnancy of "things," or the placing of high value on the
logical approach in its intuitive visual form. Bruno overturns the basic theses of
the humanists and will come to reevaluate the Schoolmen's metaphysics. Certainly he does not absolve Aristotle, who remains a conceited theoretician of
scarcely known matters and of hardly any practical use. Moreover, Aristotle stole
ideas from his predecessors—not just from Plato but from the pre-Socratics as
well. Bruno holds the latter in the highest esteem precisely because their wisdom
was not striking for its elegance but was very substantial.

During his stay in England, Bruno dares to extol Oxford at a time when its
fame was a thing of the past, precisely because that university had addressed the
issue of metaphysics "despite impurities and blots, with certain empty conclusions and theories"; he has a higher opinion of it than he has of "all . . . Ciceronian eloquence and . . . declamatory arts . . . of the present age."[18] They are
two evils, but when one must choose, it is better to search after truth, although
the means may be filthy and coarse, rather than to follow the humanistic orgy of
"lovely little elegancies" (p. 74). The fact is that truth is best pursued away from
the crowd, in the solitude of one's conscience, and in the deepest, most intense
silence. Words are rejected because their sound flatters the ears of the public, and
this of course sanctions a radical rejection of rhetoric. Also, the individual developing a demonstration must be allowed full powers, and must enjoy a special
status; one should not press him or argue with him: "When learning proceeds by
degrees . . . the listener must remain silent and, before having completely heard
and understood, must believe that, with the progress of learning, all difficulties
will cease."[19] The exact opposite was expressed in the doctrine of probability of

Cicero's followers, "who since they profess that nothing can be known, are always asking and searching without ever finding" (p. 45).

Nobody better than Bruno provides evidence of the change that takes place and that involves a shift from the sense of hearing to emphasizing the sense of sight: the immediacy of light substitutes the slow mediation and the allures of hearing: "The degrees of contemplation are like the degrees of light."[20] And the higher contemplation soars, aiming at God, the more it is struck by the divine irradiation: the divine truth "allows itself to be absorbed as promptly as the light of the sun renders itself present to him who turns and opens himself to it" (p. 251). To our senses light is the most rarefied element, close to a total loss of materiality. For this reason it is well suited to express truth, which Bruno calls "an incorporeal thing." As a consequence there follows the forthright contempt for the philosopher's external appearance: we are poles apart from the dignity and propriety in one's clothes that Valla thought necessary, in the name of the elevated task the orator was to accomplish. On the contrary, it is now a sign of success and a guarantee that one is on the right track if the body of the "hero" (of the one who can intuit the divine) is "lean, undernourished, extenuated" or is "deficient in blood and overcome by melancholy humors" (p. 166). This implies the absolute suppression of aesthetic allures; it is an invitation to give up the features that make us sociable, pleasant, and liked in a community. There is a passage in which Bruno pursues these two motifs: one concerns the properties that make an individual well adjusted to the environment: this is what makes one "vulgar, ordinary, civic" (by now we know that these are the values of rhetoric); the other motif shows the opposite features the hero must acquire to become "as free as a deer and an inhabitant of the wilderness" (p. 225).

Once again we encounter the image of the woods, as at the dawn of humanism, when Petrarch and Boccaccio opposed it to the pedantic gymnasium of the logicians. The humanists and Bruno may seem to share a positive view on the use of story or myth to veil a truth that otherwise would be too crude. But this similarity is very superficial and hides a fundamental difference: to the humanists the woods and the *fabula* enhance the possibility of gathering and filtering the pleasure of a truth, which always presents itself in rich garments and with never-ending sensual attractions. For Giordano Bruno they are tools that keep away the despised multitude—tools to put people on the wrong track, and so allow the "heroes" to have the ultimate face-to-face encounter with truth, without mediation, and at the speed and intensity of light. Bruno even rebukes Petrarch for having loved Laura without making his readers aware that she was only a pretext to ascend to a higher knowledge.

Chapter 5
Early Modernity

Rhetoric during the Baroque

We have seen that in the late Renaissance the fortune of rhetoric is running out. Its space is eroded on three fronts: by Ramus's "reformed" logic, which aims at simplicity, good sense, and "naturalness"; by the Platonic coupling of mathematical apodeixis and poetic furor of Patrizi; and finally by Castelvetro's theory of verisimilitude, which calls for the imitation of nature in sober, discreet forms. Although quite different from each other, these three lines agree precisely when it comes to limiting the role of rhetoric.

Nevertheless, in the first half of the seventeenth century the old discursive arts of the trivium, particularly rhetoric and dialectic, enter a phase of energetic last-ditch counterattack. They manage to take up for themselves a new and wider maneuvering space and even succeed in outlining a faculty devoted entirely to their own use: *ingegno*;[1] altogether they deeply influence baroque culture. Certainly the latter is born out of the awareness of the phenomenon T. S. Eliot calls the "dissociation of sensibility." In short, it comes down to the old divorce, always feared by the most tenacious supporters of rhetoric, of things from words, of *docere* from *movere*, of the senses from the intellect, of knowledge from the will. At the beginning of modernity each of these moments is on its way to setting up its autonomy and is eliminating any intrusion of the others within its sphere. On one side stands the search for truth that is becoming ever more rigorous and has acquired its own techniques; on the other side the moral sciences founded on prudence are gathering strength. This state of affairs almost anticipates Kant's pure reason and practical reason, with their inability to communicate with each other and their agreeing only when it comes to rejecting the good offices of the discursive arts.

Also, the baroque foreruns Kant's role in the attempt to fill that increasing gap and to join two modes of knowledge that were moving away from each other; it provides a kind of *Mittelglied*, an *ante litteram* middle ground, and functions as a connecting device between the two by appealing to the synergic and contextual character that *docere, delectare*, and *movere* enjoyed in the golden age of rhetoric. In particular, the task of clearly theorizing the need for unity was undertaken by some Italian scholars. After the Renaissance, to which the contribution of Italian scholarship had been outstanding, the baroque is the last time Italian scholars are in the limelight. The most interesting figures are Emanuele Tesauro (*Il cannocchiale aristotelico*), Matteo Peregrini (*Delle acutezze*), and Matteo Sforza Pallavicino (*Trattato dello stile e del dialogo* and *Del bene*). Here we can only briefly summarize their main ideas. All of them recognize the increasing importance acquired by analytics, made strong by the faculty of judgment, whose function is to distinguish and to bring out differences, in essence, to divide and separate, which is also the aim of prudence. But along with the differentiating moment, they protect the rights of *ingegno*, that is, the faculty that traces resemblances, relationships, affinities, and that does not hesitate to "transport" us from one context to another. Thus they praise tropes, in particular, metaphors that are the most productive among them. On the whole, they underline the importance of the "comparative" processes that Castelvetro and Patrizi, in their preference for "absolute" words, had denounced as dangerous because of their lack of a precise correspondence between words and things. Instead, Tesauro denounces "Socrates' foolish anger":[2] Plato refers to Socrates' wish that human beings had a small opening on their chest through which one would be able to see their thoughts directly, without having to resort to the mediation of language and its misunderstandings. On the contrary, for Tesauro that lack of immediacy is very precious; the comedy of errors opened by the gap between words and things is positive, since it allows ideas to circulate. This amounts to a praise of the circle, rather than of hitting its center with the first shot. And please do not accuse the usual limits of the human condition and complain that we are forced to move within linguistic ambiguities. For Tesauro such ambiguities are so valuable that even God would miss something if he did not have access to them. According to Tesauro, even God aspires to the role of *ingegnoso*.

To be *ingegnoso* in fact means to be endowed with perspicacity, which is the ability to "penetrate the most removed and minute aspects of every subject" (ibid., p. 82). In essence, this relaunches the *inventio* of rhetoric and dialectic, and in fact according to Tesauro one must avail oneself of a list of categories. By this he means that every subject must be questioned on the basis of Aristotle's ten categories, or the "places" of his *Topics*. With this help one performs a sort of digging up that brings out the features that in everything "lie coiled and hidden" (p. 82). *Ingegno* has another property: *versabilitá*. This is the ability to make comparisons fast: "It rapidly compares these aspects . . . it links or divides them; it increases or decreases them; it infers one from another; it mentions one through another; and with wonderful dexterity it sets one in the place of another, as jugglers do with their figures" (p. 82).

Of course all this follows the best rhetorical tradition. However, in the context of rhetoric some provisions were promptly added that would take care to maintain a certain balance: from Aristotle on there was the invitation not to exaggerate in the "transfer"; that is, one should not link things that were too far apart. On the contrary, the theorists of the baroque are aware of living in a critical time during which the universe of knowledge is rapidly growing. To keep knowledge together one must be twice as daring: for Tesauro "the most 'ingegnoso' individual will be one who is able to know and to join the most removed aspects (p. 82). According to Sforza Pallavicino, one must be able "to connect by means of shrewd apprehensions objects that might seem totally unconnected."[3] In addition to the heroic overcoming of enormous cognitive distances, there is the need to do so quickly (with *celeritas mentis*) and to offer dense and synthetic results, to offer a lot of knowledge, to make the mind roam through vast expanses, but starting from a few short words or sentences.[4] This view is the opposite of the long and slow analytic procedure that employs scholastic syllogisms (the type of logic our theorists are still dependent on) or the new "geometrical" process of Descartes's reform.

Our theorists know that they must act quickly, that they must replace with the dexterity of jugglers supports that unfortunately are about to disappear. They know that time is working against them: the true and the useful are on the increase, their territory is expanding rapidly; therefore, the activity of the *ingegnoso* must make up for it with twice as much speed and virtuosity, and must try to create an enchanted, suspended atmosphere that delays the moment of verification. Herein, however, lies the difference between Tesauro's extreme views and the moderation of the other two scholars. The former invites the *ingegnoso* not to fear the Aristotelian rules on decorum and to be always daring, especially when intervening in the free context of poetry rather than in oratory. Of course this challenge to common sense results in folly—in the inability to distinguish between life and the written work, in the application of metaphors taken from the page to life, in disrespect for norms of prudence. The result is that, instead of acquiring dignity and riches, our *ingegnoso* ends up in an asylum, but at least after being generally admired and praised. The other two theorists, although very close to Tesauro's position in their conception of the space for *ingegno*, assign to it a less heroic role, or at least they are more cautious about it, and proceed to draft a long list of instances in which one should not employ *acutezze* (conceit), that is, dangerous transports of *ingegno*; they restrict their use to a very limited number of "genres." Peregrini is the most drastic of the three in indicating the two forces that reduce the maneuvering space of conceit: on one side is "the powerful arm of necessity"; on the other, "the desire to do good to others,"[5] that is, naked truth in all its strength, and the good and useful, just as naked and directly pursued. This points to the realms of pure reason and practical reason, between whose borders *ingegno* has to open a difficult space for itself, and must defend it without openly challenging its strong opponents, who would like to do away with it.

What term should one use to describe the *Mittelglied*, which in order not to crash against the true or the good must steer a course between them? Peregrini identifies it with the beautiful, but Sforza Pallavicino, perhaps more properly, insists on the notion of novelty, astonishment, and marvel. What is certain is that it is "something more," a totalization of different aspects. Undoubtedly a consummate and exceptional ability is necessary to attain such synergism. Thus Peregrini criticizes the traditional school curriculum according to which rhetoric is taught to students in early adolescence (rhetoric occupies the second place in the trivium). This amounts to putting the cart before the mules that should pull it: the teaching of the splendid edifice of conceit must be postponed to a more mature age, when students have the full power of their faculties.[6] This observation is an important one because shortly after, with Vico and the Scottish theorists, rhetoric, to save itself, must take almost the opposite path, and "climb" down the steps of the curriculum in order to become the "first" art that is taught. Not so with the baroque theorists: here for the last time rhetoric affirms its role, more Ciceronian than Aristotelian, of the superior and final synthesis of all arts and sciences, which situates it at the very top of the curriculum instead of having just a propaedeutical function.

On this point, however, we do not have the complete agreement of Sforza Pallavicino, who splits the function of rhetoric. One function is the joining of diverse things and belongs to the line of "perspicacity" and *versabilitá* of *ingegno*. The other function corresponds to the necessity of obtaining *enárgheia*, the evidence of the senses, the abundance and richness of detail: "The pleasure of apprehending is born out of the liveliness of the latter and the splendid colors with which it is painted. . . . Poetry takes care to set in front of the eyes [the successes], protraying them as if alive with their minute circumstances and coloring them with the ultramarine taints of metaphors and similes."[7] This is no longer the high-voltage intellectual play obtained through the application of logical categories, but the perceptual and pictorial reconstruction of objects, reached with a minute and detailed use of rhetorical figures. It is an anticipation of the fusion of rhetoric and sensualism that will actually occur only after a century.

Another considerable contribution to the baroque comes from the Spaniard Baltasar Gracián (1601–58). In his treatise *Agudeza y arte de ingenio* he says nothing new, but rather reaffirms the ideas we have seen. "The concept is an intellectual operation that expresses the correspondence obtaining between objects."[8] (It is the idea of linking diverse things, which is absolutely central to the baroque). "*Ingegno*, unlike judgment, is not satisfied with truth only; rather, it aspires to beauty" (p. 54). (This is the "something more," the contextuality, the conjunction of truth and beauty, *docere* and *delectare*, on which the Italian theorists had insisted, except that they would not all agree that this superior synthesis should be brought back to the beautiful.) And finally a "concept" to express emphatically the very nature of conceit: "Understanding without *agudeza* or concepts is like a sun without light, without rays" (p. 50). But these dense and precise statements are bogged down in an overflowing analysis in which Gracián examines the modes of production of tropes and concepts, illustrating them with numerous examples taken from ancient and modern poets (Gongora above all). In a way, his selection of aphorisms entitled *Oraculo manual y arte de prudencia* is a better work, quicker and denser: here baroque poetics leaves the written page, to become a norm for life, as if to demonstrate that prudence not only has its realm in the useful and the good, but may be grounded on a talent for originality. Here Gracián employs the image of the juggler, which Tesauro also had used, but in the safer context of literature. It is true, though, that the Italian had warned us, half-complacently and half-hopelessly, that *ingegno* applied to practical life leads to the asylum. Gracián tries to outline rules for a life of *ingegno* that may not end so dangerously. The result is an indictment against "playing with one's cards on the table," which is certainly boring and does not bring any pleasure, two evils in baroque culture, but neither does it offer particular guarantees of a peaceful life, since "it is easy to kill a bird on the wing that flies straight."[9] As one can see, adopting an original life-style, "new" and unpredictable, has its good points. There is also the praise of brevity and synthesis ("The quintessence of the matter is more effective than a whole farrago of details,"[10] with an example taken from physiology: a very tall individual is rarely intelligent![11] The Italian theorists also had recognized that the products of *ingegno* are present not only in art but in nature as well.)

Finally, with regard to England, this was perhaps the most prolific and intense area of production of baroque literature (let us only recall the Metaphysical poets), but there are no literary treatises to provide an adequate theory. For this reason we have to address the works of the founder of empiricism, Francis Bacon, with whom we will deal later in this chapter.

Descartes, Pascal, and Leibniz

It is time to deal with rationalism, the philosophical doctrine that is usually analyzed in association with and in opposition to empiricism. With rationalism modernity arrives at the most radical divorce from rhetoric. Descartes (1596–1650) hits the core of rhetoric when he rejects probability, which is the very concept on which rhetoric hinges: "We reject all such merely probably knowledge and make it a rule to trust only what is completely known and incapable of being doubted."[12] At the social level, one consequence of this attitude is the disappearance of a space for dialogue, a space, that is, in which individuals aware of their limits may fairly test and compare their opinions. In fact, even before rhetoric, it is dialectic that comes out defeated, both as the Platonic search after truth that takes place through dialogue, and even more in the Aristotelian sense. Actually, Descartes chooses one of two possible ways indicated by Aristotle, as we mentioned earlier. In no lesser degree than Descartes, in the *Organon* Aristotle had been concerned with the problem of foundations, that is, with the impossibility of infinite regress, and the necessity of stopping at a "primary" datum. But Aristotle had hesitated between dialectic, according to which the foundation lies in the debate among human beings, and a more rigid intuitive solution of self-evident, self-grounded principles. For Descartes the second alternative becomes the only viable one and gives rise to the cult for "clear and precise notions" (by the way, it is one more example of a simile employing the perceptual strength of light and the sense of sight, as privileged over hearing). With this we do not mean that Descartes derived his theories from Aristotle. On the contrary, he breaks away from the conceptual framework of the *Organon*, including the *Analytics*: he rejects the categories (i.e., a qualitative type of logic), and sets forth a quantitative logic based on mathematics, especially on geometry, on the possibility of an infinite breaking down not only of matter, of the *res extensa*, but also of *res cogitans* and of its reassemblage following the rules of calculus. It is also the rejection of all the sensual, emotional components (*delectare* and *movere*) that dialectic and rhetoric had tried to reconcile through logical processes. Now philosophers do not have to worry at all about being boring and do not have to avoid obvious, taken-for-granted passages. On the contrary it is good practice to explain every intermediate passage, and to leave nothing implicit.

This opens the well-known duality that characterizes modernity, the gap between the senses and the mind, between feeling and understanding, between pure reason and practical reason. Indeed, Descartes deals also with the opposite side, the senses, the body, and passions; but he identifies them precisely as the other side, the other sphere of being, in relation to which he traces two solutions. Either he attempts to inscribe it within the sphere of geometrical figures ("it is certain that the infinitude of figures suffices to express all the differences in sensible things").[13] Or, as in the *Passions of the Soul*, he recognizes that it is an irretrievable otherness, the negation of the clarity and preciseness on which the truths of the intellect are founded: "It seems to me that we may define them generally as perceptions, feelings, or emotions of the soul which we relate specially to it, and which are caused, maintained and fortified by some movement of the spirits."[14]

Descartes can bear the weight of this huge gap quite well, but for Pascal (1623–62) it becomes a painful and irremediable problem. He will express it in two different ways of knowing: on one side, the Cartesian *esprit de géométrie*; on the other side, *esprit de finesse*, which is the answer of the rational front to the *Mittelglied* the baroque had identified in *ingegno*. It is a much less flamboyant equivalent; it too is interiorized to the degree that suits "modern" needs, but perhaps exactly for this reason it is not completely fit for the task of bridging the gap.

Only the *esprit de géométrie* is capable of carrying out a demonstration, of being convincing, and therefore of attaining "truth." But its truths unfortunately consist in very simple and somewhat obvious figures; moreover, they are pedantic because of the need to state principles, repeat definitions, list all passages — to the point that the followers of this approach can become ridiculous, especially when they leave the field of geometry. On the whole, this is a certain method, but slow and condemned to remain on the surface. In contrast, the *esprit de finesse* penetrates things in depth, is fast and synthetic; unfortunately it is seldom a certain method since it cannot give rules as to how to proceed: it is *atechnon*, artless. In the end it addresses only other "fine" people, individuals who can understand it and can apply it intuitively. Its aim is the same evidence as the *esprit de géométrie*, but in the vague realm of feelings, rather than in the clear sphere of geometrical principles.

What justifies the presence of Pascal in a text about rhetoric is a work that he felt the need to write: *De l'art de persuader*. Unlike Descartes with his inflexible radicalism, Pascal at least outlines the space that should belong to the counterpart of apodeictic-mathematical logic. However, conditioned by the "modern" anxiety to define rigorously and split up elements, he makes it a typically aporetic locus, marked by lack, and to be treated only with the uncertain ways of *finesse*. He acknowledges that, besides being able to convince, one must please others, and that to please is "more difficult, more subtle, more useful, and more admirable."[15] But this praise remains useless because immediately afterward Pascal declares his position of impotence: "The principles of pleasure are not firm or stable" (p. 595); and apart from geometry, "there is scarcely a truth upon which we have always agreed" (p. 595). Pascal almost overturns Descartes's position when from the pride, the full confidence in the preeminence of the logical-mathematical method he moves to a position that shows the limits, the "inadequacies" of the method. He is perfectly aware that alongside it there is a much vaster and more interesting continent, which belongs to the "practical" reasons of the heart, pleasure and feelings. But about it there is almost nothing one can say. It must be left to the finesse of the unexpressed, to a psychological intensity that does not tolerate external measurements and cannot be equipped with techniques. Thus the famous Pascalian maxim "La vraie éloquence se moque de l'éloquence"[16] finds here all its relevance. I had referred to it in Chapter 1 when dealing with the anonymous *Sublime*, and rightly so, because the stress on the emotions becomes the inevitable counterpart of rationalism. It is not by chance that in 1674 Boileau, author of a Cartesian *Art poétique*, translates into French the text of Pseudo-Longinus, which once again is the focus of attention, after having been revived by the Italian Patrizi in the sixteenth century. Thus Pascal's is a negative rhetoric; it needs silence so as not to disturb the intensity of intuitions; it is rich in insight, but remains essentially mute. From its perspective, the precepts of rhetoric manuals, with their attention to verbal forms, become futile. For example, "Those who indulge in the scheme of antithesis are like those who make sham windows for the sake of symmetry."[17] At stake is not so much the use of the right figures of speech, but rather "fair speaking." The reader will have noticed also the unpleasant repetition, in this quotation, of the demonstrative pronoun "those," which is against all stylistic rules. But this transgression fits the antirules made necessary by Pascal's contempt for *elocutio*.

Thus also for Pascal reality remains divided into two zones that do not communicate. Later on, Leibniz (1646–1716) tries to fill the gap within rationalism. Empiricists and sensationalists arrive at the same result but by means of different paths. Some aspects of Vico's theories will be similar, too. What we see emerging is a kind of eighteenth-century *koine*, grounded on points of correspondence that may have very different origins. Leibniz's ingenious solution is to avoid the opposition between feelings and the rational, or probability and truth, and to affirm that they are consubstantial: "The modes and degrees of perfection vary infinitely. Meanwhile the ground is everywhere the same"[18] — to the point that it is not worth it to institute separate disciplines (for example, it is not worth it to separate physics from moral philosophy and logic). There are only "different arrangements of the same truths."[19] All that is needed is to set up a progressive scale that, following the metaphor, will have ascending steps ranging from the confused and obscure to the clear and precise. Thus the two Cartesian pairs would no longer collide head-on but would arrange themselves serially, precisely in a series of small gradual passages. However, this does not lead to a full rehabilitation of the confused and the obscure, because if these qualities now achieve the same ontological dignity, they pay for this right by occupying a lower position on the scale. They are recognized as belonging to the same family, but their role is a subordinate one: they are relegated to the lower part of this vertical hierarchy. With respect to the *ingegno* of the baroque, there is incalculable progress in the "modernity" with which the rational and psychological faculties are refounded; at the same time, however, there is a regress since synergy disappears, and above all the synchronic moment that gave unity to various human aspects and concerns disappears. Some of these are downgraded and must take an "inferior" position in the new topology. This can easily be verified in the works of Alexander Gottlieb Baumgarten (1714–62), an indirect student of Leibniz's through Christian Wolff. In 1750 Baumgarten introduces the term "aesthetics" and defines it as *scientia cognitionis sensitivae*, the science of sensuous cognition, which destines it to remain *gnoseologia inferior*, an inferior form of knowledge. When dealing with Vico later in this chapter, we will come back to this enormous catastrophe befalling the perceptual-emotional faculties that are downgraded and actually undergo a diachronic repositioning according to which they are ascribed to the primordial phase of human history.

For Leibniz, then, sensory experience is made up of a band of "small" perceptions, which are various and numerous, practically infinite, and therefore cannot lend themselves to "clear and precise" knowledge. After all, this minute soil of sensory ideas is the goal of rhetorical figures, in their manner of intervention ever quicker and on a small scale, as Sforza Pallavicino had described. But there is a perceptual threshold beyond which figures as such can no longer be distinguished, and seem entirely blended with sensations. This is the death of logical-rhetorical techniques to the advantage of a "modern" psychology of perception. In fact, Leibniz is very harsh toward rhetoric in its traditional forms, and on several occasions denounces its untenability. It is true, though, that he tones down the strictness of the original Cartesian project by assigning considerable space to the sphere of probability, the ambiguous, the sensual, and by applying also to these areas the criteria of infinitesimal calculus.

Bacon and Empiricism

Before we deal with empiricism, which is traditionally contrasted with rationalism, we should be aware of a significant time gap in the lives of their respective founders. Bacon (1561–1626) is almost two generations older than Descartes; thus the fact of belonging to a post-Renaissance culture makes him more yielding toward rhetoric. From his enormous corpus, focusing especially on *De augmentis scientiarum* and *Novum organum*, we will try to select the issues most related to our inquiry. On the whole the contributions of the founder of empiricism can be summarized as follows: (1) outright rejection of scholastic and pseudo-Aristotelian dialectic, when it claims to deal with natural sciences; and (2) acknowledgment that dialectic has validity, and even more so rhetoric, when civic and practical matters are at stake. On this point he is perhaps the first to outline the topological-diachronic "fall" of rhetoric that will be developed by Vico (it is well known that Vico was an admirer and a follower of Bacon's) and by eighteenth-century sensationalists. Rhetoric, in a more or less close alliance with poetry, is located in the zones of fancy and the imagination: "Rhetoric certainly is at the service of imagination . . . the function and duty of rhetoric is to apply and commend the precepts of reason and imagination."[20] Of course this is a legitimate function, but on the other hand it is "inferior" to that of the intellect, whether the latter employs the "old" dialectic or, better, the "new organ": "eloquence is . . . without doubt inferior to wisdom" (p. 438). This gives rise to a division, and a consequent hierarchy, that also involves the opposition between the particular of rhetoric and the universal of logic (ancient or modern). In fact, the audience addressed by an orator is concrete, well defined, and actually present (here Bacon is accepting one of the most traditional notions of rhetoric), whereas a logician addresses so wide an audience that it becomes abstract and universal. This is very important because it leads Bacon to identify different ways of making history, depending on whether one remains within the "particular" of a people, or whether one wants to trace a general framework, leaving aside actual cases. This already contains the opposition, which will be taken up and further developed by Vico, between what is certain and what is true, and also, I want to stress it once more, the firm belief that the first mode (i.e., that of the particular and fancy) is rhetorically more effective; but exactly for this reason it must come "before" in the school curriculum, to be supplanted only later on by a system of logic that employs universals.

Bacon's position is really a complex one, however, since, as Luciano Anceschi has convincingly shown, in his works there are also traces of a proposal that anticipates the ideas of the Italian baroque theorists. Also, to remain within the domain of British culture, he merges the Elizabethan with the Jacobean period of the Metaphysical poets, and develops theoretical principles that, as I have said, one would be unable to find in the poets of the time. In fact, the products of rhetorical imagination (besides the terms *fancy* and *imagination* there is also the word *wit*)[21] are not always more primitive and in an inferior position with respect to the operations of logic and science. They may also situate themselves "beside," in a competitive position, equivalent to the *acutezza* and the *ingegno* of the Italian baroque theorists. This consists in a freewheeling search for the most far-off similes, in the name of a *felicity*[22] of insight that avails itself also of chance, and therefore is active on a horizon of immanent, worldly comparisons. This path is conducive to "illegal unions," unlike marriages consummated with the official blessings of legitimation provided by the natural sciences, which preserve differences very carefully.

Thus with Bacon empiricism accepts the concept of "wit," which falls within the psychological faculties of which perception is an articulation. But after Bacon this area is progressively eroded; it becomes the victim of the widening "modern" gap, and also of the increased need for rational control, along paths not too different from those followed on the front of rationalism. Satisfactory enough is the arrangement proposed by Hobbes (1588–1679). In the eighth chapter of the *Leviathan*, he starts by acknowledging that there is a *natural wit*, which corresponds to a *celerity of Imagining*,[23] as a result of which some people are able to grasp rare similes that escape the majority. This is the basis for determining who has good wit or fancy (it is extremely difficult to differentiate between the features of the two). But alongside the individuals endowed with wit, there are also individuals Hobbes praises for the opposite quality, that is, for their ability to grasp differences, described as "distinguishing', discerning, and judging," and this constitutes on the whole the ability to judge well. This quality Hobbes values more highly, more "positively" than the others. Also, this offers the opportunity to trace a casuistry about the use of the various abilities. Wit is allowed to dominate the sphere of poetry, as long as it is kept in check by judgment. In the field of history, judgment must prevail. To fancy (which is the locus where rhetoric has ended up) is assigned the task of embellishing style.

At the time, the "ornamental" purpose was a very important one and should be stressed, as Wimsatt and Brooks remind us in their comprehensive *Literary Criticism: A Short History*. In fact, in early modernity, that is, starting from the second half of the seventeenth century, rhetoric does not fare well at all on the theoretical level, whereas on the level of "diction" its role is still safe. Every classical writer, from Corneille to Racine, from Dryden to Pope, recognizes the importance of rhetoric in relation to stylistic ornamentation. However, its role is limited to defining the texture, and certainly does not reach poetic structure. In this more significant domain the precepts of Aristotle's poetics rule, accompanied by various warnings to intervene with the reins of discretion: it is the triumph of "verisimilitude" and control, as formulated by Castelvetro a century before.

Sir William Davenant, a friend of Hobbes's, in the preface to his heroic poem *Gondibert* (1650), a work written according to the "new" classicist taste, stigmatizes the excesses of baroque poets who with no restraint give themselves up to the allures of wit: "Like young Hawks they stray and fly farr off; using their liberty as if they would ne're returne to the Lure; and often goe at check ere they can make a stedy view, and know their game."[24] If the need for restraint emerges in the practice of poetry, which by universal assent is the area that can most indulge in the temptations of wit, one can imagine the extent to which the "new" and "modern" sense of *austerity*[25] imposes itself on scientific discourse. We have but to look at one of the founding documents of the Royal Society, whose goal is scientific research: it proclaims a crusade to free language of "those spacious *Tropes* and *Figures* of imaginative writing which result in only mists and uncertainties."[26] The colorful operations of rhetoric and the plays of fancy become the adversary from which one has to defend oneself. There is also the exhortation "to return back to the primitive purity, and shortness, when men deliver'd so many things, almost in an equal number of words" (p. 39). This is again the dream of the little window that allows one to see inside human beings so as to eliminate the space of ambiguity and comparison, which Tesauro had already critiqued. Obviously, the position of the Royal Society is one of absolute rigor. Poetic diction still survives alongside it and actually strengthens itself, as writers are tied to it by the very nature of their field.

John Locke (1632–1704) is another good witness to the fact that in English culture wit and the related faculties conquered a space for themselves that could not be passed over in silence. Indeed, Locke records it in his *Essay Concerning Human Understanding*. This work constitutes the best introduction to the eighteenth century; it contributes to the refounding, in the key of elementarism and psychological associations, of the entire range of human faculties, and definitely dissolves the Aristotelian framework of purely verbal forms of discourse. There are no longer hollow and full parts, but only "ideas," small particles of content that can be combined in a variety of ways. This is the tendency to homogenize that we met in Leibniz, and that he had actually derived from Locke, thus drawing closer, at least in this aspect, empiricism and rationalism, and laying the ground for the eighteenth-century atomist-sensationalistic-infinitesimal *koine*.

The section in the *Essay* (II, XI, 2) where Locke expounds the features that oppose wit and judgment should be quoted in its entirety for its clarity and conclusiveness. However, it is but the ultimate, and most effective, synthesis of what had already fully emerged in Bacon and Hobbes, and even in the Italian baroque theorists. Locke traces the usual opposition between assembling ideas quickly and recklessly, a rather misleading procedure, and distinguishing between ideas and things in a more rational and precise way. Although *ingegno* and wit are still allotted some space, there is almost no awareness of their rhetorical origin. Thus, when Locke tackles the issue of education in *Some Thoughts on Education*, he gives very little space to rhetoric. He makes but a brief and limiting mention, where only Cicero as usual escapes unscathed: he is the one author worth reading. The gentleman,[27] that is, the proper bourgeois addressed by Locke in his pedagogical treatise, should be versed in many practical skills, including even gymnastics and sports, as well as in scientific disciplines. Of course he should also have a good knowledge of grammar and language, but this should not include the complications of conceited discourse. A few decades before Locke, Pascal's *honnête homme* had in the same way given up the seductions of speaking well for speaking rightly. And Molière, through Alceste, had strongly condemned Oronte's poetic composition, drawn according to the rules of preciosity, while praising a direct and precise way of speaking that draws inspiration from nature and common sense, and of which the people are the repository. It is true, though, that Alceste is the misanthrope par excellence. The bareness of rigorous discourse, typical of the Royal Society or of the logic of Port Royal, becomes totally inappropriate in the context of social life, where on the contrary one should stick to a moderate attitude. A compromise is needed in such a way that wit will be controlled by discretion and judgment: in other words, figures should be used only for the scope of ornamentation. This propensity for moderation is to be found also in Joseph Addison (1672–1719), who in an article in *The Spectator* (March 12, 1711) suggests a mutual adaptation: "to keep alive morality with wit, to temper wit with morality."[28] However, the suspicion against purely verbal adventures is still alive and widens, so much so that Addison proclaims as "false" the kind of wit that does not find its equivalent in things.

Vico: The "Particular" of Rhetoric and the "Universal" of Logic

Recent scholarship has toned down the idealistic interpretation that Croce and Gentile gave of Gian Battista Vico (1668–1744): they had seen him as a solitary figure moving against the current. Of course Vico's originality is not in question, but it actually emerges in all its strength when one considers the profound ties he always maintained with rhetoric, not only on a theoretical level, but professionally as well, as a teacher of eloquence. In fact, Vico is a good heir to Cicero in the determination to defend the primacy of human concerns (law, politics, morality, poetry, etc.) over physical sciences: it is of course the opposition between practical reason and pure reason. Although tenaciously opposed to Descartes, Vico however accepts the Cartesian method, and believes that one must start from apodeictic, indubitable premises. Consequently, Vico's great task will be that of founding an apodeixis not only of what is "clear and precise," of analytic logic and geometry, but also of what is "confused and obscure" in practical matters, including emotions and feelings. On several different fronts too it was soon understood that the drastic Cartesian division could not be sustained (we have seen the alleged solutions proposed by Pascal and Leibniz). Therefore Vico's novelty does not lie in affirming the rights of the confused and obscure, but rather in attempting to ensure that they too receive a methodological foundation equal in dignity to that of mathematics.

In this pursuit the works of Bacon help by suggesting the reactivation of a particular property that had always been intrinsic to rhetoric. In fact, rhetoric has always offered a ground where one may discuss uncertain matters, trusting one's ability to persuade others and drawing on their sensual pleasure. What takes shape is a *paidéia* relying on the power of fascination of what strikes the senses and the imagination and availing itself of the particular, concrete character of examples, so that it is well suited for a popular, unspecialized public, unlike the universal and abstract language of logic. However, in antiquity the two approaches lived side by side, in complete synergy and synchronicity. To resort to one or the other depended on the compatibility of the subjects treated and on the audience one was addressing, but they always remained joint tools. Already Bacon had had the idea of separating in time the study of rhetoric from that of logic (dialectic), and of assigning them to two different pedagogical stages. Vico institutionalizes with the utmost strength this model of diachronic repositioning, and in doing so he breaks with antiquity, including its last offshoot, the age of the baroque. Recently there has been the tendency to consider Vico as part of baroque culture. Of course on the stylistic level, in the use of certain figures, from metaphor to emblem, the relationship is one of closeness and contiguity. But in terms of general project, of system modeling, one encounters an unbridgeable difference, which is precisely revealed by the different topological destiny of rhetoric. As we saw earlier, Peregrini complained that rhetoric was taught to adolescents, whereas he believed that it was the summit of the entire *cursus*. In Vico's system, in contrast, rhetoric becomes the "providential" tool through which God teaches human beings, in their primordial phase (the dawn of both the individual and the group), certain truths that they would not be able to understand in a bare form. So God must present them in the garb of *fabula* and examples, dressed in imaginative language. Only later, when the psychological evolution is completed and human beings have reached the stage of adulthood, will they be able to understand the direct language of logic, so the general movement proceeds from philology to philosophy.

This diachronic model holds for at least two centuries, since it will be resumed by Hegelian idealistic historicism. A very strong reaction will be necessary on the part of our culture to shake it off and restore the right of presence of all human faculties, without these having to undergo hierarchical arrangements and alternations, according to which it would be possible to go from one faculty to another only through a sort of "death" or sublimation of one of them. Notwithstanding his deep fondness for rhetoric, Vico strikes a heavy blow against it. Surely he rescues it, but at the price of "lowering" its position, and making it impossible for rhetoric to exist alongside mathematical apodeixis. We can clearly see how mathematics, over two centuries, was able to condition also the partisans of the human sciences, like Vico, who although they felt obliged to protect the rights of sensual persuasion, did not dare deal with it as an equal, but preferred to alternate it with its strong rival, so that it would not have to sustain a direct confrontation.

It must be stressed once more that the idea of alternating the two models of knowledge is not at all exclusive to Vico: already outlined by Bacon, it pervades the second half of the eighteenth century, and is resumed, in a different key, by Hegelian historicism. But Vico's originality lies precisely in the strength with which he was able to shape this diachronic repositioning, ensuring, so to speak, an apodeixis of the mobile and an axiomatics of the dynamic. Above all, for our inquiry, it is important that he comes to this proposal by means of the traditional features of rhetoric. From an instrument of discourse, rhetoric is almost raised to the responsibilities of ontological hinge. It becomes the tool through which Providence regulates the flow of history, in its various recurrences, teaching people and guiding them in a process of growth and maturation. In essence, it is the same metaphysical role that a century later Hegel will assign to dialectic, the other discursive art and ever-present counterpart of rhetoric.

Sensationalism: Words versus Terms

We must acknowledge that from the eighteenth to the nineteenth century the attention Vico pays to rhetoric is virtually unparalleled. The two models dominating the scene are those that I identified in the Renaissance in the discussions of

Castelvetro and Patrizi. The first model is marked by the primacy of Aristotelian poetics, classicism, moderation: in it rhetoric has a strictly ornamental function. The second model, which is the dialectical counterpart of the first, rediscovers the sublime and pathos. English writers such as Sir William Temple, John Dennis, and the Earl of Shaftesbury belong to the second model, while a powerful English representative of the moderate front is Doctor Johnson (1709–84), who officially applies the label "Metaphysical" to the poets of the Jacobean period. The label is born out of dislike and is intended to condemn the abstruse usage of conceit, of extreme linguistic peculiarities, and the lack of common expressions. For him, "The business of a poet is to examine, not the individual, but the species; to remark general properties and large appearances":[29] a view contrary to the direction that poetics and rhetoric are about to take (we may add aesthetics too, since it will emerge soon).

I have mentioned that from the second half of the eighteenth century one can observe, in the works of writers born in the first part of the century, the emergence of a *koine* within which a variety of tendencies are eclectically fused. There is the Lockian model, a direct descendant of empiricism, with its distinction between primary and secondary ideas, and the concept of association; this model is strengthened by Hume, the last great representative of empiricist tradition. The position occupied by Leibniz's system, the latest development of rationalism, is not too far off, thanks to the arrangement of the confused and the clear on a continuum. In this way, the particular and the universal, the sensory and the intellectual, on both the empiricist and the rationalist fronts, become homogeneous; the Cartesian duality can be overcome, but what remains is that diachronic gap we discussed when we dealt with Vico. What is confused, particular, and sensual is compelled to situate itself in primitive times, with respect to both the individual and the species. This implies a one-way direction, a historical vector that starts from the imagination and arrives at logic. Vico's solution, which is the result of a solitary, heroic project with strong chiaroscuro colors in relation to the philosophical climate of the time, will impose itself after a few decades through a creeping growth, so to speak, without traumas, and with universal unanimity. Also the emotionalist front linked to the sublime contributes to the picture. Pathos stops presenting itself as *atechnon*, artless energy, wild and uncontrollable: it goes along well with the "obscure" and the particular; actually, it becomes their spring, or their fuel. Given that the confused, the perceptual, the sensual, etc., speak the language of rhetoric, as a consequence rhetorical figures will no longer be the result of the intellectual acuteness found in *ingegno*, as happened during the baroque, but rather of the emotional tide, of feelings. This means that in some way the irrational has been rationalized, that it has become a tool.

The same configuration is to be found in France, England, and Italy, allowing of course for inevitable differences as one moves from one author to another. In France, it is represented by the sensualists and the encyclopedists, from Condillac to Diderot. Condillac (1715–80) in *Art d'écrire*, a relatively late work (1775), makes the distinction between *netteté* and *caractère*. The former describes the Cartesian *esprit de géométrie*, or Locke's primary ideas. The latter expresses the Pascalian need for finesse; in contemporary words, it is the awareness that one must contextualize, that discourse and the texture of perceptions must be opened up. In fact, Condillac observes that the individual who did not acquire the habit of enbracing a great number of ideas will be very narrow-minded. From this derives a notion that is fundamental to understanding the cultural climate we are examining, and which we meet again and again: it is that of accessory/secondary ideas, which can be acquired on the condition that one avoids the absolute use of words, linguistic bareness, or words in a vacuum; rather, words should be seen in their context, in the full relationships they maintain with contiguous, similar, opposite, etc., ideas. After all, here we find again the *topoi* and the categories to which the *ingegnosi* baroque poets resorted to "work" on their subject matter in order to make it interesting. The difference is that now contiguity, similarity, and so on, are caught not so much by virtue of a logical excursion into the *topoi*, but through sensory perceptions. The foundations are decisively psychological, and the thrust of the emotions plays a great role. Another observation: in the very idea of "supplementarity"/"secondariness" one can perceive a certain "modern," dissociated depreciation in relation to contextuality: after the process of relentless splitting up that precipitated the "bare" and the universals of logic in all their purity, there is now the attempt to cover them, to clothe them with additions through a process of aggregation. Of course Condillac also develops the theory of the three ages: infancy, maturity, and the decay of humanity.

The traces of the dissociation are perhaps more visible in Diderot (1713–84). In some passages of his vast and multifarious corpus, he opposes clarity, which "is all for convincing"[30] to enthusiasm, whose function is to move us: a task for poets, who consequently are invited to remain obscure and vague. Moreover, from a psychology of rhetorical techniques he shifts to a physiological interpretation. In this way metaphorical imagination is compared to a "sympathetic vibration of strings at unexpected intervals (p. 51). He also suggests, as the baroque theorists or even Aristotle had done, striving for "the creation of original metaphors, the yoking together of remote spheres, the apprehension of unsuspected relations": now, however, this process comes about "through the accumulation of delicate and varied experiences during the long life of an organism" (ibid.)

Passing now to the British scene, we owe Wellek the clear awareness that the fusion we described has taken place: "emotionalist concepts . . . were strongly encouraged by ideas revived from ancient rhetoric, with its emphasis on effects."[31] An exemplary case showing the merging of the two lines is *Lectures on Rhetoric* by the Scot Hugh Blair (1718–1800).[32] The work has the features of a manual, since it develops a broad and precise analysis of figures and tropes; but at the same time it provides a no less exhaustive psychological ground. "Figures, in general, may be described to be that Language, which is prompted either by the imagination, or by the passions" (I, p. 346), more or less fired by the objects that animate the mind (see II, p. 177, or III, p. 85). We must underline the distinction between the two branches of the sentimental: there is imagination, heir to baroque fancy or wit; and there is passion, the offspring of the sublime, which previously was not regarded as compatible with imagination. The reconciliation between the two is one more sign of the eclectic climate I have described: now they are set within the same theoretical framework on an equal footing, and the various rhetorical figures are distributed between them. As a result, there will be figures of passion and figures of the imagination: a most useful tool for the variety of possible applications in poetry and prose. Among the figures suggested by passion Blair lists interrogations, exclamations, apostrophe, vision (the latter "supposes a sort of enthusiasm, which carries the person who describes in some measure out of himself"; I, p.453). More relaxed and undisturbed are the figures of speech that belong to "the language of imagination" (I, p. 435), which confirms that this faculty is now seen as less subversive than it was during the Renaissance and the baroque; in fact, it includes either some well-known *topoi* (comparison, antithesis), or some well-contained constructions such as climax, hypotyposis, and preterition.

Blair's "modern" bias is revealed by the anxiety with which he stresses that rhetorical figures should not become ends in themselves; they should not be completely artificial and need the legitimation of "naturalness": "They must always rise naturally from the subject" (II, p. 2). Also, any stylistic transgression of the sound, simple rules of bare logical discourse must be justified by feelings; it must arise in a mind animated by the object that fills it, in much the same way as a bank note implies an equivalent amount of gold in the funds of the treasury department. Otherwise, without the presence of natural emotions, every eighteenth-century theorist would suspect fraud, deception, empty pseudological acrobatics. The other inevitable "modern" bias, to which Blair is liable through the spirit of the times, just like any of his contemporaries, is what we may call the "Vico effect," that is, the diachronic separation of the age of passions and the age of *logos*: it is a shortcut to avoid the irreconcilable duality of the Cartesian system. It must be understood that Vico has little to do with it; it is an unavoidable measure many eighteenth-century theorists take by force of models, but it is not possible and even unnecessary to conclude that they had direct knowledge of Vico's *Scienza nuova*. Thus Blair, too, believes in the myth of the "native original language of Poetry, among the most barbarous nations," so rich in emotions that it makes broad use of "those turns of expression, which we now distinguish by the learned names of Hyperbole, Prosopopoeia, Simile, & c" (III, p. 89). Rhetoric belongs to the beginning; it is identified with the strong emotions that arose in primitive times.

We chose Blair as representative of the Scottish school as well as of a broader and very fertile British ground to which belong figures like Henry Home, Lord Kames, with his *Elements of Criticism* (1762); George Campbell, author of *Philosophy of Rhetoric* (1776), which stresses that the function of rhetoric is to aim at the particular and at the individual evidence of the object in view; Alexander Gerard, author of *An Essay on Genius* (1774), in which genius is the faculty called to manage the imagination, and as such it has the modern-moderate duty to direct it toward a goal, without allowing it to go astray, or to be eccentric. On the level of a general epistemology, Adam Ferguson with *Principles of Moral and Political Science* (1792) and Dugald Stewart with *Elements of the Philosophy of the Human Mind* (1792) are already trying to move the association of secondary ideas from the "modern" context of the sum to the "contemporary" one of the synthesis (Stewart puts forward the notion of their "coalescence").

Two Italians that make a relevant contribution to the issues we are describing are Cesare Beccaria (1716–81) and Melchior Cesarotti (1730–1808). Their proposals are not new (they are derived from French sensualism), but they offer a clear and effective global systematization, with some good in-depth analyses. In *Ricerche intorno alla natura dello stile* (Research about the nature of style, 1770),[33] Beccaria takes from Condillac the notion of accessory ideas and sees all the elegance and worth of style as hinging on it. Remarkable and very acute is his insight concerning the presence of a "crowd of very minute pleasures with which our life is almost continuously filled, and that are daily lost for us because of the gloomy remembrance of the past and our restless thrusts into the future" (p. 218). The psychology of the eighteenth century is so sharpened that it almost anticipates "lived experience" and the "stream of consciousness" of the end of the nineteenth century and the beginning of the twentieth, when novelists and poets attempted to capture, with epiphanies or the "remembrance of things past," such a treasure of almost elusive sensations ("rapid and passing flashes of attention that lit up in us through accessory ideas that are simply awakened/stirred and not expressed"; p. 223). Style, and the old tools of rhetoric along with it, are the only anchor for avoiding the boredom of a universe of absolute words, that is, words that deny the pleasure of the context, of associations and connections.

As with Blair's *Lectures*, with Beccaria's *Ricerche* it is very interesting to follow the transcription of rhetorical figures in a psychological-physiological key. For example, why is *cocchio* (coach) stylistically better than *carrozza* (carriage)? Not because it is rather uncommon, but "because the idea is represented by a shorter sign; so that the same effect is obtained with less expenditure of energy and time" (p. 226). The notion of saving energy and of rapid apprehension had been stressed by the theorists of *ingegno*, and we will come back to saving on the expenditure of energy when dealing with Freudian psychoanalysis. And why is the epithet "white snow" flat, while it is more effective to call snow "cold"?

Because the first description is ordinary and above all it gives the thing an obvious visual completion, while the latter, belonging to the sense of touch, is not so common or is more removed. In fact, Beccaria will theorize the systematic use of synesthesia, precisely to connect the different modes of the senses; in the same way he finds "very beautiful the combination in which a physical element is added to a moral object, and to a physical object is added a moral element" (p. 231). It is almost an anticipation of T. S. Eliot's "objective correlative," and thus it is an effort to overcome the modern "dissociation" between the different spheres of reality (but it is an effort that follows the analytic way of the dissociation, of the sum, of the atomic combination). Certainly there is a spiritual affinity with T. S. Eliot, to the point that Beccaria criticizes "the imitators of Petrarch and sometimes Petrarch himself" (p. 309), because in describing modes of feelings and accessory integrations they remained within boundaries that were too spiritual, and so a proper dose of objects and particularities was lacking in their work. In fact, Italian sensualism is backed by a sort of *ante litteram* poetics of objects; thus it finds congenial to its taste the poetry of Parini. In contrast, the Petrarchian mode is anemic, poor; it does not mix the various spheres of experience, which is negative not only on the stylistic level but on the existential level as well, if it is true that, as Beccaria believes, by increasing the number of ideas, the feeling of our existence seems augmented and amplified. These same motifs will be elaborated by Giacomo Leopardi, but in the key of a tragic clash, which the eighteenth-century Beccaria does not know. Beccaria accepts the usual diachronic model: he entrusts the passing of the ages with the task of balancing the relationship between the "poetic" times and the age of cold reason, so that any radical opposition will be avoided, unlike what Leopardi will do.

An important work that will influence Leopardi's theory of language is Cesarotti's *Saggio sulla filosofia delle lingue* (Essay on the philosophy of languages, 1785), in which a fundamental difference is drawn between terms (*termini*) and words (*vocaboli*). The former, also called memory words or numeral terms, "have with the idea only a conventional and arbitrary relationship."[34] On the contrary the latter, which for a good reason are also called figure terms, deal with the contextual and relational properties of rhetoric. This means that they do not limit themselves to "recalling the main idea," but they "depict it, dress it, shape it in a more particular, or more lively way, or they give rise to other accessory ideas." In fact, no one is more aware than Cesarotti of the importance of the context and of the "concert" that the various words give rise to, in such a way that each one of them loses its original and absolute meaning, in order to constitute a "sum total formed by their mutual interweaving" (p. 34). To be precise, one could remark that the sum is not yet a synthesis and not even a structure — but these concepts were unknown to eighteenth-century culture.

Chapter 6
Modernity

Kant's Search for a *Mittelglied*

We have already mentioned Kant (1724–1804), apparently in an arbitrary way, when we talked about the theorists of *Ingegno* and their notion of a *Mittelglied*. Indeed, the link is arbitrary if one considers what is to be used in the "space in between" by Kant and the theorists in order to bridge the gap. As an heir to the eighteenth-century philosophical tradition based on sensationalism, nothing could be more removed from Kant's taste than the conceptual linguistic play dear to the baroque. Nevertheless, the space opened, and the need to fill it, to a great extent overlap: what is at stake is the need to reconcile knowledge with morality, the laws of nature with human freedom. The similarity obtains also for the negative attitude toward Vico's diachronic model. Actually, for baroque theorists it is not even a question of rejection: they simply ignore such a possibility, which lies outside the ancient conception of a full, perfect synergism between the different arts and discursive faculties, within which each has its specific function, but all are placed on the same level. For his part, Kant strongly rejects the diachronic model. In this respect he is the great forerunner of our contemporary age: with it he sets up a direct line that overcomes the once-again historicist and diachronic deviation, which Hegel will officially introduce within a few decades.

However, if Kant is fully aware that imagination and aesthetics must be brought to a level of full synchronicity with the understanding and reason, he is not of the opinion that they should be grounded on rhetoric. Actually, he does not hold the latter in much esteem. One may say that he outlines a space for its function, while the organ is lacking: Kant is very sensitive to the introduction of tools that may join sensory experience with understanding, outward necessity with interior freedom. This was a task that rhetoric had performed in the past, but Kant is more inclined to assign it to a discursive faculty close to poetry, or more generally to the arts and aesthetic judgment. To be sure rhetoric does not leave the stage entirely; at the last minute it is able to join the beautiful arts, more specifically the subgroup of the discursive arts, with a function very close to that of poetry. The leading force in the group, however, remains poetry, which is conceived as pure, disinterested, and independent of the understanding. In fact, there is a sort of inversion of roles between rhetoric and poetry, something that on one side demonstrates that they are located in the same space with similar functions, but on the other confirms that poetry is privileged. Rhetoric is "the art of carrying on a serious business of the understanding as if it were a free play of the imagination,"[1] which means that it remains tied to pure reason and the cognitive faculties and thus is oriented toward precise goals. In contrast, poetry consists in the free play of the imagination, and the mark of "business of the understanding" bears on it in the free, not binding, form of an "as if." We could also say that rhetoric makes a good start but finishes badly: at first the orator "gives something which he does not promise, viz. an entertaining play of the imagination (p. 165). But then he fails to supply something that instead should have been one of his goals, since rhetoric is still connected with knowledge: he fails to provide the "purposive occupation of the understanding" (p. 165). In conclusion, rhetoric remains a half-measure, an unsatisfactory solution, a compromise. This will lead Kant to declare his preference for the clearer and more straightforward ways of poetry: "A beautiful poem has always given me a pure gratification, while the reading of the best discourse, whether of a Roman orator or of a modern speaker . . . has always been mingled with an unpleasant feeling of disapprobation of a treacherous art" (p.172n). Actually, what is taking shape here is a distinction between eloquence and oratory: the former reveals the free play between imagination and understanding, while the latter is the practical end of rhetoric. We find here one more point of similarity that Kant shares with the model of theorists of *ingegno* had been led to develop: exactly like *ingegno*, the free play of poetry or eloquence may weave its suspended magic space, as long as it does not collide against knowledge and necessity. Confronted with the latter it will miserably sink, or at least it must give up its place: "If we are dealing with civil law, with the rights of individual persons, or with lasting instruction and determination of people's minds to an accurate knowledge and a conscientious observance of their duty, it is unworthy . . . to allow a trace of any luxuriance and imagination to appear" (p. 171). And again, more clearly, "It is unworthy of so important a business to allow . . . any trace of the art of talking people over and of captivating them for the advantage of any chance person (p. 171).

In sum, Kant must be credited with the great merit of having forcefully inserted between pure reason and practical reason, the two big blocks modernity has inherited, a third space for their reconciliation through imagination and aesthetics. Moreover he introduces it on an equal footing, in full synchronicity, and without resorting to the device of progressive growth, or the diachronic-genetic-historical axis, to which had resorted the philosophers of the second half of the eighteenth century who were searching for a mediation. But Kant's *Mittelglied* is fragile and insecure, and in fact he dealt with it somewhat late in the elaboration of his philosophical system, when it was already difficult to find an adequate space for it.

On the contrary, Friedrich Schiller (1759–1805) tries to strengthen that mediating link considerably, while fully respecting Kant's theoretical watermark. He actually raises the Kantian system to dramatic proportions by conceiving the two "modern" spheres of necessity and freedom as "drives" (he employs the term *Trieb*, the same word Freud will use for psychoanalysis). On one side is the drive toward material sensory experience (the manifold, the diverse); on the other side is the drive toward unity through form. One more drive provides the "mediating link": it is the drive toward play. We are no longer in the presence of Kant's tactful sailing in dangerous waters, where he had to carefully avoid being caught by the rocks of understanding, usefulness, and morality, and skillfully simulated them with the stratagem of an "as if." Schiller's concept of play presents itself as a powerful synthesis that unifies and totalizes in itself the other two thrusts; it almost becomes a categorical imperative for human beings and society: only in the aesthetic unity reached through play can there be health and happiness, for both the individual and the collectivity.

But perhaps precisely because of his high stakes on aesthetics and play, Schiller is forced to fall back in part on this historical-diachronic model. This is also the result of his interest in the history of poetry, which Kant almost totally ignored. The climate of Schiller's time was far from giving him hope that the drive toward play would soon succeed. Actually, the dissociation was very deep, and he could not be satisfied by the hope that the free play of imagination was a modest side field among the stronger fields. The only possible solution was to set one's hopes either in a suspended uncertain future, or in the past, whose historical certainty could serve as a guarantee for the future. If at one point a state of aesthetic felicity has already manifested itself, one may cherish the hope that it will reappear. Hence the praise for an ancient age, in which "natural" poetry had flourished, which Schiller sets against his time.

But it would be a mistake to assimilate this type of diachronic solution into the one proposed by the eighteenth-century Vichian model, which is taken up by Hegel. As I have said, Hegel believes in the optimistic possibility of overcoming the dangers of the "modern" dissociation by situating the sentimental-emotional and the logical-conceptual phases within a cyclic development. These phases show very marked differences: the realm of poetic imagination belongs to the origins, whereas the age of maturity is dry, but functional and efficient. A choice between the two does not make sense, since one takes over the other according to a necessary and inevitable logic. This is not the state of affairs in the Kantian model, and even less so in the historicized and more dramatic resumption that Schiller makes of it. The origins, the classical age, or age of naive poetry, are not at all a beginning totally out of balance and tipping over under the weight of feelings and emotions: rather, these are seen as times of supreme balance, where one could find "the tacitly creative life, the serene spontaneity of their activity, existence in accordance with their own laws, the inner necessity, the eternal unity with themselves."[2] These features were usually found in close connection with rhetoric and its tools, a fact that legitimizes our dealing with such issues here, even though, just as did Kant, Schiller also tends to pass over to poetry the "function" that had belonged to rhetoric. But his conception of poetry precisely because it aims at a great synthesis, at the fullest balance, does not at all submit itself to the striking of the sublime feeling and Platonic enthusiasm. Be that as it may, Schiller's attitude is not to resign himself to dreaming from afar of the model of antiquity, nor does he regard it with the Olympian indifference and detachment afforded by a historical perspective. The longing must transform itself into action so that the model may come to life again. For the time being it offers the right arguments to denounce the problems and the limitations of the present, which witnesses the triumph of sentimental poetry. The latter is regarded as a state of unbalance, ill-proportion, and as extremely removed from the Kantian *Mittelglied*, from the great dream of a synthesis between the various human faculties. In fact, the mode of sentimental poetry is such that "imagination crowds out sense and thought feeling, and they close their eyes and ears to sink into internal reflection."[3] Later on Hegel will recognize these features as pertaining to modern or romantic poetry, with the big difference, however, that he will see them as a positive and necessary step in the development of the Spirit toward self-consciousness. In contrast, for Schiller modern or romantic dissociation and ill-balance are an evil, against which one must tirelessly oppose the longing for the classical or natural ages.

Around the positions of Kant and Schiller a great number of talents gravitate more or less closely. In Germany there are first of all the Schlegel brothers; in England there are Wordsworth and Coleridge, and in Italy Giacomo Leopardi: they all produce vigorous aesthetic theories that are far from easy to summarize. To call these figures romantic may be a simple way to accept current definitions; this label, however, clashes with the fact that to them the romantic present was a time of unacceptable lacerations. Moreover, that same label will be applied to very different positions, for example, the one that will begin with Hegel. We must also stress the considerable similarity between the proposals advanced by this group of thinkers and poets, and those to which our age has arrived. From this perspective that group situates itself at the beginning of the contemporary age, not only in terms of historical periodization, but above all because of deep intrinsic aspects, the first of which is the great desire to overcome the dissociation caused by modernity. And yet, it is significant how our avant-garde poets and critics, as we will see, evince a clear preference for the synthetic, synchronic configuration that emerged during the baroque. Once again our interest in rhetoric will allow us to understand the reasons for such a preference. The Metaphysical poets, writers of conceits and preciosity, had shown themselves to be well equipped (with the tools provided by the rhetorical-dialectical tradition) to bridge the open gap of the middle function. In contrast, the post-Kantian poets and theorists, although affirming the need and legitimacy of that function, do not know how to implement it. Grown intolerant of the old rhetorical figures, they try to overcome them by appealing to genius, feelings, or the imagination. They run the risk of falling into the trap of the *atechnon*, of the absence of structure, and thus they may find themselves back in the position, which they reject as romantic, of the irreparable split between the claims of truth and those of sheer emotionalism.

In this sense their attitude toward rhetorical figures is typical: they do not reject them (unlike Benedetto Croce, a later systematizer of Hegelian romanticism). Actually, they list them with precision, careful not to leave out even wit, plays on words, conceit, irony, and so on. But they believe that to treat rhetorical figures extensively or to give them too much weight will stop short the totalizing thrust, with a consequent fall into analysis. This fear especially affects allegory, but metaphor also does not come out unscathed, whereas it is the symbol that gains ground because it allows the encounter of the natural with the spiritual, of the inward with the outward, almost without technical mediations. What is of the utmost importance for all these writers is to go beyond the present: the synthesis is located in the future, but it is never about to realize itself; or it may be found in the past, in mythical golden ages of poetry, or otherwise it is tied to practically unattainable ideals. To return to the object of our inquiry, rhetoric does not disappear from such programs, even if it is seen as something to be overcome: as Kant pointed out, it is poetry that takes over.

Thus we come to the well-known definition given by Friedrich Schlegel (1772–1829) in fragment 116 of the *Athenäum*: the aim of romantic poetry is "to reunite all the separate species of poetry and put poetry in touch with philosophy and rhetoric."[4] But in practice how is one supposed to tackle such a totalizing task? This is the question contemporary poets and theorists raise: for them Schlegel's proposal to entrust the relationship between subject and object to a sort of play as in a hall of mirrors, falls into the *atechnon*; it cannot be considered a solution, since it expresses only a wish. In other words, we could say that this proposal employs an alternating current, where the same and opposite pulsations rapidly change sign: a "wonderfully perennial alternation of enthusiasm and irony.''[5] Above all, what prevails is the need to project all of this to infinity, to keep removing the possibility of a realization, in the name of "the infinite play of the universe, the work of art which eternally creates itself anew."[6]

Clearer and more precise, less striking or contradictory, are the theories of Wordsworth and Coleridge, the two English poets whom we ascribed to this same cultural climate, although ultimately they too agree on the necessity to postulate a final unity of the manifold. For example, in his preface to the *Lyrical Ballads* published in 1800, Wordsworth defends its choice of subjects and techniques because they allow "the passions of men . . . incorporated with the beautiful and permanent forms of nature,"[7] or because through them "our continued influxes of feeling are modified and directed by our thoughts" (p. 19). There is also the famous praise of "emotion recollected in tranquillity," (p. 27), which means that the emotion is reexperienced in an atmosphere of suspension and virtuality. In short, this is what in more recent times has been called the "philosophy of rhetoric" (the agreement between the intellectual level and the sensory), although the external aspects of rhetoric come out defeated because Wordsworth rejects "poetic diction" and "traditional colors." For him emotions find their support in verse, while a prosaic style is suitable for expressing the everyday, which intervenes to moderate emotional excesses.

Coleridge (1772–1834) also traces something similar to a *Mittelglied*, under the philosophical influence of the Kantian system: "Art itself might be defined as of a middle quality between a thought and a thing, or as I said before, the union and reconciliation of that which is nature with that which is exclusively human."[8] He also revives the notion of the coalescence of ideas, which belongs to the eighteenth-century English theory of association of ideas: for example, Coleridge defines beauty as "the unity of manifold, the coalescence of the diverse" (p. 221).

Earlier I said that Giacomo Leopardi (1798–1837) should be included within the broad boundaries of this context, even though he had scant knowledge of Kant, Schiller, or the Schlegels. He belongs here because in his own way and by employing other sources, he reaches a similar theoretical position, although he formulates it much later with respect to the authors examined here. On the other hand, rhetoric contributes fully to the development of Leopardi's ideas, since his education was profoundly imbued with classical philology. In the *Zibaldone*, he describes the great, dramatic Schillerian conflict between the age of nature and a romantic age that is sick and divided within itself. The former was a marvelous time of contextual balance, in which reason did not annihilate with its cold beams the rights of the senses and the imagination, but neither did it leave the stage totally to irrational values. On the contrary, reason knew how to present itself in the proper garment of a *mezza ragione* (half-reason). (This view of Leopardi may be linked to Cicero's notion of probability, which suits well a philosophy of nature not rigidly dominated by mathematics, nor radically opposed to human concerns.) This was also a time in which one knew how to employ "proper" words that were rich in a variety of references, and open to those nuances of meaning that the eighteenth-century sensualists had described and called accessory ideas. On the contrary, Leopardi sees his time dominated by the need for precision, for univocal definitions (what John Stuart Mill will later call denotation). The aridity of "terms" (a notion borrowed from Beccaria and Cesarotti) prevails over the contextual fullness of proper words. The dissociating evil of specialism is the rule, instead of a relaxed and serene way of speaking, popular and natural at the same time, that would be close to common sense (the ultimate judge, in every system recognizing the rights of rhetoric), and to the multifariousness and pleasantness that belong to a conception of nature not numbed by the anxiety of scientific knowledge.

The Italian theorists at the end of the eighteenth century had already described this scenario. But while they dealt with this state of affairs with cold scientific detachment, Leopardi passionately takes side for one face of the coin. In the same way he lives in a state of paroxysm and competition in the linguistic battle between French and Italian. The former is the champion of rationalistic dryness, of the modern taste for univocal, denotative terms, devoid of context or references. In contrast, Italian, as the true heir to Greek and Latin, is rich and multiform. This qualifies it to take on stylistic flourishings, which intervene only in the presence of linguistic stratification: thus is opened the possibility of choosing also "strange" solutions, slightly "removed" from current usage.

So we understand why Leopardi does not like languages in their primitive or archaic state, since in these phrases there would not be available any reservoir of stylistic possibilities. If Homer is great, one must suppose that he wrote when there already existed a rhetorical tradition that granted him a solid ground of expressions and lexical variations. Generally Leopardi does not like simple unilateral solutions, or the ages that adopted them. Thus his preferences go neither to the Vichian primordial times nor to "modernity," an age in which the romantic aspirations of the heart offer themselves as miserable compensation for the invasion of an overpowerful "truth." From this perspective, Leopardi, following a path of his own, rediscovers the Kantian need for a *Mittelglied*. But, like Schiller, he projects it retrospectively onto the naturalness of the classical age. He wields it as an ideal with which to oppose all the evils of his time, and draws from it the strength to envisage a future in which the various faculties will be newly integrated.

All this has interesting consequences on the level of practical reason: here Leopardi detaches himself from the Kantian model to which he adhered unaware and to which, for other aspects, we thought he could be linked. Upholding the values of antiquity, he affirms his rejection of modern egalitarianism, of a notion of society understood as atomlike individuals all equal and homogenized, or at best united by that vague and generic adhesive supplied by the idea of universal brotherhood (the ideal of the Enlightenment as proclaimed in 1789). Against them, Leopardi evokes the weight of the full-bodied communal values of antiquity, a time when one knew the difference between a neighbor and a stranger, between one's country and its enemies; a time when conflicts and disputes were accepted, and not only on the discursive level, but also in terms of taking up arms. Among the citizens solidarity was an actual bond, powerful and warming. Also, cities were on a human scale; they had not reached the enormous size of the modern megalopolis, where "solitary crowds" gather, squalid aggregates of numberlike individuals, who try to overcome their sad condition by squeezing out sentimental elegies in the romantic taste. (Wordsworth, too, had denounced the evils of urbanization: one of his goals had been to fight them by adopting rustic themes in his works.)

Hegel and the Overcoming of Rhetoric

We already noted that G. W. F. Hegel (1770–1831) marks the passage to a model considerably different from the one I described as freely derived from Kant, although the materials, the interests, and sometimes even the terms and the concepts employed by the two philosophers are to a great extent the same. But Hegel forcefully relaunches the diachronic model that had been traced by Vico and the eighteenth-century theorists, and gives it a vectorial direction that does not at all end in favor of poetry. Poetry is identified with one stage in a development that inexorably leads to its overcoming. A similar fate befalls rhetoric: in the Hegelian system, although not neglected, it becomes an inhibiting and disturbing element.

The three moments of Hegel's periodization for what concerns poetry and rhetoric have the following configuration: (1) the first is a "natural" age, characterized by the inadequacy between subject and object; (2) the second stage is characterized by a full adequacy between subject and object and corresponds to the classical age; (3) finally, in modern times this perfect marriage breaks up, and the subject prevails over the object and nature. So far Hegel's analysis corresponds to that of the Kantians. However, for Kant's followers this situation is an evil, a perverse tendency, against which one must react by retracing one's steps and relaunching the need for the classical requirements of totality and balance. In contrast, Hegel interprets it as the taking off of the superior stage of self-consciousness, the Spirit on the way to the short circuit with itself.

In such a design, rhetorical figures occur mostly in the first stage, which is generally marked by the distinction between subject and nature. More specifically, they appear during this stage when the subject becomes conscious of such distance, and tries to bridge the gap by applying a series of devices that can be brought together globally under the figure of comparison. Rhetorical figures are seen as comparisons varying in degree and effectiveness. Hegel's classification is comprehensive; he is able to move from a mere descriptive taxonomy to a historical development (in fact, the history of literary genres is one of the great vocations of the romantic age, starting with the Schlegels, who, however, while tracing it, aim at its possible overcoming in a great final synthesis). Hegel deals with "comparisons originating from the external object,"[9] such as the fable, the parable, proverbs, and the apologue; he then progressively moves to more internal figures, such as the riddle, the allegory, and above all the metaphor, the image, and the simile. He also considers "plays on words" (*ingegno*, wit) in Shakespeare and baroque poets. However, notwithstanding the careful analysis of his classification, Hegel regards all these comparative or periphrastic operations with deep suspicion since they may end up offering not "the free life of the matter in hand in its concrete appearance, but the prosaic separation of concept from reality" (p. 991).

This danger disappears during the stage of classical poetry, when a perfect adequacy between subject and object is reached. For Hegel's objectives, such a goal is even overreached, whereas the Kantians would ask for nothing else than to remain in that felicitous balance, Hegel intends to move forward and overcome this state whose deficiency lies in keeping hooked together consciousness and the external object. Fortunately the modern dissociation intervenes to bring about the romantic situation. This state of affairs would prompt Kantian thinkers to postulate an even more difficult, tightrope-like totalization between elements and faculties dangerously diverse (although they are sensitive to the seductiveness of such difficult reconciliation of opposites). On the contrary, this gives Hegel the opportunity to put aside once and for all the *caput mortuum* of natural phenomena, of external appearances. In romantic art, "the spirit, which has as its principle its accord with itself, the unity of its essence with its reality," finally finds "its correspondent existence only in its native spiritual world of feeling, the heart, and the inner life in general."[10]

Between Romanticism and Positivism

The view that modernity is an age of progress because it is closer to the truth is shared by a great many writers, poets, and critics, who, given their diverse areas of interest, are far from reaching the theoretical complexity of Hegelian idealism. For example, in France, Victor Hugo (1802–85), in the preface to *Cromwell* (1827), shows his adherence to the Vichian hypothesis of the three stages. He prefers the third one because it is marked by the advance of Christianity. Hugo believes that Christianity "leads poetry to truth,"[11] and therefore the poet "must take advice only from nature, from truth and from inspiration, which is also a truth and a nature" (p. 32). Under the circumstances rhetoric is regarded as a curb, a delay, almost a residue of the ancien régime, to the point that in the much shorter preface to *Hernani* (1830), he defines romanticism a form of liberalism in literature.[12] However, it would be a mistake to believe that Hugo favored a bare style, or, a common and vulgar language that would be closer to nature. On the contrary, he sees the distance between art and a flat, deceptive naturalism; he also claims that the true has to be taken into good account, in a way not that different from Wordsworth's. The stance of the romantics toward rhetoric is not too removed from the attitude that emerged in the second half of the seventeenth century and the first half of the eighteenth: excessive use of rhetorical devices is rejected, especially when rhetoric tries to impose its rules and structures. However, its good offices are tacitly accepted, provided common sense remains in control. Thus rhetoric survives — actually it will enjoy a long life as poetic diction, and it will be all the stronger the less it undergoes critical analysis. It is the symbolists and twentieth-century avant-garde poets who will do away with poetic diction, while at the same time they paradoxically draw attention to the structural role of rhetorical figures — but obviously it is always the case that one is impressed by what seems rather unfamiliar.

The formulations of Hugo had already been expressed ten years before by the Italian romantics who gathered around the magazine *Il Conciliatore*. It is not surprising that Leopardi, as an unwitting follower of Kant and Schiller, engaged with them in harsh debates. For example, Ludovico di Breme, like Hugo, defends modern times for their sentimentality and pathos and for their tendency to set up a direct relationship between emotions and things. If mythology and rhetoric have to be fought (there is a close connection between them because most figures and tropes arise from a mechanical application of attributes befitting "false and lying" gods), this depends on the fact that they interpose "a material filter between us and things."[13] This is the delaying factor, the impediment produced by exteriority that the romantics want to exorcise (whereas baroque and twentieth-century poets see this as a good opportunity to enrich the context with periphrastic connotations). Di Breme is not against the poetical-rhetorical search for resemblance, but he finds metaphors impaired by their necessary ties with mythology. They must be replaced with "poetically similar ideas" taken outside all codes so that "to feel them deeply is proper only of those sensitive and generous souls that are called and are poets" (p. 270).

The condemnation of the baroque for its immoderate use of rhetorical devices not backed up by feelings acutely developed by Alessandro Manzoni (1785–1873). In the foreword to *I promessi sposi* (The betrothed) he composes a piece of prose in the style of the seventeenth century that he ascribes to the anonymous author of the manuscript. Even in this case, however, rhetoric is not rejected totally. On the contrary, Manzoni is ready to admit that in a narrative there may be passages that "call for a little eloquence, but it should be discreet, subtle and in good taste."[14] Of course in the faked baroque manuscript this requirement does not obtain (and its critique purports the stylistic and moral condemnation of the entire period), whereas for his part Manzoni will respect it. In fact, it is enough to think of one passage: "Addio ai monti" (Farewell, mountains).[15] There Manzoni admits that he has put himself in Lucia's place, and that the description of her thoughts is developed with an artistry that does not just flatly reflect nature. As we noted, romanticism always retains some degree of "poetic diction." This concession, though not amounting to much, will be harshly condemned by Benedetto Croce, who distinguishes himself, as we will soon see, for carrying out one of the most ruthless and radical critiques of rhetoric ever: "Italian Romanticism with Manzoni at its head . . . dealt a blow at rhetoric: but was it killed by the stroke? Apparently not, judging by the concessions unconsciously made by the scholastic treatise-writer Ruggero Bonghi."[16]

In the short treatise in epistolary form *Perché la letteratura italiana non sia popolare in Italia* (The reason why Italian literature is not popular in Italy, 1855), Bonghi observes that in the middle of the nineteenth century the tendency is to move toward a *koine* within which the "positive" reasons of common sense and adherence to truth coexist with the idealistic and romantic reasons of feelings: an evidence that subject and object are in good balance. Bonghi is an heir to Lombardic Enlightenment, which was inspired by the French; this accounts for his praise of the clarity and lightness of the French language. His view is exactly the opposite of Leopardi's, although the latter, together with Manzoni, is acknowledged as the only outstanding writer of prose in Italian at that time. Interesting and unusual is the "feminist" argument in defense of French: the reason for its clarity and adaptability lies in the larger role women writers are allowed to play in France. French women have introduced into their language their spontaneous good sense and quick intuition. However, Enlightenment and positivism are not all there is to Bonghi's text: he is concerned with a defense of style, too. For him style is "an individual, intimate thing" that corresponds to a kind of Hegelian concrete universal in a simplified version, almost for the use of the ladies. He even excludes from the domain of style many subjects, "all those that lack a universal, being limited either in their concrete particularity, or in abstractions" (p. 68). His choice is a middle course that avoids one-sided extremes. The famous saying of Buffon, *Le style c'est l'homme*, must be matched with Voltaire's *Le style c'est la chose* (this is precisely the synthesis between subject and object, between words and things). One must avoid disparaging art in the same way as one must avoid paying homage to artificiality. On the whole, Bonghi suscribes to Manzoni's view that certain occasions in a story call for "a little eloquence, but . . . discreet, subtle, and in good taste."

Very interesting is his analysis of rhetorical figures, in particular his treatment of inversions. Also on this occasion Bonghi is far from proclaiming that the only proper way is direct construction as practiced by the French Enlightenment. Inversions are necessary, or better still, "they exist"; they are made familiar by usage. In a way, Bonghi anticipates the paradoxical position that Jean Paulhan will take a century later: Paulhan's opinion is that the worst way to defeat rhetoric is terror, that is, the attempt to abolish clichés and stereotyped expressions. By so doing one would only be conditioned by rhetoric, although in a negative way. It is better to accept these expressions openly, and start from the assumption that they are necessary; thus one can try to forget them through usage, instead of making their presence more conspicuous by a maniacal rejection.

On this subject Bonghi espouses Manzoni's well-known views on language, and extends them from lexicon to syntax. He identifies a problem in the lack of an average Italian language that could be generally accepted: this would lay the ground for constructions, such as inversions, from which to start out. He sees the Italian language and literature as having been affected by a stylistic and rhetorical obsession for the very reason that there was no fixed, stable rhetoric. Therefore, to put an end to the battle of dialects and idioms, Florentine should be taken, not because of intrinsic qualities, but by convention. Only by accepting a proper body of clichés will Italian literature be able to "forget" words; by not being so self-conscious, it will be able to concentrate on things, and will please its readers' modern tastes.

Croce's Severe Critique

Bonghi's adoption of a middle course is shared by a whole nineteenth-century *koine*, for which a "subtle and discreet" rhetoric must manage its way between the "positive" demands for clarity and the demands stemming from the feelings of the individual. But at the beginning of the twentieth century this compromise is rejected by Croce in his *Estetica*. It is actually the whole century that seems to present itself under the sign of dissociation, in favor of an outright cutting of the Gordian knot. Following this direction Croce (1866–1952) comes to perfect the indications implicit in the Hegelian system and will take the radical steps that his predecessor had refrained from taking. This may be due to the fact that the diachronic interval between the stages of the spirit in Hegel's philosophy was not just ideal, but maintained a good dose of historicity. In contrast, in Croce the diachronic moments of the spirit are freed of any historical necessity, and become purely theoretical; paradoxically, we could say that they become synchronic, or perhaps better, atemporal, hinging on an implacable chain of distinctions and a strategy of mutual exclusions. In the case of poetry, the synthesis between feelings and intuition, form and content, matter and expression, is absolute and without residue, nor is there space for mediations, for circumlocutions. Above all Croce insists on the struggle, which he sees as irremediable, between two cardinal concepts of rhetoric: convenience and ornamentation. He accepts the former, and in fact the aesthetic synthesis he evokes is a total convenience (congruence, adequacy) of form and content; but then there can be no place for the ornament, for a supplement. Also, if by "convenience" is understood the bare form, devoid of imaginative components, one falls into the moment of truth, of logic. The imaginative cannot be an addition, but must find its internal "convenience."

However, after this radical stance, due in part, as he will later admit, to the extremist positions he took in his youth, when he wrote the *Estetica* (1902), Croce felt compelled to move toward a more compliant attitude. The fact is that "poetic diction," as I have said, continued to survive, notwithstanding all the official condemnations that sometimes were even expressed by the very same poets who used it: in many cases they were poets close to Croce's taste, essentially moderate and misoneist. In fact, those who have the courage to follow Verlaine's precept "Take eloquence and wring its neck," are the new poets who try symbolist experimentation, and toward whom Croce does not waste any good feelings. In a later work, *Poesia* (1936), he reaches a compromise and grants some space to "literary expression," that is, to eloquence. However, the system is not shaken, because for this discursive zone there still exists no category that would correspond to a form of the spirit, which would then grant its autonomy. Eloquence must be happy to be an intermediate stage, an aside, inferior in status, only half-recognized, and unable structurally to interfere with poetry, with which it will only be entitled to have a relationship of contiguity: "Poetry and literature, although they touch each other on one side, remain two different things."[17]

However, even to Croce's very cautious attention, literature seems to be in a phase of clear expansion, while to identify the authentic presence of poetry becomes increasingly difficult. To a great extent Croce's method is a subtracting procedure; one of the first operations he performs is precisely the clearing up of the field from the cumbersome layers of eloquence besetting any literary work. The danger is that poetry may become some kind of polarity at the limits, almost unattainable, almost unrealizable, never experienced as actually existing, if it is not accompanied by an inevitable dose of eloquence.

It should be kept in mind that precisely in this cultural climate Giovanni Gentile, who is at the same time an ally and an adversary of Croce's, carries out the reform in the Italian education system that bears his name: rhetoric and its rules are decisively eliminated from it. This concept of aesthetics stressing feeling and a direct relationship between subject and object emerged in the eighteenth century, and it has taken it almost two centuries to eliminate its hated and chief rival. The compromise between the two had held out for a long time.

Chapter 7
The Contemporary Revival of Rhetoric

Critique of the "True" and the Return to Probability

We have just seen how the twentieth century starts out very negatively biased against rhetoric. It is a state of affairs reminiscent of the climate that, almost three centuries before, had dominated early modernity at the time of the emergence of the new scientific method. In fact, it is not only in the post-Hegelian system of Croce that one can verify such a negative attitude, but also in other philosophical currents that in many respects are quite different. By this I mean the front of logicism, analytic more than ever before, and heavily influenced by mathematics, which is considered the preferential model of reasoning (see Russell, Frege, Peano). The same model is adopted by the various schools dedicated to the analysis of language (the Vienna Circle with Wittgenstein and Carnap; the Oxford school, after Wittgenstein moves there). With Croce these schools shared the objective of eliminating the degenerative use of associationism and genetic causalism that developed in the second half of the nineteenth century, in a mixed climate of post-Hegelianism and narrow-minded positivism, absorbed by the decomposition of logical processes and their consequent degradation into "mental chemistry." Also the final results of that antipositivistic revival show some points of convergence with Croce: an opposition is produced between two separate and noncommunicating islands. On one side is the domain of truthfulness (based on an analytic linguistic model for the Vienna Circle and the Oxford school, or rather on the synthesis of the Hegelian concrete universal in the case of Croce). On the other side is the domain of the emotions (to which Croce gives a structure, an a priori form, whereas for logical positivism it is an irrational, almost inexpressible residue). Whichever of the two theories one may follow, the general picture remains one of dissociation; thus it does not appear compatible with the spirit of rhetoric, that is, one of conciliation and integration, as by now we have had ample occasions to verify.

It would be a mistake, however, to believe that these philosophical theories, dissociated and structured according to the principle of differentiation, give the tone to our time. On the contrary, we may call them neomodern, since they return to the initial inflexibility and hardness of the seventeenth century, and complete the circle, so to speak. Instead, the most promising contemporary thought emerges with other goals, out of an acute need to undermine the presumptuous claims to truth of analytic systems. The main front for intervention in fact is identified in the logical-epistemological area: here the linguistic, analytic truths of formal logic, physics, and mathematics must be questioned by showing that they are only "working hypotheses," useful and convenient formulations, which must undergo not only an internal test but also and especially an external test, in terms of operativity and effectiveness in accounting for natural phenomena as well as for psychological and anthropological ones. Nature and life are "open," they are in a state of continuous transformation; therefore any statement about them can only be partial, provisional, and hypothetical. In short, this is the return of probability, skepticism, and "suspension of judgment"—those various theoretical positions that in other ages had favored the development of rhetoric and had provided the ground for its luxuriant growth.

The labels to be assigned to the movements that contribute to such a climate may be found in any good philosophical textbook: pragmatism in North America; in Europe, empiriocriticism, or the philosophy of contingency developed by Emile Boutroux; Henri Bergson's theory of intuition; Georg Simmel's vitalism. We also may include Husserl's phenomenology, since it undeniably takes part in the antipositivistic logical enterprise, as opposed to the theory of psychological associationism of the late nineteenth century, and insists on eidetic intuition (ideas come as wholes and in one time); but on the other hand it provides them with a vast background of renewing material: the *Lebenswelt*. In the beginning there are obscurity, confusion, totality, complexity, and certainly not the clarity or the evidence of principles, postulates, and axioms, as analytic reasoning has always claimed. To this package of theories about the obscure and the confused must be added the exceptional contribution of Freudian psychoanalysis, but we will examine its relevance for our inquiry later on.

Such a rich climate might have favored the reinstatement of rhetoric; actually, rhetoric itself could have provided the best technical tools for the advancement of the cause of "probability." But things went differently. We must wait till the 1950s for this link to be made, when Chaim Perelman's *Traité de l'argumentation* appears. Perelman, a Belgian, starts out *in partibus infidelium*, since he is among the followers of analytic logic. His project is to apply logical procedures to a context that is very resistant to them: the philosophy of law. After ascertaining the impossibility of making such a field the object of a totally formalized and axiomatic discourse, he is reluctant to leave it prey to subjective arbitrariness, to the unverifiable nuances common to the human sciences (against which in the 1930s also the Danish linguist Hjelmslev, a follower of Carnap and of the analytic method, had expressed very negative views). Perelman wants to overcome the "modern" split between the two cultures, the two ways of knowing. He believes the human sciences must be equipped with techniques of their own (of course they must be "open," adaptable, and variable techniques). Thus he goes back to Aristotle, who had been the founder of the fortune and logical dignity of rhetoric. It is now appropriate that the author of the *Topica* becomes the springboard for a relaunching of rhetoric on the part of a thinker dissatisfied with a philosophical tradition stressing only the *Analytics*. This may be the main road to a return of rhetoric, understood as one of the great articulations required by a logic broad and flexible enough to adapt itself to the different spheres of human activity. Moreover, we will also examine two other paths that led to such a reflourishing of rhetoric. One focuses on linguistic and stylistic devices, and is strictly linked with the operations of the poets of our time, who are obsessed by the need to use language consciously. The other pays attention to the great changes introduced by technological innovations, and the way they affect all other cultural aspects.

Perelman's Theory of Argumentation

Perelman may be considered a neo-Aristotelian who propounds the rightness of dialectic and rhetoric for certain areas that concern all human beings, such as law, politics, ethics, and aesthetics. On the whole, after more than two thousand years, he relaunches the well-balanced and harmonious views that had been put forward by the Stagirite. For Perelman it is not a question of eliminating analytics in favor of dialectic and rhetoric, or vice versa, but rather of assigning the proper place to each. There are contexts such as mathematics and the exact sciences related to it in which it is legitimate to use the terminology of demonstration, since the goal here is convention and truth (this is the formal axiomatic discourse). But in other contexts, where the aim is persuasion, one is authorized to use argumentation. It does not follow, however, that the domain of argumentation is inferior to that of demonstration: it is simply grounded on different rules.

From this premise one may easily determine for the two domains their parallel series of distinctive features. Demonstration postulates a universal audience, believing in some axioms that are unanimously accepted. Also, it is an audience located in an atemporal dimension, in a sort of closed system with no entry or exit, so that the axioms do not undergo any process of change. Moreover, only the intellectual faculties of this audience are stressed, with no interference from the physical or moral aspects of the individuals who constitute it. The very opposite obtains for the audience of an argumentative discourse: it is placed in a specific time and space; it holds beliefs that cannot be formalized, and to ascertain them is one of the first tasks of the orator. Also, these opinions are far from rigid, but instead have a high degree of plasticity. Thus in the beginning there are the "confused notions" referred to by Gonseth, the sociologist of knowledge who, with E. Dupréel, is one of the major influences on the "new rhetoric" of Perelman, as he himself openly admitted.

The same degree of plasticity that invests notions—the *doxai*, which are far from self-evident, since it is always possible to dig around them, and engage them in a regressive movement of search for the beliefs from which they derive—invests facts too. The procedures for definition, description, and narration become "open" interventions that may be expanded or contracted according to what is required by the argumentation. The latter must obey a global and finalized strategy, in relation to which there can be no free zones relying on a predetermined development. The altogether logical role Perelman assigns to the "new rhetoric" leads him to privilege its first two parts, *inventio* and *dispositio*. But he is far from rejecting *elocutio*, and above all he does not give it a role apart, as happened when the unfortunate separating tendencies prevailed, bringing about so many evils for rhetoric. The separating approach stems from those scholars who want to move the axis in favor of the analytic or dialectical pole, of a narrow and impersonal logicism (Ramus), or on the contrary it is the approach of those who stake everything on *elocutio*, on the ornamental function, as will happen in so many linguistic and stylistic projects, especially those inspired by semiotics, as we will soon see. Perelman, on the contrary, firmly refuses to "study stylistic structures and figures independently of the purpose they must achieve in the argumentation."[1]

The comprehensive enhancement of the parts of rhetoric rightly advocated by Perelman does not include the last two components, *memoria* and *actio*, because he believed they were not suited to a culture like ours, where discourses circulate above all through the printed word. But today this limitation is not at all necessary. When Perelman was trained in the 1940s and 1950s, he could not take into account the influence of new technologies such as the tape recorder and television—tools that made possible the rediscovery of the importance of pronunciation and gestures, as we will see more clearly when analyzing the third group of factors that made possible the new fortune of rhetoric.

The limitation that, in a somewhat unnatural way, Perelman applies to his project is dangerous inasmuch as he accepts the "classical" belief that persuasion addresses not only the "minds," the abstract intellectual faculties of the audience, but also their senses and their emotions. There exist values that Perelman attributes to "presence"; however, since he proceeds to exclude gestures from his inquiry, he must evidently refer to a symbolic presence, mediated by writing or by stylistic devices. In his overall rearrangement of the vast repertory of rhetor-ical figures, he classifies them under three general headings: figures of choice, which undertake to define facts, to give form to the plasticity of matter, trying to find a basis for agreement with the audience; figures of presence (onomatopoeia, hypotyposis), which stress the senuous aspect of things (what the Greeks called *enárgheia*); and figures of communion, such as apostrophe and rhetorical inter-rogation. The last two groups are obviously connected in attempting to supply a surrogate for the values of *performance*, which get lost when discourse is filtered by the printed word. It is a sort of presence in absence that cannot be overlooked, since, as any good rhetorician knows, a discourse addresses people, and in gen-eral it deals with other people; meanwhile the rhetorician is a person too and cannot neutralize his or her personal history, his or her past. As Perelman aptly remarks, in a rhetorical situation one cannot overlook the fact that "the person is the best context for evaluating the meaning and the significance of an assertion."[2] Once again, we encounter the idea that in an argumentation it is im-possible to identify and isolate pertinent elements from those that do not belong to it: the context can always open up and slip away. And just as actors and their clients are human beings, so are the listeners, since not only their mind but their body as well must be taken into account. To be sure, they cannot be satisfied with *docere* only: *movere* and *delectare* will be necessary as well. Therefore the order that the arguments should follow is not only a question of logical design, of good internal economy, but is a psychological and emotional strategy as well. Persua-sion is also a psychagogy.

The Italian Giulio Preti in his *Retorica e logica* (1968) reaches results similar to Perelman's after recognizing the limits of the strictly analytic models offered by neoempiricism and logical positivism. Significantly, in a previous work, *Praxis e empirismo* (1957) he had identified praxis as the context within which one could legitimately oppose the "analytic" claims. More specifically, the agreement with Perelman can be seen in Preti's acknowledgment that in the ter-ritory of rhetoric the difference between judgments of fact and judgments of value disappears. Judgments of fact too, as Perelman saw, when dealing with human concerns, enter a horizon of choice, and therefore interfere with the pa-rameters adopted in selecting and molding them. Of course the parameters will be functional to the goals one intends to reach.

The Microrhetoric of Freud and Saussure

The epistemological revolution that occurred between the end of the nineteenth century and the beginning of our century has found one of its most powerful strongholds in Freudian psychoanalysis. Although the very word that constitutes it contains the word "analysis," no theoretical stand questions more than psy-choanalysis the "analytic" claims, taking the word in its logistic meaning.

Truthfulness becomes a matter of economy of psychic energies within the sphere of the Ego or of the reality principle (which to produce its cultural edifice needs useful and essential formulations, at the cost of sacrificing a whole fringe of other aspects and values that are connected with the sphere of libido). In short, psychoanalysis also advances arguments in favor of a revision of epistemology and logic on conventional and utilitarian grounds. Furthermore, it forcefully introduces a double-track logic, a sort of biaxial organization of our psychic activity: one axis obeys the horizontal economy of the reality principle, but on it interferes at every step the vertical axis of libido, eros, which is able to invest with peculiar importance elements on the first axis: thus it makes them symptoms of its different logic. In this respect, Freud's thought belongs to the philosophies that Perelman would call "regressive" because they allow one to dig, in a search for primal causes not yet thematized and that are to be considered particularly suitable for rhetoric. But from our point of view, the most interesting fact is that Freud does not certainly leave the vertical axis of libido in an *atechnon* state run by loose, ineffable emotions, but rather assigns to it precise possibilities on a technical level. This occurs in a major work like *The Interpretation of Dreams*, but also in other texts that may ideally be considered preliminary stages to it, *The Psychopathology of Everyday Life* and *Jokes and Their Relation to the Unconscious*. In these last two works the technical tools that regulate the interference between the Ego and the Id are decisively verbal, and therefore they bear on rhetoric. Thus Freud ensures a powerful switch from the first to the second group of motives that we placed at the origin of the contemporary return to rhetoric: in his work, the logical-epistemological reasons are welded to those aspects that address a careful analysis of linguistic material.

One of Freud's greatest intuitions was to suppose a contiguity between the class of comic phenomena (including jokes) and the dream work. It follows that the typical techniques of dreams, condensation and displacement, will also be found in the context of the former. In dreams, condensation is a process that sets up connections between images, or fragments of images not linked by a horizontal type of logic that would follow the utilitarian demands of reality; rather, what is at work is the "other" logic, that of libido. In the case of jokes, condensation produces a peculiar type of metaphor that allows the coexistence in the same linguistic material (or in a linguistic material that has undergone only slight literal modifications) of both the original meaning and of the meaning that substitutes it because of some degree of affinity (according to the relationship of genus to species, or of species to species, which Aristotle had already described). In an ordinary metaphoric process, for example, "The meadows are laughing," there is no relationship between the signifiers "laughing" and the more justified "turning green." It is possible, however, to reconstruct the chain of semantic associations that sets up a logical link between the two (they are turning green because the grass is beginning to grow, therefore they are young. Young people are cheerful, therefore they laugh). But if the resemblance between literal meaning and transported meaning is provided by the signifier, that is, if there is an actual literal coincidence of two different words, no logical legitimation is needed. What this means is that the "horizontal" logic can be set aside, while its place is taken by the vertical logic of libido, which for a moment can escape the mesh of censorship. "Base" meanings related to sex or aggressiveness may short-circuit higher, nobler, or just ordinary meanings, which usually follow a different path. For a moment the former may come into the open, exploiting precisely the legitimation enjoyed by the latter. One consequence is that some of the energy that usually is employed for repression may be saved and can be spent laughing.

What we generically called metaphoric processes are in fact instances of double meaning, or expressions that exploit the resemblance in sound of consonants and vowels at the phonetic level of the signifiers (sometimes also at the graphic level): alliterations, assonances, rhymes, slight anagrammatic inversions, substitutions of a single letter in a word, fusions (crasis), or on the contrary, occurrences of apocope, of apheresis. Here are some examples taken from the rich collection Freud displays in *Jokes and Their Relation to the Unconscious*. In French *vol* means both "flight" (high meaning) and "theft" (low meaning). The two meanings are accidentally linked by their phonetic identity. Exploiting this fact, during the reign of Napoleon III it was possible to express an opinion that otherwise would have been improper and subject to censorship: the sentence "C'est le premier vol de l'aigle" (It is the eagle's first *vol*) referred to Napoleon III's thefts rather than to his flights of glory.[3] One more joke on Napoleon: the name Buonaparte in Italian makes sense even when cut into two parts, "buona-parte," in English "a good part." Thus to a tactless remark by Napoleon I, "Tutti gli italiani danzano si male" ("All Italians dance so badly"), an Italian lady revenged herself by answering "Non tutti ma buona parte" ("Not all but a good part") (p. 31). Another example: the French name Rousseau also can be divided into two parts, each with full sense: *roux* is "red" and *sot* is "silly." One can use the whole word and the two parts to describe a stupid red-haired young man, with the pretension of being as talented as Jean-Jacques Rousseau was (p. 30). Here is another joke: a millionaire treats a poor man familiarly, that is, with the condescension characteristic of his status. The poor man says that he has been treated quite "famillionairely" (pp. 16–17). King Leopold of Belgium had as mistress a woman whose first name was Cleo: thus the cruel joke in calling him Cleopoldo (p. 20).

Another important group of jokes employs the second crucial technique of the dream work: displacement. In linguistic terms this means that one plays on a displacement of the accent from the whole to the part of a statement (it can be a sentence, an idiomatic expression, a cliché). The procedure leads to a recovery of figures derived from metonymic operations: metonymy proper and synecdoche.

The following joke is a good example: one Jew meets another Jew near the bath-house and asks: "Have you taken a bath." But the interlocutor breaks it down and applies a literal meaning to the verb "to take," understood as "to appropriate, to gain possession of." Thus his answer: "What? Is there one missing?" (p. 49).

What we have seen so far gives us the opportunity to make at least three different observations. (1) Already in Freud's work there emerges a movement following which the vast repertory of rhetorical figures tends to converge around the two poles of metaphor and metonymy, one acting along the vertical axis and the other on the horizontal axis. Roughly at the same time, Ferdinand de Saussure gives them the name that will be generally recognized: the paradigmatic and the syntagmatic axes. (2) Freud goes a step further. In his analysis of jokes he relaunches a vast complex of figures that occupy a space between grammar and rhetoric—figures that often violate the materiality of the word, like condensations proper, crases, apocopes, anagrams, and those that produce intraverbal practices, so to speak. These practices deserve careful consideration nowadays, not simply because of their application in the context of plays on words, puzzles, and the like (a field that has always been recognized and organized), but also for the more demanding and responsible applications in poetry and poetic experimentation. (3) Furthermore, the logic of libido is offered as a strong motivation for the most random semantic associations (what Marinetti will call "wireless imagination") without falling into irrational or unjustified vagaries.

Although Freud and Saussure ignored each other, there is almost perfect synchronicity between the psychoanalytic project of the one and the institution of structural linguistics of the other, with the two fundamental axes of paradigm and syntagm. In a way, Saussure's project does not propose anything new: in it one can detect the recuperation of the eighteenth-century theory of associations, which was based precisely on the two poles of similarity and contiguity. But between the two-century-old model and the "contemporary" one of Freud and Saussure, there occurred a movement from an age that was grounded in analysis and psychic atomism (the "ideas" of empiricism, and also Leibniz's infinitesimal rationalism) to one that relaunches a priori synthesis, thus revealing its descent from Kant and its preference for general processes, structures, global and unitary behavior. Besides his general and very important theoretical contribution (exceeding the boundaries of linguistics, as we well know), Saussure makes a very particular and more specialized contribution in a sphere listed under point 2 in the preceding discussion of Freud. I am referring to his meticulous attention to intraverbal figures and techniques such as the anagram and the paragram (this term refers to the construction of a new word obtained through the partial application of verbal elements from another word). In relation to paragrams, Saussure has described a mysterious and fascinating discovery that perhaps cannot be completely demonstrated, or perhaps it is unverifiable: he hoped to find "words beneath words" (following the title of Jean Starobinski's study dedicated to Saussure).[4] This means that in poetic discourse a deeply buried logic can be traced to be at work, in addition to the horizontal logic of common language. Saussure starts out by analyzing some examples from Latin poetry, like the Saturnian verse, but then opens up the field to include Seneca's prose, or even the Latin poetry of the Italian poet Giovanni Pascoli. In all these cases he discovers that some theme words recur "paragrammed," and form a web of echoes, rhymes, internal assonances, and so on, without respect for boundaries, for lexical or syntactic divisions. This suggests that there is an *elocutio* of the deep, acting below the verbal threshold—a microrhetoric. As I said about Freud, this opens up new territories for inquiry and above all provides contemporary poetry with new ground for experimenting.

Rhetoric and Literature: The Synthetic Line of Anglo-American Criticism

I described how in the nineteenth century the *koine* between romanticism and positivism, with its emphasis on feelings and common sense, sets up a climate of indifference or hostility toward rhetoric. This resistance, however, does not prevent poets from employing rhetoric in very conventional ways: actually, they are led to use it in conventional ways, according to the classicist canon of "poetic diction," precisely because they disregard it. From this perspective, Alessandro Manzoni and Victor Hugo, Swinburne and Tennyson, Carducci and Pascoli are not too far apart from each other: they all share a common attitude amply codified by their time, even if each of them obviously adapts it to his particular needs.

This state of affairs changes with the emergence of the "tradition of the new," that is, the terrorism of the avant-gardes. On one hand, avant-garde writers reject the generic notion of poetic diction, and therefore somehow help bring about the divorce of poetry from rhetoric (the latter taken in its conventional sense). But on the other hand they dismiss the sentimental and emotional bias of an immediacy between language and external objects; therefore, they get rid of the belief in the transparency of language and reintroduce the idea of its opacity. By doing this they end up emphasizing language, which will shake rhetoric from its fixed routine and force it to rethink tropes and schemes, or to fish out with more boldness from its millenary storage house.

Charles Baudelaire (1821–67) may be considered the first representative of the historical avant-garde. This statement of his is a good example of the attitude just described: "I am sorry for the poets who are guided only by their instincts. I consider them incomplete. . . . Everything beautiful and noble is the result of reasoning and calculation."[5] To Stéphane Mallarmé's poetry (1842–98) may be applied the following more specific and technical observations: "Rhymes and alliterations on one side; figures, tropes, metaphors on the other side, are no longer . . . discursive details and ornaments that may be eliminated: they are essential properties of the work: the « substance » is no longer the *cause* of the form but one of its effects.''[6] Thus the object is no longer seen as a target to hit: on the contrary, one moves around it; one looks for ways to replace it with the periphrastic itineraries that a certain romantic sensibility intensely disliked (the romantic proper, excluding the line that derives from Kant). Precisely this attitude will become the ground for poetic experimentation in the twentieth century; the process will even go so far as to reject any relationship of dominance by content, understood as the old opposition between bare and embellished style. The content of poetry is the context with its infinite series of ornamental devices. On this point hinges the *koine* of our century. Of course the accent will vary from one writer to another and there will be quite different theoretical standpoints: our task will be to isolate their differences.

Finally, in the twentieth century the line of Baudelaire and Mallarmé is adopted by Paul Valéry (1871–1945), who observes that rhetorical figures are unjustly neglected by modern critics although they play a role of primary importance in poetry.[7] But one may suspect that the continuity soon breaks down when postsymbolist poetry, an *ante litteram* hermetic *trobar clos* strongly tinged with sacredness, is succeeded by the decisively desecrating vein of Breton's surrealism: Breton, the real terrorist, as Paulhan aptly called him. However, also in this case at the last minute at least the paradigmatic-metaphoric axis remains. Actually, it is emphasized beyond all limits, in the wake of the thinking by binary oppositions that we have noted. In fact, Mallarmé's poetry may be described as having prevalently metonymic intentions; or, we should say, syntagmatic (since later on the opposition between metaphor and metonymy will have to be toned down). Indeed, the primary feature of Mallarmé's style lies in syntactic displacement; that is, it uses figures rather than tropes, in agreement with a periphrastic aim. In contrast, Breton believes that ''in relation to [metaphor and comparison], the other 'figures' that rhetoric persists in enumerating are absolutely devoid of interest. Only the analogical trigger excites us: it is exclusively through it that we can act on the engine of the world.''[8] Of course the analogies to which the chief theorist of surrealism refers are derived not from baroque *ingegno* nor from romantic feelings, but from the logic of the Freudian unconscious. As I have said, this is a way to provide with technical tools the operations of the powerful libidinal drive, of the primary *Trieb*, which consequently is not left at the mercy of blind affects.

Another trend of the poetic avant-garde, this time in the English-speaking world, is set by two figures that make significant contributions in the area of our inquiry: T. S. Eliot and Ezra Pound. In both, the militant engagement in poetry is grounded on far-reaching historical theories. Actually, between the two moments is supposed an integral relationship: according to Eliot's famous principle the latest poet that comes to the fore obliges us to reread Dante with an entirely different awareness: the old and the new condition one another. So, Pound rereads Dante and the poets of the Stil Novo, while Eliot reproposes the Metaphysical poets, emphasizing their structural wit[9] and contrasting it with the purely ornamental wit of the Elizabethans. I owe to Eliot a felicitous expression that I have used often in this work: for him the seventeenth century, the early modernity that sees the emergence of the new science, consummates an unfortunate "dissociation of sensibility"[10] that separates thinking from feeling and disdains all the intermediate pathways, which traditionally were implemented by rhetoric. The merit of the Metaphysical poets resides in their unfolding of a way of thinking that is made concrete in objects, while sensual objects for their part are full of intellectual significance. Eliot discovers this happy fusion already in Shakespeare; to be precise, in an analysis of *Hamlet* he finds the principal figure that exemplifies his views: the "objective correlative."[11] It will be remembered that we had already come across an antecedent of this idea in the eighteenth-century Italian writer Beccaria. Trying to define it in the context of a manual, it is difficult to determine whether the figure of the objective correlative is related to metaphor (association by resemblance) or to metonymy (contiguity), or whether it is part of the general case of *enárgheia* (evidence) and example. It can be objected that unlike the ingenious comparisons of baroque and Metaphysical poets, Eliot's objective correlative does not seem to find its origin in the logical features of rhetorical topics, but is closer to the psychoanalytic associations dear to the analogies of Breton and the surrealists. Undoubtedly with the latter there are points of contact, keeping in mind, however, that Eliot's aim is to bring about an integration with the elements of thought. On the whole, his search is for a totality, for a comprehensive context, and certainly he was not planning to lead the revolt for the affirmation of the unconscious against the surface level.

For his part, Pound exemplifies this situation in a simile: the poet is like a centaur that while galloping at high speed, must shoot an arrow at a distant target:[12] the gallop corresponds to the emotional or deep aspects; hitting the center represents the operations of the intellectual level. The two parts must combine closely, but without canceling each other, in such a way that it must be possible to distinguish, at least in an ideal way, the various components present in the poem. More specifically, in the language of poetry Pound identifies three moments: melopoeia is the rhythm and meter, or microrhetoric; phanopoeia is clarity and precision of word; logopoeia is the conceptual framework.[13] Although these are three different tracks, they must meet and combine "on the run," and form a harmonic whole, a process that is very different from a sort of mystical sinking, since the various components remain identifiable: the poem can be dissected and reassembled under our eyes.

The movement known as the "New Criticism" emerges in the United States in the 1930s and 1940s influenced in part by Eliot and Pound. The name derives from an essay by John Crowe Ransom, in which the conflict between the understanding and the senses, so well exemplified by Eliot and Pound, returns in the form of a polar tension between *structure* and *texture*. On the whole this dialectical couple suggests once again the old *querelle* between bare (rational and controlled) and embellished style. These two moments must enter the conflict on an equal footing; the more the conflict is hard and endured, the more the poem will be valid if it is able to portray the struggle dramatically, while a falling and consequent appeasing of the tension would be detrimental. It is very interesting that in this essay Ransom goes back to Kant's *Critique of Judgment*, confirming that in a historical outline of aesthetics the work of Kant represents the stage that succeeds the baroque, especially in the light of the development Kantian aesthetics will find in Coleridge: nature offers the sensory material on which the understanding inserts itself as a watermark, "as if" between the two there were an agreement. To this encounter nature provides the pleasant variety of phenomena, while the understanding supplies unity and rigor: respectively, they constitute the flesh and blood necessary to a healthy organism.

At least two other new critics must be mentioned: Allen Tate and Cleanth Brooks. The former, a poet and novelist (Ransom was a poet too), insists on the concept of tension. He shows that tension may derive from the falling of the prefixes "in" and "ex" in the words extension and intension (this is a witty application of the grammatical-rhetorical figure of apocope). Both in ordinary language and in the technical language of logic, the word "extension" designates a set of concrete individuals, of particular cases, whereas "intension" indicates the application of concepts, collective notions, ideas. Thus we are back to the old conflict between the general and the particular, the flesh and blood that poetic tension (in a close alliance with rhetoric) must be able to manage and orchestrate wisely. To Tate must be given the credit for having pointed out the "communicative" bias in the modern dissociated way of thinking, according to which communication would take place only when "clear and exact" ideas are transmitted, that is, isolated notions bearing a univocal meaning (in the eighteenth-century debate they would have been called terms, that is, words devoid of the gratifying halo of accessory ideas). From this perspective poetry does not simply "communicate" but creates states of "communion"; in other words, in addition to the *docere* its aim is also to move and please (*movere* and *delectare*). As usual it offers the totality of experience, rather than breaking it up into its various parts.

Of the group we are examining Cleanth Brooks is the only representative who dedicated himself exclusively to criticism (the others were also poets or novelists). Brooks forcibly introduced a series of notions that up until the 1950s were well known and widespread, and not only in English-speaking countries: for example, in Italy his work was introduced after World War II. Today, however, he is unfairly overlooked and neglected. Brooks denounces the prejudice that poetry would be a matter of direct communication, as the partisans of dissociation claimed, both those on the rational front (those who believed only in a scientifically rigorous and controlled language) and those on the emotional front (those who underscored a language of feelings, as straightforward and univocal as the previous one). To this view he opposes the rights of obliquity, of circumlocution, and periphrasis: not the text, but the context, which is a texture, a strategy of occurrences. To some extent poetry is always built around ambiguity because it plays on a plurality of meanings; it is paradoxical because it avoids plain statements and makes us see things with different eyes; it is ironical because it never unfolds in the way one would have expected, but always introduces a degree of surprise and displacement. Confronted by a weaving of such complexity and mastery, the claim to lay bare only the logical structure would do violence to the poem. In other words, it would be like reducing it to a skeleton; one would fall into the trap that Brooks calls "the heresy of paraphrase," which is perhaps his best-known formula.

In connection with the tradition of the New Criticism, we must mention other figures close to the group. One is the English poet and critic William Empson, author of *Seven Types of Ambiguity*, a classic text of literary criticism in the 1930s, and a work that, as its title indicates, focuses on the central notion of ambiguity. It is above all with Ivor Armstrong Richards that we must briefly deal. At the beginning of his long career Richards favored the theories radically opposed to the "philosophy of rhetoric" that he developed in his maturity. In fact, his well-known *Principles of Literary Criticism* was a mixture of all the possible "neomodern" heresies: psychological atomism and "mental chemistry," dissociated emotionalism, "communication" prejudices. His *lectures*[14] on rhetoric delivered in the 1930s and published as *The Philosophy of Rhetoric* (1936), mark a happy landing on the side of the context, now considered of primary importance, and no longer derived, like a "compound" sum of its parts. In the beginning there is complexity, both in ordinary language and in the discourse that makes use of rhetorical and evaluative devices. As to the univocal dimension of scientific discourse, it is the result of an artificial polarization, and is far from being at the origin of language. The title Richards chooses for his lectures is a very felicitous one, and for this reason I would like to extend it beyond his text. The whole movement of the New Critics and of their associates can be seen as trying to propose a global philosophy of rhetoric, set against the scientism of the time, and in defense of the values of integration, harmony, and humanism that seem to have collapsed under the weight of the modern industrial revolution. Of course these are also ethical and ideological implications that lead the new critics to condemn individualism and capitalism. To the northern states of the Union, founded on the worship of economic success, they oppose the "Old South," still anchored in the values of a rural way of life, and of patriarchal communities. It is also the Catholic or Anglican faith that is contrasted with the Protestant and Calvinist Reformation. But we will come back to these issues when dealing with

Marshall McLuhan, when we will examine a third group of motives that lie at the origin of the present return to rhetoric.

Before leaving the critical tradition of the United States I must mention that there were a vast number of historical contributions, some of them a little narrow-minded and strictly academic, and devoid of the broad perspective a "philosophy of rhetoric" may offer, but all very well informed: I refer to the Chicago school and to the works of people like Richard McKeon and Bernard Weinberg, or isolated figures like Rosemond Tuve.

Returning to our inquiry, I want to deal now with the Frenchman Jean Paulhan, since his concerns are similar to those we just saw, and his critical contribution is outstanding. Paulhan is perhaps the sharpest critic to grasp the importance of ambiguity intrinsic in a philosophy of rhetoric, the latter taken in its fullest sense and not just as a body of technical rules. He has skillfully indicated the possibility of a "third alternative" that keeps its distance from Croce's short-circuit synthesis, where form and content perfectly pass one into the other, and in fact neutralize each other, and also from the dissociation resulting in a sumlike coexistence of separate, unrelated parts. Paulhan borrows from algebra the formula for the binary system of equations with two unknown quantities that are connected to come to a mutual solution. Words and things, rhetoric and terror against it, constitute a system of this type. The assertions that only the content counts, or, vice versa, that style is preeminent, must be conjugated (which does not mean that they become identical or totally overlapping). Paulhan develops his views in a number of sparkling and paradoxical texts tinged with rhetorical wit, such as *Clef de la poésie, De la paille et du graine*, and the most famous of them all, *Les Fleurs de Tarbes*. I mentioned them when discussing Ruggero Bonghi, the follower of Manzoni, who is a pale precursor of Paulhan. The terroristic exclusion of the flowers of rhetoric, or indeed their repression, if we want to use a Freudian term, may become an obsession that can turn into neurosis (Breton is a case in point). It is much better to accept them, since this is the way to forget and overcome them. In the public garden of Tarbes a sign should be posted telling visitors to come in with flowers: only in this way will people be immune from the temptation to pick the flowers from their beds.

Among the thinkers who have some degree of affinity with the "philosophy of rhetoric" of Richards and the New Critics we must mention the Italian Galvano della Volpe, who himself admitted being influenced by Brooks and other British and American critics. In his *Critica del gusto*, one of the best Italian works on aesthetics in the second half of the twentieth century, he constructs a model that identifies three types of discourses. The first is found in ordinary language; it may be applied to all contexts and is equivocal; the second is scientific discourse, which is univocal and contextual but not organic; and finally poetic discourse (as usual we set rhetoric alongside it), which has multiple meanings, is contextual and organic. One positive feature of this model is that it does not posit the univocal discourse of science as the degree zero: this was the scientific prejudice of what Perelman called "progressive philosophies." On the contrary, for della Volpe the degree zero resides in the confusion and ambiguity of ordinary language, where rhetorical figures and tropes may be present, but are used without any conscious aim or technique. Therefore, figures and tropes are not "deviations" or the by-products of a privileged and originary type of communication. The discourse of poetry and rhetoric is not subordinated to that of logic and mathematics; it is not an exception or an abnormality derived from them. And just as figures are not secondary or derived from scientific discourse, they also are not a prerogative of the discourse of the origins, the idea dear to romantics; rather, their locus is to be found in a use of technique aware of its applications to a specific kind of discourse.

Still in the context of Italian culture, I must mention the contribution of militant criticism to the climate I have been describing. The critic Luciano Anceschi has identified two trends or lines in twentieth-century Italian poetry. Actually, he calls them *istituzioni*, borrowing the term from Quintilian's *Institutio oratoria*, with a view to underscoring his belief that classical rhetoric is the best repository in which language can be equipped with technical tools. The two institutions, or poetics, are grounded respectively in analogy and in the object. To be sure, if we recall the picture outlined at the beginning of this section, it will be apparent that these are the Italian homologues of the postsymbolist line of Mallarmé and Valéry, and of the line of Eliot, Pound, and the objective correlative. What is suggested is again the oppositions between metaphor and metonymy, between paradigm and syntagm. Better still, since we saw that these definitions can be taken only so far, on one side is a poetry that twists the syntax and relies on melopoeia and logopoeia (to use Pound's terminology): it produces a musical and sacred aura, such as one finds in the lyric poetry of Giuseppe Ungaretti, the major representative of the "analogic" line. On the other front is a poetry that stresses the semantic richness of things, phanopoeia (according to the circumstances metaphor, metonymy, synecdoche — all the associations by similarity or contiguity — will be used). One possible consequence of this line is that, from a balanced and classic use of the poetics of objects, such as is found in Eugenio Montale's poetry, it may transform itself, as in fact it does with the Novissimi, i.e., the contemporary poets, the avant-garde of the 1960s, into a return to wild asyntactic associations, or to the very high semantic density advocated by the surrealists: in other words, the reign of terror that, however, does not lack its own figures, as Paulhan taught us.

One more remark: the historical approach of T. S. Eliot, that is, the belief that contemporary interests necessarily lead to new interpretations of the past, can be traced in a number of Italian works. Some examples: Anceschi rereads the aesthetics of English empiricism between the baroque and the restauration; Paolo

Bagni writes on the medieval *artes*; finally, I may include here this text, in which I am attempting to offer a comprehensive interpretation.

Still in Italy, but in the context of historiography, I must mention Eugenio Garin and the Florentine group around him that includes Cesare Vasoli and Paolo Rossi: their work is fundamental to an understanding of the role and incidence of rhetoric on the history of ideas and of civilization in general, from the Middle Ages to the Renaissance and beyond.

Rhetoric and Literature—the "Analytic" Line: From the Russian Formalists to the *Nouvelle Critique*

Another movement that in its fervent research addressed the question of a new treatment of the linguistic material manifested by literary language is that of the Russian formalists, who were tied to the futurist and constructivist avant-gardes, and who belonged to the 1920s dynamic climate that immediately followed the Russian Revolution. On the whole it can be objected that, unlike the criticism of Eliot, Pound, and the New Critics, the formalists did not develop an adequate "philosophy of rhetoric." They did not grasp the knot of ambiguity, or the system with two variables, to use Paulhan's formula, that binds words and things, form and content (the ambiguity that Aristotle had perceived when he located rhetoric midway between discursive arts and moral sciences). With the Russian formalists the formal movement is privileged, as their very name indicates. Their approach will have both positive and negative effects. The first consequence is that *elocutio* is separated from *inventio* and *dispositio*, for the reason that it lends itself better than the other parts to a rigorously scientific analysis relatable to that of other formalized discourses. This project is carried out under the aegis of linguistics, which in those years was itself acquiring scientific status. Paradoxically, this approach brings to bear upon rhetoric analytic tools, so that there may be a danger of misinterpreting it or at least leaving out considerable areas of ineffability: too much light is thrown on certain parts while other parts are passed over. One of the main thrusts is the isolation of the specific literariness of language, and therefore of rhetoric as well. However, this search is pursued exclusively on a linguistic level: della Volpe would call it an organic contextual finality but purely internal, a sort of autorevelation of language, which in order to reach this level gives up on lived experience, external reality, the real world outside. In a way, the formalists internalize content; they treat it as one element among others, with no different status. The procedure seals off literature and makes it into a separate field in all its purity and autonomy. Then the question arises as to what kind of interaction is possible with other fields, like ethics or politics, once any originary, constitutive relationship has been denied or rejected (this problem was dealt with particularly by Yuri Tynianov).

Nevertheless the research of the Russian formalists produced excellent studies; actually their analysis of specific writers has been more incisive than that of the Anglo-American line precisely because of the scientific rigor they strived to reach, and because they did not have to broaden their scope—they did not have to include too many elements. Victor Shklovsky takes from Aristotle the category of the "making strange," starting from its very etymology, that is, the search for meanings that are outside common usage, and that are characteristic of barbarians and strangers. But if at the beginning *elocutio* is the level at which estrangement is applied, the technique soon opens up to reach psychological and epistemological levels; it becomes a way of perceiving and thus of describing reality. This is also facilitated by the fact that Shklovsky deals mostly with prose. His analysis of Tolstoy's fiction is particularly well known: he shows that Tolstoy's search for the estrangement effect is achieved through the use of metonymy and synechdoche, or perhaps better, of functions corresponding to these traditional tropes, since the units Shklovsky takes are really long descriptive passages that are typical of a novelist like Tolstoy, who "focuses" on part of a face or of behavior, rather than giving the whole.

The concepts of the formal method are further developed and systematized by Roman Jakobson, who, as we briefly noted, arranges all tropes on the basis of the Saussurian dichotomy. Relations of similarity, which give rise to metaphors, pertain to the paradigmatic pole, whereas to the syntagmatic pole belong the relations of contiguity, from whose alterations stem metonymies. Jakobson, whose range of interests was extensive, tackles this opposition also from the point of view of language psychopathology. He considers two types of aphasia: in one type the aphasic is unable to find synonyms; in the other, the aphasic cannot organize sentences. From this dichotomy Jakobson derives also a model of general, transhistorical application: he puts forward the hypothesis that literature can be arranged according to two recurring poles: the romantic pole, which is metaphorical and primarily displayed in poetry, and the realistic pole, which is metonymic and mostly used in prose. Such an impressive division has been commented on, criticized, and applied by a variety of thinkers, but for now it appears too schematic and not easily verifiable.

Jakobson has been one of the leading vehicles through which Western culture, especially English-speaking countries, was introduced to the Russian formalists and the Prague Linguistic Circle. His role in spreading and launching the linguistic concepts of these movements has been very important, especially in the 1950s, when the impact of the New Critics was slowing down. His work contributed to the strengthening of the analytic approach, which anyway was inherent in the formal method. Finally, an increasing awareness of their similarities led to the merging between formalist poetics, with its baggage of stylistic and critical concepts, and linguistic structuralism, the latter being further revised and formalized by the Danish linguist Hjelmslev. Both approaches were developed in the specific framework of a global discipline of signs: semiotics.

In the 1960s the French *Nouvelle Critique* is undoubtedly the hot spot around which all these fusions and reelaborations take place. The label is ambiguous on purpose, but in any case it stands for a group of thinkers who on the whole are influenced by "analytic" principles, and who borrow from the Russian formalists the idea of a scientific approach to rhetorical and literary textual devices.

One issue of the journal *Communications* (number 16 of 1970) allows us to take a comprehensive view of the situation. Bearing in mind the economy of our discourse, the following positions may be identified.

1. Claude Bremond, editor of the issue, remarks that "of the four or five parts of traditional rhetoric, only *elocutio* is enjoying an actual recovery."[15] This observation clearly betrays the typical formalist or analytic prejudice, according to which only stylistic and ornamental devices constitute the specificity of a rhetorical discourse, separating it from the solid and usual prerogatives of a rigorous logic. Bremond totally ignores, or represses, the work of Perelman, who more than ten years before had already relaunched the argumentation stressing the relevance of *inventio*, with the warning not to separate *elocutio* from the body of the other parts.

2. Next we have to consider the positions of the French linguist Jean Cohen, author of *Structure du language poétique*, and of the Belgian Groupe μ, which produced *Rhétorique générale*. They all seem to prove Bremond's assertion that only *elocutio* is encountering new fortune, because their researches were almost exclusively dedicated to it. Their investigation is very attractive and up-to-date, but it locates itself within the theoretical framework that suffers from the "analytic" prejudice: we may call its mode the "philosophy of antirhetoric," since it takes back with one hand what it gave with the other. In fact, both Cohen and Groupe μ agree on one point at least: they conceive of style as a deviation from the norm. The norm is provided by scientific discourse, understood as univocal in meaning, denotative and direct, that is, a discourse within which every signifier corresponds to one signified, and one only; and whose constructs and syntax are straightforward, regular. What crops up once again is the modern dissociation of sensibility that we described at the beginning of the twentieth century, situated between the position of a paramathematical logic on the one side, and Crocean intuitionism on the other side: truth and imagination are opposed; actually, they are separated, alternated. In fact, the theory of the deviation, or transgression of the norm, had been upheld at first by post-Crocean critics (Leo Spitzer first of all) in the attempt to conciliate the importance of the subject, the unique and unmistakable character of personal creation, with the fact that language is an impersonal code of general usage. Of course in Cohen the impressionistic, divinatory aspects of Spitzer's stylistic analysis disappear; the analytic approach prevails, and with it the aim of measuring the transgression scientifically.

In and of themselves the results are remarkable. Among other things, they stand out for demonstrating the untenability, under close scrutiny, of the opposition between metaphor and metonymy that Jakobson had set up. Contrary to appearances, the one does not go without the other. The metaphoric deviation is seen first of all as an irregularity, an anomaly, an abuse perpetrated on the order of the syntagms. Actually, paradigmatic resemblance, once discovered, allows the deviation to be absorbed, to be made normal again. But the fact remains that for Cohen the use of figures (whether it is tropes or schemes, arbitrary operations on the paradigmatic or syntagmatic axes) is a privilege of subjectivity, contrasted with the objectivity of scientific discourse. He never suspects that it is instead the difference between two systems organized differently, but both objective (that is, public, verifiable in the same way, if not with the same tools). By the time he comes to the end of his analysis, Cohen actually nurtures the doubt that to assume scientific language as the basic standard, the measure, may be a historical and cultural bias that must be seen in the context of Western culture. But in the 1960s there are already enough signs to realize that a redistribution of the parts is under way, that Western culture is criticizing and demolishing its Cartesian, scientific, and analytic options, which after all go back only to the seventeenth century. For example, the same issue of *Communications* contains an excellent essay by Pierre Kuentz, "Le 'Rhétorique' ou la mise a l'écart." This essay succeeds quite well in pointing out and correcting the prejudices we saw. Furthermore, the persistence of and the return to rhetoric and its parts is seen as a Freudian return of the repressed tied, in recent history, to the desire to undermine the place that rhetoric, with its roundness and softness, held, only to replace it with efficient forms of communication.

Groupe μ is more cautious than Cohen. They understand the difficulty of establishing a degree zero of language in a "natural" way. For one thing they are aware, as della Volpe was, that ordinary language is not at all the realm of denotation, but it is quite rich in figures of speech. Already the rhetorician Du Marsais, who is quoted a great deal by all contemporary French linguists, had wittily observed that more figures are produced in a day at the open market than in long years of sophisticated academic research. This amounts to saying that the degree zero is already an artificial construction, "the ideal that scientific language aspires to achieve."[16] Simplicity is not a primary, originary feature, but rather a construction: as a consequence, like Perelman, the group rejects "progressive" philosophies.

Notwithstanding their excellent theoretical stand, Groupe μ cannot but ground the whole rhetorical edifice on univocal communication. Thus rhetoric is given a secondary derived status, at least from a logical point of view, if not on the level of evaluation. This is perhaps an inevitable result reached every time *elocutio* is sealed off from the other parts and then set up as a science, overlooking the general goals of argumentation: that is, this state of affairs obtains every time rhetoric is turned into a mere science of tropes.

Given these limits, from the point of view of a global "philosophy of rhetoric" it must be acknowledged that the classificatory enterprise of Groupe μ is still today most valuable and exhaustive. Three general levels are identified that move away from the degree zero: addition, suppression, and permutation. The "analytic" stance is confirmed when the idea is borrowed from Hjelmslev of conducting distinct investigations both on matter and form, on expression and on content levels. In essence, this corresponds to the old distinction, always present in every traditional classification, between figures that only affect the signifiers (*verba*), and those that involve the signifieds (*res*).

One of the most remarkable achievements of *Rhétorique générale* is its powerful study of metaplasms, the transformations that the signifier can undergo within a single word (apocope, apheresis/aphesis, ellipsis, crasis, plays on prefixes and suffixes, metathesis, anagram, etc.). The aim of such an accurate taxonomy is purely neutral: an inventory of suggestions is provided that everybody may then apply to various kinds of discourses and various historical situations. We saw that metaplasms are particularly relevant in humor and jokes, and that they find a considerable application in poetry, from the classics to the latest avant-garde, if we are ready to accept the striking indications of Saussure's paragrams.

Metataxis is the label that Groupe μ, resourceful and ingenious in the way they renew traditional terminology, gives to figures that act on the structure of the sentence, such as asyndeton, polysyndeton, and parataxis. The general term "metasememes" is applied to tropes proper, that is, figures that modify the meaning. As in Cohen, here too the contrast that usually is so well marked between metaphor and metonymy is considerably attenuated. They show how metaphor (the substitution of one meaning for another that "resembles" it) at first relies on a synecdochic phase; that is, it zeroes in on an aspect of the meaning one starts from, which in its turn will make manifest the resemblance with an aspect of the meaning one arrives at, and then it allows one to regain it in its totality. Finally, "full" figures of content—litotes, aposiopesis (reticence), hyperbole, paradox, etc.—are called metalogisms.

3. The last position I want to isolate from issue 16 of *Communications* is that of the famous French structuralist critics/*Nouveaux Critiques* Barthes, Genette, and Todorov. Actually, if we start with the oldest, Roland Barthes, who was already well known in the 1950s, it is at first hard to trace a boundary with respect to the scholars already reviewed, since in France Barthes was one of the leading figures who helped establish the "analytic" approach by adopting Hjelmslev's structuralism and semiotics. The compendium of ancient rhetoric that he published in *Communications* is further proof of this. He was attracted to ancient rhetoric, in fact, inasmuch as it seemed to be the repository of a wide systematic

literary discourse, a perfect theoretical and taxonomic grid at the same time, which at most could be revised, rewritten, renamed from the standpoint of the scientific expertise of our times. At stake was the formalization of the connotative level, as Hjelmslev had already tried to do, when he was separating every kernel of content into two parts: form and substance, almost hoping to see substance itself diminish or at the limit disappear. Indeed, this is what Barthes attempts to do when, for example, he proceeds to construct *the fashion system*. He soon realizes, however, that rhetoric is the undermining moment and the breaking point of any analytic attempt at systematicity; it is the territory where reemerge the confused, the informal, the discordant, with the sphere of ideological evaluations, and the consequent movement from theory to praxis. In fact, Barthes, and with him the whole *Nouvelle Critique*, postulates the confluence of the new semiotic methodologies with the stronger foundations of Marxian praxis and Freudian psychoanalysis. But by starting out from euphoric analytic premises, doesn't one condemn oneself to experience the return of rhetoric as a "return of the repressed," as Kuentz lucidly observed? With respect to the claimed innocence of those who support a theory of rhetoric as deviation from the norm, Barthes has the advantage of being aware of the "bad conscience" of repression provoked by the analytic viewpoint. Nevertheless, he is not better equipped with technical instruments: with him rhetoric runs the risk of becoming the "other," the open void that threatens the excessive clarity of the citadel of denotative language.

In brief, what is required is the global perspective of a "philosophy of rhetoric" so that one will no longer have to deal with isolated units in sparse order, and one will be able to reverse the tendency that, in the same issue of *Communications*, Gérard Genette rightly describes as a progressive and relentless shrinking of rhetoric, in such a way that its whole field is now reduced to *elocutio*, and this too is limited to metaphor and metonymy. The need for a global outlook is no doubt correct, but also in Genette persists a limitation that from the very beginning forces him to move in the direction of the analytic: he adheres to the formalist line that restricts analysis to verbal aspects only. Against the primacy of denotation Genette's only remedy is to postulate an absolute connotation, connotation for its own sake. Rhetoric and literature would refer only to themselves; they would constitute themselves as a continuous deviation between signifier and signified, a space in-between, a distance, an open gap. The figure that emerges at this point and that I must mention because it was very influential on the French structuralists is Maurice Blanchot, and through him a "certain" reading of Heidegger. For example, Blanchot is quoted by Tzvetan Todorov in *Littérature and signification*, in the chapter "Tropes et figures." There the "new function of rhetoric" is seen as "making us aware of the existence of discourse."[17] In other words, the poetic function signifies itself, in accordance with the theories of the Russian formalists, and of Jakobson in particular. This makes possible an agreement with the Heideggerian "being for nothingness" of Blanchot: a proud act of self-foundation that at the same time is self-destructive; an absolute statement coupled with an equally radical erasure. Todorov interprets all this also in terms of the contrast between transparency and opacity of language, which corresponds to the polarity we saw in the "philosophy of rhetoric" of the New Critics and their followers. For the New Critics, however, opacity was not self-sufficient; rather, it served the purpose of winning over to the strategy of poetic-rhetorical discourse plurivocal meanings, or it brought about the balance between knowledge, pleasure, and the emotions. In other words, it was a space where a full integration was realized, rather than being a strong concentration on the formal aspect only.

Rhetoric and Technological Media: Marshall McLuhan

In investigating the present revival of rhetoric, we have dealt so far with the "weak" motives, characteristic of the movements that exclusively stress *elocutio*; and with the "medium" motives of Perelman's logical approach. Now we must examine the "strong" motives: the factors belonging to the material, economic, and technological order. The most persuasive suggestions in this direction come from the Canadian critic Marshall McLuhan in his well-known *Gutenberg Galaxy* (1962) and *Understanding Media* (1964). From these works emerges a very stimulating outlook, and the circle we have been tracing in our survey comes full: through the great technological changes we are led to understand why rhetoric underwent its most serious crisis at the beginning of modernity, in the seventeenth century, and why for a quite a few years now it has enjoyed a significant revival. The crisis finds one of its causes in the introduction of printing by movable type: the invention of the mythical Gutenberg. McLuhan applies the name of Gutenberg to characterize an entire epoch, a galaxy actually, a system of aggregations that touch all the spheres of culture, although they find their prime kernel in the material technology of the printing process. Of course print did not produce all its effects immediately; it actually took a long time before its technique imposed itself, before it shaped Western consciousness, and this result was reached almost through a patient subliminal process. Printing decisively brought about the prevailing of writing over the spoken word. It brought to an end the age of orality, since thanks to the new technology writing became easily reproducible, and thus economically advantageous. The book is the first object produced according to the laws of industrialized mass production, the first example of a consumer commodity distributed on a large scale. Communication no longer focuses on the mouth-ear circuit: it now shifts to the "silent" visual modality of the eyes. Everybody who has a book in hand can read it in the silence of his or her room. In contrast with communal values, silent individual reading puts the stress on individualism; it strengthens the claim to act on one's own, to judge with one's own head by appealing to reason, and it also favors a disregard of authority, of the persuasive power of speakers who offer their words in person, with the support of their moral authority and their very presence. To a conception of rhetoric that made it one of the pillars of the Roman Catholic church, is now opposed the possibility of direct communication with God, as sustained by Protestant reformers. The accent moves away from the sensuous musical character of eloquence and falls on the logical aspects of language.

This process is also facilitated by the material characteristics of the printed page: type is arranged following the geometrical regularity of lines and columns in a way that strongly emphasizes atomistic fragmentariness (the single type is isolated from the others and at the same time is ready to be reproduced in its stereotyped form), lineal seriality, succession by contiguity. All of these aspects will be introjected by the "new science" and the new philosophy of the seventeenth century, and we can trace them in the internal operations of mathematics, logic, and psychology. To be sure, they originate in the conditioning effects that Western civilization experienced with the introduction of books and a reading practice subjected to the Gutenberg modes. Even the modern dissociation of sensibility, on which we insisted so much, perhaps is grounded in the fact that communication processes increasingly came to rely on that *ante litteram* "Cartesian" grid, or even before, on the Euclidean model. The prerogatives of the emotions, imagination, and affections do not filter through the mesh of the typographic cage: they are left out and excluded, whereas in a world where orality was the norm there were not separate channels for *docere* and *movere*: both were spontaneously mixed, to the point that the attempt to distinguish between them would have been considered an abstract and derivative undertaking. McLuhan goes so far as to say that through these processes of fragmentation "modern" civilization has created the unconscious; that is, it has legitimized the repression of an entire instinctual area, which is contrasted with the geometrical and rational spaces expressed through the Gutenberg technology.

McLuhan's theses coincide in part with the views of left-wing Freudianism, which came to take a Marxian stand and was most effectively represented by Herbert Marcuse. From this perspective the crisis of rhetoric after the Renaissance and during modernity appears less and less "innocent": it is not simply provoked by choices at the cognitive level, and in fact very strong practical, political, and social implications will derive from it. The Gutenberg human being is at the same time the bourgeois individualist, the future protagonist of the industrial revolution, the master of a vast control over nature, from which resources are endlessly drawn with a view to rapid progress. But for all this there is a high price to pay in the strong repression of aesthetic elements, sensual pleasure, and emotions, which points to Freud's unhappy scenario about the inexorable deepening of discomforts brought about by civilization. The "modern" individual is condemned to pay for material comfort and technological power with a progressive increase in social and collective neuroses that constitute the return of the repressed, i.e., some distorted and indirect attempts to satisfy libidinal sensual aesthetic drives (among which is also the pleasure of orality) too rigidly inhibited.

A certain technological order, print, has caused this disease. A different technology may provide the liberation, the way out of this state of affairs. This is in fact the opinion of McLuhan and Marcuse: we are moving away from the mechanical outlook of the Gutenberg era; its place is taken first of all, in the domain of communication, by electric and electronic media such as the telephone, radio, television, tape and video recorders. These technical possibilities radically revolutionize the Gutenberg framework. It is no longer true that *verba volant scripta manent*. Now oral communication can be "kept"; it can be stored and transmitted long distance; it can be reproduced at affordable prices, in the same way as writing. Its advantage is that it also and above all "keeps" the physicality of discourse, like sounds, gestures, mimicry, at least in the case of video recording. What reemerges is the possibility of a way of speaking that includes all of its aspects, speaking in the fullest sense of the word: the speaker may be entirely present in body and soul, intellect and senses. This marks the return not only to the first three parts of rhetoric, those that bear a more cognitive relevance, as was expressed already in Perelman's logical system and by the stylistic-linguistic analysts. Now rhetoric returns also as *actio*, as a mode of delivering words, of managing and acting. It is a *performance*, an action that has a not insignificant degree of well worked out artistry. It is the reemergence of sounds, and not only of sight, that in fact had accompanied the strong development of rhetoric throughout antiquity. This return is also an attempt on the part of our civilization to undertake a sort of psychoanalysis of itself in order to recover the sensory dimension, the libidinal erotic pleasure of the word—its "presence," to borrow a term from a scholar close to McLuhan: Walter Ong.[18]

Conclusion: The Present Vitality of Rhetoric

Our short journey through a good two millennia of rhetoric and its vicissitudes comes to an end on a hopeful note. Indeed, rhetoric now enjoys good health: this is true not only of one of its traditional parts, *elocutio*, as the editorial of *Communications* issue 16 claimed, but of its other parts as well. In fact, thanks to Perelman *inventio* and *dispositio* have been reinstated in the role they once had. Overcoming the reduction or actually the repression within the Cartesian attitude of modernity, we noted that forensic and political debates had continued to be lively, and in ways not so different from the classical ones. In any trial whatsoever the interventions of the prosecution and the defense follow in the steps of forensic Ciceronian oratory today just like in the past, and one can draw useful advice from *De inventione* as well as from any other classical manual. Indeed, there has been a remarkable increase in opportunities for deliberative oratory made possible by the expansion of a democratic orientation that has spread to many areas of social life. I am thinking of the phenomenon of assemblies, which apart from their traditional official space (the House of Representatives, the Senate, and other legislative and governmental organs) are being set up in many social contexts, for example in high school and university life, in unions, in a variety of groups. These assemblies emerge whenever a collective body must take decisions in common (we may take as the minimum, unicellular level a condominium meeting). In all these cases the old rules still apply that teach us how to convince others, or how to conduct an argumentation in a context where there is no possibility of using a logical-mathematical (analytic) demonstration.

It may seem that if these two parts of rhetoric are thriving and always renewing themselves, epideictic rhetoric, also called demonstrative or laudatory (which in traditional classifications is the third part), would definitely be dead, the reason being that it is too tied to the verbosity of antiquity, to the cult of authority, to the necessity of praising the virtues and denouncing the vices of public figures. Today these are redundant attitudes that would not find a welcome place in our sophisticated, more democratically oriented times. Apart from the fact that eulogies, panegyrics, and encomia still exist, and actually seem to justify the negative meaning of rhetoric itself, we must not overlook two relatively new fields that today are engaged in producing laudative discourse. The first is, in general terms, the evaluation of art: the vast area of criticism of literature, film, theater, music, the visual arts, etc., in the great variety of places that today are open to such a genre, that enjoys significant circulation and consumption (for example, in newspapers, magazines, and journals). As a matter of fact, this type of discourse intersects with the judiciary, as the etymology of the word suggests (*crinein*, to judge), but on the whole it may be better placed with epideictic rhetoric, since an aesthetic judgment implies not a verdict and a punishment but an increase or decrease of ethical and psychological values, such as praise, virtue, glory. Certainly if we had the space to move on to some applications of the historical and theoretical survey carried out so far, a considerable part would be dedicated precisely to showing that literary criticism is a perfect case of rhetorical discourse: it contains qualitative components such as the choice of topics, their strategic arrangement, and the choice of stylistic devices; it also contains quantitative components: how to start; how to sum up the plot of a book or a movie, selecting aspects that are significant and that can be used in the final judgment to avoid boring the reader with excessive descriptions; moreover, one must proceed to ''confirm'' one's thesis while refuting that of one's adversary; and one has to conclude, summing up and defending one's point of view.

The other area in which epideictic rhetoric is booming is the realm of commercials, which direct our attention to products with the goal of persuading us of their good qualities. The first requirement of advertising is brevity, since it is not something requested by the public, but rather fills up ''dead'' space and time and is situated in almost subliminal zones. If boredom is always negative to any rhetorical intervention, it must be particularly avoided in the context of advertisements, which must invest a lot of energy in bringing about the effect of *delectare* in the recipients. Thus enthymemes will be suitable (the shortened syllogisms that skip over obvious middle passages), but also examples, with their sensuous appeal, or finally, witty remarks and jokes in general. In relation to the latter, Freud has shown that success depends on speed, on catching the moment in which the Ego is off its guard and the brakes of censorship are let up, so that a libidinal or aggressive meaning may get through using as its vehicle a noble, irreprehensible meaning, before censorship is able to separate the two and send back the illicit guest.

Jokes, anagrams, plays on words such as metaplasms (as the members of Groupe μ would call them), which are among the operations most exploited by commercials, finally summon up the third part of rhetoric: *elocutio*. It goes without saying that it is in full growth: it may actually be overgrowing, with the danger of claiming autonomy for itself and of putting in the shade the other parts. Granting that it has many responsibilities, it must nevertheless wisely act in close cooperation with the other parts. To start with, *elocutio* may provide the first arrangement of metaplastic phenomena and figures of content (litotes, rhetorical questions, irony) that are precisely at the origin of wit and jokes, and may be used in advertising or more generally in ordinary discourse; they may actually become effective and fearful weapons in judiciary and deliberative rhetoric, and in criticism as well, whether literary, of the figurative arts, etc. Second, we have ascertained that *elocutio* finds its way in ordinary language, too. The idea that ordinary language is the degree zero of communication, that it is linear, direct, and devoid of rhetorical figures, is no longer acceptable. On the contrary, the degree zero is a derivative product obtained through complicated processes of reduction, by applying a sort of rigorous self-censorship. Tropes are "there," so to speak: they are part of language; they inhabit it spontaneously and are far from being a deviation, a derived outcome. No linguistic intervention, however immediate and practical, is without rhetorical devices, and therefore an analysis in this direction is always appropriate. Third, *elocutio* carries huge historical responsibilities toward literary discourse (prose and poetry), or else discourses produced with the intention of accounting for rhetorical techniques, of not overlooking them. More complex is the relationship with contemporary poetry. As we noted, the latter starts off with a terroristic critique of "poetic diction," that is, with a radical rejection of a mannered *elocutio*. However, according to the logic of the equation suggested by Paulhan, by doing so one ends up giving an extremely careful consideration to linguistic material and its properties, so much so that it is in fact contemporary experimentation in poetry and militant criticism that have focused attention again on the crucial issue of figures, for no other reason than that it seemed necessary to introduce new ones, or to revise and modify those in use. This opens up a whole new landscape: the revision and adaptation of the old illustrious metaphor and metonymy in the light of the new tasks they are required to perform. Moreover, contemporary poetry is becoming increasingly interested in "intraverbal" figures, that is, figures related to changes within the signifier of single words, or single lexical or morphological fragments. Vast perspectives are opened up in the direction of microrhetoric, which was announced by Saussure's paragrams and by Freud's study on jokes. In the not too distant future, poets might no longer be working on the breaks between words, but mainly within words themselves.

Actio also markedly partakes in the recent success of rhetoric. It had been neglected by the "weak" and "medium" approaches that either analyzed only *elocutio* or followed Perelman's theory of argumentation, since both perspectives stopped at the written, or rather, the printed word, print being until recently the only official way in which writing circulated. This is no longer the case, since thanks to photocopying and collotype handwriting can also be kept and reproduced. If we then take into account the theories of McLuhan about the incidence of technology, we must recognize that today any form of discourse, whether ordinary, political, literary, judiciary, of advertising, etc., is maintained and diffused by means of the general availability of electronic media. Therefore pronunciation, affective impact, emphasis, regain the importance they had in antiquity, when there was no choice, or the only modest alternative was the still uncommon technique of writing. Certainly in all ages these features had had a role, but they were relegated to the minor setting of communication "in the presence" of an audience. This was considered a lower context precisely because of its precariousness and scarce diffusion in comparison with print, a fact that added to the mistrust in rhetoric, conceived as an art typically addressing an almost private and occasional channel. On the contrary, now a speech can have vast resonance and reach thousands of millions of listeners. This imposes on everybody, and especially on people with public responsibilities, the need to pay renewed attention to *actio*. What regains all of its relevance is the question, the "ancient" anxiety, of being eloquent, of being a skillful orator, and not only in the sense of writing well, which is a mediated and virtual feature, but in the immediacy of direct contact, which also is mediated, but by high-fidelity electronic audio and video systems. We should also note the line of development that led first to a revival of sounds (the radio) and then, and increasingly so, to the integration of the visual, of gestuality, the elements tied to presence, facial features and mimicry, attractiveness (television). To have a beautiful voice is no longer enough: one must be good-looking, or at least pleasant. It must be added that electronic technology beside high-fidelity recording and transmitting has shortened the distance between the place of emission (of course a virtual point where one locates one's radio or television) and that of the reception. In the past the recipients of a speech were at a considerable distance from the speaker: the crowd would gather in a room or in a square. The distance still survived at first when radios were an expensive novelty, and not yet a cheap commodity one could listen to in the privacy of one's home. In the beginning the radio was mainly a piece of public property, and this meant that one was obliged to listen to it in big crowds. Apart from material economic reasons, this was the outcome of a skillful orchestration on the part of propaganda operators during fascism: through a high concentration of people and the maintaining of a safe distance between listeners and the point of emission, remarkable psychagogic effects could be obtained. Hence the dictatorial eloquence of the 1930s, as McLuhan notes, whether it was delivered from a platform, or from a close and yet distant radio message diffused through loudspeakers. But from the 1950s on, television introduces the need for a more colloquial style and, becoming a commodity, it penetrates on tiptoe into the family. Since the group of viewers is smaller, there is more space for discussion and exchange of views.

The powerful revival of *actio* has enhanced research into a number of fields related to it: proxemics is the study of the position and distance between people involved in social interaction, whether communicative or other; kinesics and paralinguistics study the role of the motor function of the body, of the voice, etc., isolated from the linguistic moment. Moving in a different direction, the gestuality of a speaker is related to the performance in visual arts such as dance, music, recitation, and mime. In short, there are enough reasons to rewrite an *Institutio* for our time as comprehensive as Quintilian's, and one in which special care should be given to all the classical parts of rhetoric, overlooking none of them. Even *memory* is enjoying a comeback, in close connection with *actio*: now there are frequent occasions to deliver impromptu speeches in the direct presence of an audience. Memory had fallen almost completely in disuse under the advance of the Gutenberg galaxy: in this context the usual way to memorize something was by means of a printed book, a manual of easy consultation. Above all, it was oral speech itself that had fallen into disuse. Now that almost anyone can find him- or herself in the position to give a speech, whether it is in the humble situation of a small group making a decision, or in front of crowds of listeners and viewers, we must return to the skill of memorizing an outline of our topics, arranging them in the order in which we want to give them. In the same way we are obliged to remember notions that, even if momentarily forgotten, would seriously damage the dignity of our self-image.

Suggested Reading

Historical outlines on rhetoric embracing Western culture from the origins to our time are extremely rare. Chaignet is quite dated. The classic *Traité de l' argumentation* by Perelman and Olbrechts-Tyteca contains a wide range of materials from various historical periods, but they are mainly used to support a discourse that remains largely theoretical. Short and concise but quite powerful in its incisive historical insights is the outline by Florescu, to whom we will refer again. Indirectly, Wimsatt and Brooks also trace a history of rhetoric. For a systematic and synchronic classification we can avail ourselves of the well-versed compendium by Lausberg, or of the expository study by Groupe μ that is lucidly constructed on a semiotic foundation. The recent *Dizionario* by Marchese is also useful. To the contemporary revival of rhetoric the publication of the journal *Philosophy and Rhetoric*, edited by W. J. Johnstone, bears witness, as does the existence of the International Society for the History of Rhetoric, founded in the summer of 1977 in Zurich, on the occasion of a conference whose proceedings should appear soon. Also very interesting are the colloquia held annually in Bressanone by the Circolo Filologico-Linguistico Padovano, directed by G. Folena.

The Greeks

The historical outline by Riposati is very broad and detailed. That of Funaioli is rather outdated. Plebe's *Breve Storia* is lively and fresh, but it sustains questionable views. Barthes's compendium, although rich and knowledgeable, aims first of all at a systematic and synchronic classification. Very useful are the contributions by Baldwin and Clark. Untersteiner's study on the Sophists has become a classic; it attempts a generous rehabilitation, but contains subtleties that are sometimes a little tortuous. Viano has written a well-balanced work on Aristotle, whereas the theses of Plebe are well versed but questionable. Levi is useful on Isocrates. The best reconstruction and interpretation of the "question" of the *Sublime* is that of Rostagni.

The Romans

Leeman's examination of Latin rhetoric is broad and well documented. On *Rhetorica ad Herennium* see the information in the critical edition of G. Calboli. On Cicero, in addition to the sections dedicated to him in the works already mentioned (in particular Baldwin and Clark), the editors' introductions to each rhetorical work in the series Belles Lettres (Courbaud, Bornecque, Martha) are also very helpful. For a more in-depth analysis of the interpretation of Cicero developed in this work, see Barilli (1969). On Quintilian, in addition to the information contained in the *Institutio Oratoria* edited by R. Faranda, Lana is also interesting.

The Middle Ages

Gilson (1944) offers a very lively, chiaroscuro historical outline of medieval thought from the church fathers to the beginning of humanism. Effective considerations on the trivium and the quadrivium and the significance of the shifting in their mutual balance are formulated by Florescu. The attempt at periodization suggested by McKeon, although very learned and analytic, does not seem thoroughly functional or verifiable. As to Augustine, the church fathers and their relationship with classic Latin culture, a study of great insight is that by Marrou. For dialectic during mature Scholasticism, the framework traced in Garin (1958) is very subtle. Curtius remains a classic on poetics and its problematic; see also the contributions of the young scholar Bagni. The essays by Gilson (1939) and Nardi are helpful for understanding Dante's philosophical views.

Humanism and Renaissance

The movement from the dialectical spirit of the thirteenth century to the revival of *humanae litterae*, and thus of rhetoric, in the fourteenth century is traced very acutely by Gilson (1944). To Garin and Vasoli we owe fundamental studies on the humanists' conception of rhetoric and dialectic. For the theories of the Renaissance (sixteenth century), some useful suggestions may be derived from the classical but dated general histories of Spingarn, Saintsbury, and Toffanin. The careful scholarship of Anglo-American criticism on Renaissance rhetorical-poetical traditions has been rejuvenated in our time by Weinberg, to whom we refer for detailed information on the Italian theorists (see also Barilli 1973). The issues at stake in the humanists' debates on the preeminence or rejection of rhetoric (from Agricola to Vives and Nizolio) have been rigorously examined by Vasoli and Rossi. On Ramism the monograph by Ong (1958) is fundamental, as well as for the light it sheds on a general history of culture and technology. Very effective considerations are offered also by McLuhan (1962). On Bruno and in general on esoterism, Platonism, and the art of mnemonics in the late Renaissance, the studies by Yates have an invaluable significance.

Early Modernity

On the Italian theorists of *ingegno* see F. Croce and Raimondi. For the poetics of the baroque set in a larger European framework, see Eliot, Bethell, and Anceschi. The rise and development of French rationalism and classicism, with reference to literary questions, is followed by Bray; a wide range of suggestions also come from Wimsatt and Brooks. Specific analyses tracing the significance of rhetoric on British ground, in the Metaphysical poets, Bacon, and empiricism, are offered by Tuve, Howell, Brooks, Anceschi, and Vickers. An updated view on Vichian criticism may be found in *Omaggio a Vico*; K. Lüwitz, S. Moravia, P. Rossi, and G. Semerari, among others. The themes of seventeenth-century criticism are developed in Wellek's powerful fresco, and Bate gives an exhaustive description of the beginnings of the preromantic attitude.

Modernity

For the literary and stylistic conceptions of German romanticism, still fundamental is the second volume of the study by Wellek, to which we already referred and which follows also the interferences and connections on English, French, and Italian grounds. A recent and in-depth contribution is Todorov (1977). For an interpretation of Kant's link with baroque theories, see Ransom. The possible relevance of Schiller's views to our time is upheld by Marcuse. On Wordsworth and Coleridge there are very insightful chapters in Wimsatt and Brooks. On the old-modern, reactionary-progressive aspects of Leopardi see Luporini and Barilli (1969).

The Contemporary Revival of Rhetoric

Decisive contributions to a critique of the epistemology of logical positivism, and in general of the "analytic" spirit of the twentieth century, implicit in the perspective of rhetoric, come from Perelman's works, and also from Preti's essay. On Freud's and Saussure's rhetoric see the stimulating chapters in Todorov

(1977). On jokes, and in general on humor and its relationship with rhetoric, see the recent essay by Olbrechts-Tyteca. Saussure's study on paragrams is illustrated by Starobinski. The organic contextual conception of poetical-rhetorical discourse in Anglo-American criticism is elucidated by the very poets and critics who practiced it (Eliot, Pound, Ransom, Tate, Brooks). On the Russian formalists see Erlich and Ambrogio; on R. Jacobson, see Cohen and Groupe μ. The most important contributions of the *Nouvelle Critique* to rhetorical issues come from Barthes, Todorov, and Genette. Eco's and Marchese's interest in rhetoric is developed in a semiotic key. The classic studies by McLuhan and Ong analyze the tie between rhetoric and technological media.

Notes

1. The Greeks

1. *The Collected Dialogues of Plato*, ed. Edith Hamilton and Huntington Cairns, Bollingen Series 71 (Princeton, N.J.: Princeton University Press, 1980), p. 420.

2. *The Older Sophists*, ed. Diels-Kranz (Columbia: University of South Carolina Press, 1972), p. 10.

3. Ibid., p. 10.

4. See *The Collected Dialogues of Plato*, p. 872.

5. *The Older Sophists*, p. 42.

6. Ibid., p. 52.

7. See Isocrates, *Against the Sophists*, trans. G. Norlin, Loeb Classical Library 229 (London: Heinemann; New York: G. P. Putnam's Sons, 1929), p. 171.

8. Isocrates, *Antidosis*, trans. G. Norlin, Loeb Classical Library 229 (London: Heinemann; New York: G. P. Putnam's Sons, 1929), p. 335.

9. *Gorgias, The Collected Dialogues of Plato*, p. 239.

10. *Protagoras, The Collected Dialogues of Plato*, p. 320.

11. *Gorgias*, pp. 246–47.

12. *Phaedrus*, in *The Collected Dialogues of Plato*, p. 513.

13. *Prior Analytics*, trans. Hugh Tredennick, Loeb Classical Library 325 (London: Heinemann; Cambridge, Mass.: Harvard University Press, 1973), Book 1, p. 199.

14. *Topica*, trans. E. S. Forster, Loeb Classical Library 391 (Cambridge, Mass.: Harvard University Press; London: Heinemann, 1976), I, i, pp. 273–75.

15. Ibid., p. 277.

16. Aristotle, *The "Art" of Rhetoric*, trans. J. H. Freese, Loeb Classical Library 193 (Cambridge, Mass.: Harvard University Press; London: Heinemann, 1975), Book 2, p. 297.

17. *The "Art" of Rhetoric*, Book 3, p. 347.

18. *The Poetics*, trans. W. Hamilton Fyfe, Loeb Classical Library 199 (Cambridge, Mass.: Harvard University Press; London: Heinemann, 1982), p. 81.

19. *The "Art" of Rhetoric*, Book 3, p. 407.
20. *I frammenti degli Stoici antichi* (Bari: Laterza, 1932), p. 29.
21. [Longinus], *On the Sublime*, trans. W. H. Fyfe, Loeb Classical Library 199 (Cambridge, Mass.: Harvard University Press; London: Heinemann, 1982), p. 125.

2. The Romans

1. *Rhetorica ad Herennium*, H. Caplan trans., Loeb Classical Library 403 (Cambridge, Mass.: Harvard University Press; London: Heinemann, 1954), p. 5.
2. In English in the text.—Trans.
3. *Tusculan Disputations*, trans. J. E. King, Loeb Classical Library 141 (Cambridge, Mass.: Harvard University Press; London: Heinemann, 1966), vol. 33, pp. 458–59.
4. To wobble in Latin is *clodicare*.—Trans.
5. *De oratore*, trans. E. W. Sutton and H. Rackam, Loeb Classical Library 349 (Cambridge, Mass.: Harvard University Press; London: Heinemann, 1977), Book III, p. 125.
6. *De oratore*, Book I, pp. 89–91.
7. At the beginning of Book VI.—Trans.
8. *Institutio oratoria*, trans. H. E. Butler, Loeb Classical Library 124 (Cambridge, Mass.: Harvard University Press; London: Heinemann, 1980), Books II, XV, pp. 34, 315.
9. *Institutio oratoria*, trans. H. E. Butler, Loeb Classical Library 126 (Cambridge, Mass.: Harvard University Press; London: Heinemann, 1976), Book IX, pp. 1, 14, 355.

3. The Middle Ages

1. Tertullian, *Apology*, trans. T. R. Glover, Loeb Classical Library 250 (Cambridge, Mass.: Harvard University Press; London: Heinemann, 1966), IV, 3, pp. 26–27.
2. Minucius Felix, *Octavius*, trans. G. H. Rendall, Loeb Classical Library 250 (Cambridge, Mass.: Harvard University Press; London: Heinemann, 1966), 15.2, 352–53.
3. *Answer to the Skeptics: A Translation of St. Augustine's Contra Academicos*, trans. D. J. Kavanagh (New York: Cosmopolitan Science and Art Service, 1943), Book III, Chapter 11, 26, p. 185.
4. *On Christian Doctrine*, trans. J. F. Shaw, in *Great Books of the Western World*, no. 18, Augustine (Chicago: Encyclopaedia Britannica, William Benton, and the University of Chicago, 1952), Book II, 37, p. 654.
5. Ibid., Book III, 40, p. 668.
6. Ibid., Book IV, Chapter 14, 30, p. 685.
7. See *Metalogicon*, ed. and trans. Daniel D. McGarry (Los Angeles and Berkeley: University of California Press, 1962), Book 1, Chapter 7, pp. 26–27.
8. "The method of demonstration is therefore generally feeble and ineffective with regard to facts of nature (I refer to corporeal and changeable things). But it quickly recovers its strength when applied to the field of mathematics." Metalogicon, Book 2, Chapter 13, p. 105.
9. *Summa theologica*, literally trans. by the Fathers of the English Dominican Province (New York: Benziger Brothers, 1947), vol. 1, p. 1097.
10. "La dialettica dal secolo XII ai principi dell'età moderna," in *Studi sulla dialettica* (Turin: Taylor, 1958), p. 127.
11. *Convivio*, in *Le opere di Dante*, ed. Barbi, Parodi, Pellegrini, Pistelli, Rajna, Rostagno, and Vandelli (Florence: Bemporad, 1921), Book III, Chapter 11, p. 230.
12. *Convivio*, Book III, Chapter 15, p. 238.
13. *De vulgari eloquentia*, trans. Warman Welliver (Ravenna: Longo, 1981), Book II, p. 91.
14. *De Monarchia*, Book I, Chapter 11.
15. *Convivio*, Book II, Chapter 2, 4, p. 191.
16. *Convivio*, Book I, Chapter 7, p. 158.

17. *De vulgari eloquentia*, Book II, Chapter 6, p. 107.

18. Ibid., Book II, Chapter 7, p. 111.

4. Humanism and the Renaissance

1. Petrarch, *De sui ipsius et multorum ignorantia* in *Prose* (Milan and Naples: Ricciardi, 1955), p. 713.

2. Ibid., p. 747.

3. Coluccio Salutati, *Fratri Iohanni Dominici: De laboribus Herculis*, in *Classici della pedagogia, L'Umanesimo*, ed. E. Garin (Florence: Giuntine-Sansoni, 1958), p. 57.

4. Albertino Mussato, *Declaratio epistulae responsivae ad Iohannem de Mantua*, in *Classici della pedagogia, L'Umanesimo*, pp. 11ff.

5. Leonardo Bruni, *De studiis et litteris liber*, in *Classici della pedagogia, L'Umanesimo*, p. 151.

6. Aeneas Silvius Piccolomini, *Tractatus de liberorum educatione*, in *Classici della pedagogia, L'Umanesimo*, p. 263.

7. Lorenzo Valla, *Elegantiarum libri*, in *Opera omnia* (Turin: Bottega d'Erasmo, 1962), p. 118.

8. *Laurentii Vallae Romani in libros suos dialecticos praefatio*, in *Opera omnia*, p. 645.

9. Ibid., p. 644.

10. Giovanni Pico della Mirandola, *Ermolao Barbaro poetae*, in *Prose Latine e altre opere*, ed. M. Ricci (Milan and Naples: Ricciardi, 1965), p. 815.

11. M. Nizolio, *De veris principiis et vera ratione philosophandi contra pseudophilosophos libri IV* (Rome: Bocca, 1956), p. 24.

12. Ibid., p. 78.

13. Rudolphus Agricola, *De inventione dialectica* (Venice: 1567), p. 111.

14. J. L. Vives, *Against the Pseudo-logicians*, trans. Charles Fantazzi, in *Renaissance Philosophy*, ed. L. A. Kennedy (The Hague and Paris: Mouton, 1973), p. 78.

15. Ibid., p. 82.

16. Peter Ramus, *De la Dialectique* (Geneva: Droz, 1964), p. 144.

17. Ludovico Castelvetro, *Poetica d'Aristotele vulgarizzata et sposta*, ed. W. Romani (Bari: Laterza, 1978), p. 127.

18. G. Bruno, *Cause, Principle and Unity*, trans. Jack Lindsay (New York: International Publishers, 1964), p. 69.

19. G. Bruno, *The Ash Wednesday Supper*, trans. E. Gosselin and L. Lerner (Hamden, Conn.: Shoe String Press, 1977), first dialogue, p. 97.

20. *The Heroic Frenzies*, trans. P. G. Memmo, Jr. (Chapel Hill: University of North Carolina Press, 1964), Part 1, fifth dialogue, p. 152.

5. Early Modernity

1. Traditionally, the power of conceiving, judging, or reasoning. — Trans.

2. E. Tesauro, *Il cannocchiale aristotelico*, ed. A. Buck (Berlin and Zurich: Gehlen-Bad Homburg, 1968), a reproduction of the 1670 Turin edition, p. 16.

3. Matteo Sforza Pallavicino, *De bene* (Milan, 1831), p. 54.

4. This sentence is a paraphrase of a quote that Barilli could not find. He told me we could delete it, but I have chosen to retain it. — Trans.

5. Matteo Peregrini, *Delle acutezze* (Bologna, 1639), p. 135.

6. Matteo Peregrini, *I fonti dell' ingegno ridotti ad arte* (Bologna: per Carlo Zenero, 1650), p. 177.

7. Sforza Pallavicino, *Del bene*, p. 46.

8. Baltasar Gracián, *Agudeza y arte de ingenio*, ed. E. Correa Calderón (Madrid: Editorial Castalia, 1969), p. 55.

9. Baltasar Gracián, *The Art of Worldly Wisdom*, trans. J. Jacobs (New York: Macmillan, 1943), maxim XVII, p. 10.

10. Ibid., maxim CV, p. 59.

11. Maxim XXVII states that "even among men giants are commonly the real dwarfs" (p. 15).

12. *Rules for the Direction of the Mind*, in *The Philosophical Works of Descartes*, trans. E. S. Haldane and G. R. T. Ross (Cambridge: Cambridge University Press, 1967), rule II, p. 3.

13. *Rules*, rule XII, p. 37.

14. *The Passions of the Soul*, in *The Philosophical Works of Descartes*, Art. XXVII, p. 344.

15. *De l' art de persuader* in *Oeuvres complètes*, ed. J. Chevalier (Paris: Gallimard, 1954), p. 595.

16. *Pensées*, in *Oeuvres complètes*, p. 1094.

17. *Pensées*, p. 1099.

18. G. W. Leibniz, *New Essays on Human Understanding*, trans. A. G. Langley (New York: Macmillan, 1896), Chapter 17, p. 575.

19. *New Essays*, Chapter 21, pp. 625–26.

20. *De dignitate et augmentis scientiarum*, *The Works of Francis Bacon*, ed. J. Spedding, R. L. Ellis, and D. D. Heath (Boston: Brown & Taggard, 1861), vol. 2, p. 439.

21. In English in the text. —Trans.

22. In English in the text. —Trans.

23. In English in the text. —Trans.

24. Sir W. Davenant's *Gondibert*, ed. D. F. Gladish (London: Oxford University Press, 1971), p. 19.

25. In English in the text. —Trans.

26. Quoted in Walter Jackson Bate, *From Classic to Romantic* (Cambridge, Mass.: Harvard University Press, 1946), pp. 38–39.

27. In English in the text. —Trans.

28. Donald F. Bond (ed.), *The Spectator* (Oxford: Oxford University Press, 1965), vol. 1, p. 44.

29. Quoted in René Wellek, *A History of Modern Criticism 1750–1950* (New Haven: Yale University Press, 1955), vol. 1, p. 85.

30. Quoted in Wellek, *A History of Modern Criticism*, vol. 1, p. 51.

31. Ibid., pp. 105–6.

32. Hugh Blair, *Lectures on Rhetoric and Belles Lettres*, 3 vols. (1785; reprint New York: Garland, 1970).

33. Cesare Beccaria, *Ricerche attorno alla natura dello stile*, in *Opere* (Florence: Sansoni, 1958).

34. Melchior Cesarotti, *Saggio sulla filosofia delle lingue*, in *Opere scelte* (Florence: Le Monnier, 1945), p. 23.

6. Modernity

1. Kant, *Critique of Judgement*, trans. J. H. Bernard (New York and London: Macmillan, 1951), p. 165.

2. F. Schiller, *Naive and Sentimental Poetry*, trans. J. A. Elias (New York: Ungar, 1966), p. 85.

3. Ibid., p. 129.

4. *F. Schlegel's Lucinde and the Fragments*, trans. P. Firchow (Minneapolis: University of Minnesota Press, 1971), p. 175.

5. F. Schlegel, from "Talk on Mythology," in *Dialogue on Poetry and Literary Aphorisms*, trans. and ed. E. Behler and R. Struc (University Park: Pennsylvania State University Press, 1968), p. 86.

6. "Talk on Mythology," p. 89.

7. Preface to *Lyrical Ballads, with Other Poems* (1800), in *Literary Criticism of William Words-worth*, ed. Paul M. Zall (Lincoln: University of Nebraska Press, 1966), p. 18.

8. "On Poesy or Art," in *The Literary Remains of S. T. Coleridge*, 2 vols., ed. H. N. Coleridge (London: William Pickering, 1836), vol. 1, p. 218.

9. *Aesthetics: Lectures on Fine Art*, trans. T. M. Knox, 2 vols. (Oxford: Clarendon Press, 1975), vol. 1, p. 381.

10. Ibid., vol. 1, p. 518.

11. Preface to *Cromwell*, in *Oeuvres complètes*, Théâtre (Paris: Imprimerie Nationale, 1912), vol. 23, p. 14.

12. Preface to *Hernani*, in *Oeuvres complètes*, p. 523.

13. Ludovico di Breme, *Il Giaurro*, in *Discussioni e polemiche sul Romanticismo* (Bari: Laterza, 1943), p. 263.

14. A Manzoni, *The Betrothed*, trans. Bruce Penman (New York: Penguin, 1972), p. 21.

15. The reference is to a famous passage at the end of Chapter 8 that Italian high school students used to memorize. — Trans.

16. B. Croce, *Aesthetic*, trans. D. Ainslie (New York: Noonday Press, 1960), p. 435.

17. B. Croce, *La poesia* (Bari: Laterza, 1963), p. 41.

7. The Contemporary Revival of Rhetoric

1. *The New Rhetoric: A Treatise on Argumentation*, trans. J. Wilkinson and P. Weaver (Notre Dame, Ind.: University of Notre Dame Press, 1969), p. 142.

2. Ibid., p. 317.

3. See *Jokes and Their Relationship to the Unconscious*, in the *Standard Edition of the Complete Psychological Works of Sigmund Freud* (London: Hogarth Press, 1960), vol. 8, p. 37.

4. Jean Starobinski, *Les Mots sous les mots* (Paris: Gallimard, 1971); the title of the English translation is *Words upon Words*, trans. Olivia Emmet (New Haven: Yale University Press, 1979).

5. Quoted in V. Florescu, *La retorica nel suo sviluppo storico* (Bologna: Il Mulino, 1971), p. 112.

6. P. Valéry, "Mallarmé," *Oeuvres complètes*, ed. Jean Hytier (Paris: Gallimard, 1957), vol. 1, p. 709–10.

7. See P. Valéry, "Questions de poésie," in *Oeuvres complètes*, vol. 1, p. 1289; first published in 1935.

8. André Breton, "Signe Ascendant," *La Clé des champs* (Paris: Les Editions du sagittaire, 1953), p. 114.

9. In English in the text. — Trans.

10. T. S. Eliot, "The Metaphysical Poets," in *Selected Essays* (New York: Harcourt, Brace, 1932, 1936, 1950), p. 247.

11. Eliot, "Hamlet and His Problems," in *Selected Essays*, pp. 124ff.

12. E. Pound, "The Serious Artist," in *Literary Essays* (London: Faber & Faber, 1954), p. 52.

13. E. Pound, "How to Read," *Literary Essays*, p. 25.

14. In English in the text. — Trans.

15. *Communications*, 16 (1970), p. 2.

16. Groupe μ, *A General Rhetoric*, trans. P. B. Burrell and E. M. Slotkin (Baltimore: Johns Hopkins University Press, 1981), p. 30.

17. Todorov, *Littérature et signification* (Paris: Larousse, 1967), p. 103.

18. See *The Presence of the Word* (New Haven: Yale University Press, 1967).

Bibliography

Bibliography

This bibliography is divided into two sections. The first lists classical sources that have made an original and outstanding contribution to rhetoric, from the beginning to the early nineteenth century. For the works of antiquity, the editions selected were those preferably combining a rigorous philological apparatus of the texts in Greek or Latin with good translations in English or another common modern language. The second section contains theoretical and historical critical contributions that belong to the twentieth century.

I

Augustine. *Answer to the Skeptics: A Translation of St. Augustine's "Contra Academicos."* Translated by D. J. Kavanagh. New York: Cosmopolitan Science and Art Service, 1943.

———. *On Christian Doctrine.* Translated by J. F. Shaw. In *Great Books of the Western World*, No. 18. Chicago: Encyclopaedia Britannica, William Benton, and the University of Chicago, 1952.

Agricola, Rudolphus. *De inventione dialectica.* Italian translation. Venice, 1567.

Alcuin. *Dialogus de rhetorica et virtute.* In *Rhetores Latini minores.* Edited by C. Halm. Lipsiae, 1863.

Anonymous [Cicero]. *Rhetorica ad Herennium.* Translated by H. Caplan, Loeb Classical Library 403. Cambridge, Mass.: Harvard University Press; London: Heinemann, 1954.

Anonymous [Longinus]. *On the Sublime.* Translated by W. H. Fyfe. Loeb Classical Library 199. Cambridge, Mass.: Harvard University Press; London: Heinemann. 1982.

Aristotle. *The "Art" of Rhetoric.* Translated by J. H. Freese. Loeb Classical Library 193. Cambridge, Mass.: Harvard University Press; London: Heinemann, 1975.

———. *Prior Analytics.* Translated by Hugh Tredennick. Loeb Classical Library 325. Cambridge, Mass.: Harvard University Press; London: Heinemann, 1973.

———. *The Poetics.* Translated by W. H. Fyfe. Loeb Classical Library 199. Cambridge, Mass.: Harvard University Press; London: Heinemann, 1982.

———. *Topica.* Translated by E. S. Forster. Loeb Classical Library 391. Cambridge, Mass.: Harvard University Press; London: Heinemann, 1976.

Bacon, Francis. *Novum Organum* and *De dignitate et augmentis scientiarum*. Vol. 2 of *The Works of Francis Bacon*. Edited by J. Spedding, R. L. Ellis, and D. D. Heath. Boston: Brown & Taggard, 1861. 15 vols.

Barbaro, Ermolao. *Iohanni Pico*. In *Prosatori latini del Quattrocento*. Edited by E. Garin. Milan and Naples: Ricciardi, 1952.

Beccaria, Cesare. *Ricerche intorno alla natura dello stile*. In *Opere*. Florence: Sansoni, 1958. 2 vols.

Beda. *Liber de schematibus et tropis*. In *Rhetores Latini minores*. Edited by C. Halm. Lipsiae, 1863.

Blair, Hugh. *Lectures on Rhetoric and Belles Lettres*. 3 vols. 1785. Reprint. New York: Garland, 1970.

Boccaccio, Giovanni. *Genealogia deorum gentilium*. In *Prose latine e altre opere*. Edited by M. Ricci. Milan and Naples: Ricciardi, 1965.

Boethius. *The Consolation of Philosophy*. Retranslated by S. T. Tester. Loeb Classical Library 74. Cambridge, Mass.: Harvard University Press; London: Heinemann, 1973.

_____. *De consolatione philosophiae*. Italian translation. Milan: Sonzogno, 1911.

_____. *Opera*. In *Patrologiae cursus completus*. Vol. 64. Edited by J. P. Migne. Paris, 1847.

Bruni, Leonardo. *De studiis et litteris liber*. In *Classici della pedagogia. L'Umanesimo*. Edited by G. Garin. Florence: Giuntine-Sansoni, 1958.

Bruno, Giordano. *The Ash Wednesday Supper*. Translated by E. Gosselin and L. Lerner. Archon Books. Hamden, Conn.: Shoe String Press, 1977.

_____. *Cause, Principle and Unity*. Translated by Jack Lindsay. New York: International Publishers, 1964.

_____. *The Heroic Frenzies*. Translated by P. G. Memmo, Jr. Chapel Hill: University of North Carolina Press, 1964.

Buridanus, Ioannes. *Compendius totius logicae*. Frankfurt, 1965.

Cassiodorus. *De rhetorica*. In *Rhetores Latini minores*. Edited by C. Halm. Lipsiae, 1863.

Castelvetro, Ludovico. *Esaminazione sopra la ritorica a Caio Erennio*. Modena, 1653.

_____. *Poetica d'Aristotele vulgarizzata et sposta*. 2 vols. Edited by W. Romani. Bari: Laterza, 1978.

Cesarotti, Melchior. *Saggio sulla filosofia delle lingue*. In *Opere scelte*. Florence: Le Monnier, 1945.

Cicero. *Academica*. Cambridge, Mass.: Harvard University Press, 1961.

_____. *Brutus*. Translated by J. Martha. Paris: Belles Lettres, 1923.

_____. *De inventione; De optimo genere oratorum; Topica*. Translated by H. M. Hubbell. Loeb Classical Library 386. Cambridge, Mass.: Harvard University Press, 1949.

_____. *De Oratore*. Translated by E. W. Sutton and H. Rackam. Loeb Classical Library 349. Cambrige, Mass.: Harvard University Press; London: Heinemann, 1977.

_____. *Orator*. Paris: Belles Lettres, 1964.

_____. *Paradoxa Stoicorum*. Paris: Belles Lettres, 1971.

_____. *Partitiones oratoriae; Topica*. Translated by H. Borneque. Paris: Belles Lettres, 1924.

Coleridge, S. T. *Prose e Poesie*. Turin: UTET, 1931.

Condillac, Etienne Bonnot de. *Traité des sensations*. In *Oeuvres philosophiques*. Paris: PUF, 1947–51.

Dante. *Opere*. Milan: Mursia, 1965.

Descartes, René. *Rules for the Direction of the Mind* and *The Passions of the Soul*. In vol. 1 of *The Philosophical Works of Descartes*. 2 vols. Translated by E. S. Haldane and G. R. T. Ross. Cambridge: Cambridge University Press, 1967.

Di Breme, Ludovico. *Il Giaurro*. In *Discussioni e polemiche sul Romanticismo*. Bari: Laterza, 1943.

Erasmus. *Ciceronianus*. Basilae, 1528.

Evrard l'allemand. *Laborintus*. In *Les Arts poétiques du XII et du XIII siècle*. Edited by E. Faral. Paris: Champion, 1924.

Fracastoro, Gerolamo. *Naugerius sive de poetica*. In *Opera omnia*. Translated and edited by G. Preti. Milan: Minuziano, 1945.

Geoffroi de Vinsauf. *Poetria nova*. In *Les Arts Poétiques du XII et du XIII siècle*. Edited by E. Faral. Paris: Champion, 1924.

Gerard, A. *An Essay on Genius*. Munich: 1966.

Giovanni da Mantova. *Epistula Mussato poetae paduano invehens contra poeticam*. In *Classici della pedagogia. L'Umanesimo*. Edited by G. Garin. Florence: Giuntine-Sansoni, 1958.

Johannes de Garlandia. *Poetria de arte prosayca et rithmica*. In *Les Arts Poétiques du XII et du XIII siècle*. Edited by E. Faral. Paris, 1923.

John of Salisbury. *Metalogicon*. Translated and edited by Daniel D. McGarry. Los Angeles and Berkeley: University of California Press, 1962.

Gracián, Baltasar. *Agudeza y arte de ingenio*. Edited by E. Correa Calderón. Madrid: Editorial Castalia, 1969.

———. *The Art of Worldly Wisdom*. Translated by J. Jacobs. New York: Macmillan, 1943.

Hegel, G. W. F. *Aesthetics: Lectures on Fine Art*. 2 vols. Translated by T. M. Knox. Oxford: Clarendon Press, 1975.

Hugo, Victor. Preface to *Cromwell* and *Hernani*. *Oeuvres complètes*. Vol. 23. Paris: Imprimerie Nationale, 1912.

Isocrates. *Against the Sophists; Antidosis*. Translated by G. Norlin. Loeb Classical Library 229. London: Heinemann; New York: G. P. Putnam's Sons, 1929.

Kant, I. *Critique of Judgement*. Translated by J. H. Bernard. New York and London: Macmillan, 1951.

Latini, Brunetto. *La rettorica*. Florence: Le Monnier, 1968.

Leibniz, G. W. *New Essays on Human Understanding*. Translated by A. G. Langley. New York: Macmillan, 1896.

Leopardi, Giacomo. *Zibaldone di pensieri*. In *Tutte le opere*. 2 vols. Milan: Mondadori, 1975.

Locke, John. *An Essay Concerning Human Understanding*. Collated and annotated by A. C. Fraser. New York: Dover, 1959.

Matthieu de Vendôme. *Ars versificatoria*. In *Les Arts poétiques du XII et du XIII siècle*. Edited by E. Faral. Paris: Champion, 1924.

Minucius Felix. *Octavius*. Translated by G. H. Rendall. Loeb Classical Library 250. Cambridge, Mass.: Harvard University Press; London: Heinemann, 1966.

Mussato, Albertino. *Declaratio epistulae responsivae ad Iohannem de Mantua*. In *Classici della pedagogia. L'Umanesimo*. Edited by G. Garin. Florence: Giuntine-Sansoni, 1958.

Nizolio, M. *De veris principiis et vera ratione philosophandi contra pseudophilosophos libri IV*. Rome: Bocca, 1956.

Ockham, William. *Summa logicae, pars prima*. Edited by Ph. Boehner. St. Bonaventure, N.Y.: Franciscan Institute, 1951.

Pascal, Blaise. *Oeuvres complètes*. Edited by J. Chevalier. Paris: Gallimard, 1954.

Patrizi, Francesco. *Della retorica*. Venezia, 1562.

Peregrini, Matteo. *Delle acutezze*. Bologna, 1639.

Petrarch. *De sui ipsius et multorum ignorantia*. In *Prose*. Milan and Naples: Ricciardi, 1955.

Piccolomini, Aeneas Silvius. *Tractatus de liberorum educatione*. In *Classici della pedagogia. L'Umanesimo*. Edited by E. Garin. Florence: Giuntine-Sansoni, 1958.

Pico della Mirandola, Giovanni. *Ermolao Barbaro poetae*. In *Prose Latine e altre opere*. Edited by M. Ricci. Milan and Naples: Ricciardi, 1965.

Plato. *The Collected Dialogues of Plato*. Edited by Edith Hamilton and Huntington Cairns, Bollingen Series 71. Princeton, N.J.: Princeton University Press, 1980.

Quintilian. *Institutio oratoria*. Translated by H. E. Butler. Loeb Classical Library 124–127. Cambridge, Mass.: Harvard University Press; London: Heinemann, 1976, 1977, 1979, 1980.

Ramus, Peter. *De la Dialectique*. Geneva: Droz, 1964.
———. *Scholae in tres primas liberales artes*. Frankfurt, 1581.
Salutati, Coluccio. *Fratri Iohanni Dominici; De laboribus Herculis*. In *Classici della pedagogia. L'Umanesimo*. Edited by E. Garin. Florence: Giuntine-Sansoni, 1958.
Schiller, Friedrich. *Naive and Sentimental Poetry*. Translated by J. A. Elias. New York: Ungar, 1966.
Schlegel, Friedrich. *Dialogue on Poetry and Literary Aphorisms*. Edited and Translated by E. Behler and R. Struc. University Park: Pennsylvania State University Press, 1968.
———. *F. Schlegel's Lucinde and the Fragments*. Translated by P. Firchow. Minneapolis: University of Minnesota Press, 1971.
Sforza Pallavicino, Matteo. *Del bene*. Milan: 1831.
———. *Trattato dello stile e del dialogo*. Turin, 1830.
Sophists. *Testimonianze e frammenti*. 4 vols. Edited by M. Untersteiner. Florence: La Nuova Italia, 1949.
Stoics. *Frammenti*. 2 vols. Bari: Laterza, 1932.
Tacitus. *Dialogus de oratoribus*. Translated by W. Peterson and revised by M. Winterbottom. Loeb Classical Library 35. Cambridge, Mass.: Harvard University Press; London: Heinemann, original ed. 1914, revised 1970.
Tertullian. *Apology*. Translated by T. R. Glover. Loeb Classical Library 250. Cambridge, Mass.: Harvard University Press; London: Heinemann, 1966.
Tesauro, Emanuele. *Il cannocchiale aristotelico*. Edited by A. Buck. 1670. Reprint. Berlin and Zurich: Gehlen-Bad Homburg, 1968.
Thomas Aquinas. *Summa Theologica*. Literally translated by the Fathers of the English Dominican Province. New York: Benziger Brothers, 1947.
Valla, Lorenzo. *Opera omnia*. 2 vols. Turin: Bottega d' Erasmo, 1962.
Vico, Gian Battista. *Opere*. Edited by F. Niccolini. Milan and Naples: Ricciardi, 1953.
Vives, Luis. *Against the Pseudo-logicians*. Translated by Charles Fantazzi. In *Renaissance Philosophy*. Edited by L. A. Kennedy. The Hague: Mouton, 1973.

II

Ambrogio, I., *Formalismo e avanguardia in Russia*. Rome: Editori Riuniti, 1968.
Anceschi, Luciano. *L' estetica dell' empirismo inglese. Bologna: Alfa, 1959.*
"Attualità della retorica." *Quaderni del Circolo filologico-linguistico padovano*. Padua: Liviana, 1975.
———. *Le istituzioni della poesia*. Milan: Bompiani, 1968.
———. *Le poetiche del Barocco letterario in Europa*. In *Momenti e problemi di storia dell' estetica*. Vol. 1. Milan: Marzorati, 1959.
Bagni, P. *La costituzione della poesia nelle "artes" del XII–XIII secolo*. Bologna: Zanichelli, 1968.
Baldwin, C. S. *Ancient Rhetoric and Poetic*. New York: Macmillan, 1924.
Barilli, Renato. *Poetica e retorica*. Milan: Mursia, 1969.
———. "Le poetiche e la critica d' arte del Cinquecento." *Storia della letteratura italiana*. Vol. 4. Bari: Laterza, 1973.
———. "Retorica e narrativa." *Attualità della retorica. Quaderni del Circolo filologico-linguistico padovano*. Padua: Liviana, 1975.
———. "Semiologia e retorica nell'interpretazione del *Decameron*". *Il Verri* 35–36 (1970), pp. 27–48.
———. *Viaggio al termine della parola. La ricerca intraverbale*. Milan: Feltrinelli, 1981.
Barthes, Roland. "L'Ancienne Rhétorique." *Communications* 16 (1970), pp. 172–229.
Bate, Walter Jackson. *From Classic to Romantic*. Cambridge, Mass.: Harvard University Press, 1946.
Battistini, A. *La dignità della retorica. Studi sul Vico*. Pisa: Pacini, 1975.

Bethell, S. L. *The Cultural Revolution of the Seventeenth Century*. London: Dobson, 1884.

Bonghi, Ruggero. *Perché la letteratura italiana non sia popolare in Italia*. Naples: Morano, 1884.

Bonora, E. *Il classicismo dal Bembo al Guarini*. In *Storia della letteratura italiana*. Vol. 4. Milan: Garzanti, 1966.

Bray, R. *La Formation de la doctrine classique en France*. Lausanne: Payot, 1931.

Breton, André. *La Clé des champs*. Paris: Les Editions du sagittaire, 1953.

Brooks, Cleanth. *The Well Wrought Urn*. New York: Harcourt, Brace and World, 1947.

Chaignet, A. *La Rhétorique et son histoire*. Paris: Bouillon, 1888.

Clark, D. L. *Rhetoric in Greco-Roman Education*. New York: Columbia University Press, 1957.

Cohen, J. *Structure du language poétique*. Paris: Flammarion, 1966.

Conte, G. *La metafora barocca. Saggio sulle poetiche del Seicento*. Milan: Mursia, 1977.

Costanzo, M. *La critica de Novecento e le poetiche del Barocco*. Rome: Bulzoni, 1976.

Croce, Benedetto. *Aesthetic*. Translated by D. Ainslie. New York: Noonday Press, 1960.

_____. *La poesia*. Bari: Laterza, 1963.

Croce, F. *Le poetche del Barocco in Italia*. In *Momenti e problemi di storia dell' estetica*. Vol. 1. Milan: Marzorati, 1959.

Curtius, E. R. *La Littérature européenne et le moyen âge latin*. Paris: PUF, 1956.

Desmouliez, A. *Cicéron et son goût*. Brussels: Latomus, 1976.

Dixon, P. *Rhetoric*. London: Methuen, 1971.

Douglas, A. E. "The Intellectual Background of Cicero's Rhetoric: A Study in Method." In *Aufstieg und Niedergang der römischen Welt*. Berlin: W. De Gruyter, 1973, vol. 13, pp. 95–138.

Eco, Umberto. *A Theory of Semiotics*. Bloomington: Indiana University Press, 1976.

Eliot, T. S. *Selected Essays*. New York: Harcourt Brace, 1932, 1936, 1950.

Erlich, Victor. *Russian Formalism: History-Doctrine*. Vol. 4 of *Slavistic Printings and Reprintings*. Ed. Cornelis H. Van Schooneveld. The Hague: Mouton, 1955.

Florescu, V. *Retorica si reahilitarea e in filozofia contemporaneâ*. Bucharest: Ed. Academiei R. S. Romania, 1960. (Italian translation *La retorica nel suo sviluppo storico*. Bologna: Il Mulino, 1971.)

France, P. *Rhetoric and Truth in France: Descartes to Diderot*. Oxford: Clarendon Press, 1972.

Freud, Sigmund. *The Interpretation of Dreams* (1900–1901). Vols. 4–5 in the *Standard Edition of the Complete Psychological Works of Sigmund Freud*. Translated from the German and edited by James Strachey. 24 vols. London: Hogarth Press, 1960, 1978.

_____. *Jokes and Their Relation to the Unconscious* (1905). Vol. 8 in *The Standard Edition*.

_____. *The Psychopathology of Everyday Life* (1901). Vol. 5 in *The Standard Edition*.

Funaioli, G. *Studi di letteratura antica*. Bologna: Zanichelli, 1946.

Garin, E. "La dialettica dal secolo XII ai principi dell'età moderna." In *Studi sulla dialettica*. Turin: Taylor, 1958.

_____. *Medioevo e Rinascimento*. Bari: Laterza, 1954.

_____. *Note su alcuni aspetti delle retoriche rinascimentali e sulla "Retorica" del Patrizi*. In *Testi umanistici sulla retorica*. Milan and Naples: Ricciardi, 1953.

_____. *L'Umanesimo italiano*. Bari: Laterza, 1952.

Gazzola Stacchini, V. *Leopardi politico*. Bari: De Donato, 1974.

Genette, Gérard. *Figures I, II, III*. Paris: Seuil, 1966, 1969, 1972.

_____. "La Rhétorique restreinte." *Communications* 16 (1970), pp. 158–71.

Gilson, E. *Dante et la philosophie*. Paris: Vrin, 1939.

_____. *La Philosophie au moyen âge*. Paris: Payot, 1944.

Groupe μ. *A General Rhetoric*. Translated by P. B. Burrell and E. M. Slotkin. Baltimore: Johns Hopkins University Press, 1981.

_____. *Rhétorique de la poésie*. Brussels: Complexe, 1977.

Haskins, C. H. *The Renaissance of the XIII Century*. Cambridge, Mass.: Harvard University Press, 1927.

Howell, W. S. *Logic and Rhetoric in England (1500–1700)*. Princeton, N.J.: Princeton University Press, 1956.

_____. "Poetics, Rhetoric and Logic in Renaissance Criticism." In *Classical Influence in European Culture (1500–1700)*. Edited by R. R. Bolgan. Cambridge: Cambridge University Press, 1976.

"Le instituzione e la retorica." *Il Verri* 35–36 (1970).

Jakobson, Roman. "Two Aspects of Language and Two Types of Aphasic Disturbances." In *Fundamentals of Language*. The Hague: Mouton, 1956.

Kennedy, G. *The Art of Rhetoric in the Roman World*. Princeton, N.J.: Princeton University Press, 1972.

Kuentz, Pierre. "*Le Rhétorique' ou la mise à l'écart*." *Communications* 16 (1970), pp. 143–57.

Lana, I. *Quintiliano, il "Sublime" e gli "Esercizi preparatori" di Ezio Leone*. Turin: Univ., 1951.

Lausberg, H. *Elemente der literarischen Rhetorik*. Munich: Hüber, 1960.

Leeman, A. D. *Orationis radio*. Amsterdam: Hakkert, 1963.

Levi, M. A. *Isocarte*. Milan: Istituto Cisalpino, 1969.

Luporini, C. "Leopardi progressivo." In *Filosofi vecchi e nuovi*. Florence: Sansoni, 1947.

McKeon, R. "Rhetoric in the Middle Ages." In *Figure e momenti di storia della critica*. Milan: Feltrinelli, 1967.

McLuhan, Marshall. *The Gutenberg Galaxy*. Toronto: University of Toronto Press, 1962, 1986.

_____. *Understanding Media*. New York: McGraw-Hill, 1964.

Marchese, A. *Dizionario di retorica e di stilistica*. Milan: Mondadori, 1978.

Marrou, H. I. *St. Augustine et la fin de la culture antique*. Paris: Seuil, 1956.

Mazzacurati, G. *Conflitti culturali nel Cinquecento*. Naples: Liguori, 1977.

Michel, A. *Rhétorique ey philosophie chez Cicéron*. Paris: PUF, 1960.

Nardi, B. *Dante e la cultura medievale*. Bari: Laterza, 1949.

Olbrechts-Tyteca, L. *Le comique du discours*. Italian translation. Milan: Feltrinelli, 1977.

Omaggio a Vico. Naples: Morano, 1968.

Ong, Walter. *The Presence of the Word*. New Haven, Conn.: Yale University Press, 1967.

_____. *Ramus: Method and the Decay of Dialogue*. Cambridge, Mass.: Harvard University Press, 1958.

_____. *Rhetoric, Romance, and Technology*. Ithaca, N.Y.: Cornell University Press, 1971.

Paulhan, Jean. *Clef de la poésie*. Paris: Gallimard, 1944.

_____. *Les Fleurs de Tarbes*. Paris: Gallimard, 1941.

Perelman, C. *Le Champ de l'argumentation*. Brussels: Ed. de l'Université, 1970.

_____. *L'Empire rhétorique*. Paris: Vrin, 1977.

_____. *Rhétorique et philosophie*. Paris: PUF, 1958.

Perelman, C., and Olbrechts-Tyteca, Lucie. *The New Rhetoric: A Treatise on Argumentation*. Translated by J. Wilkinson and P. Weaver. Notre Dame, Ind.: University of Notre Dame Press, 1969.

_____. *Traité de l'argumentation, la nouvelle rhétorique*. Paris: PUF, 1958.

Plebe, A. *Breve storia della retorica antica*. Bari: Laterza, 1968.

Pound, Ezra. *Literary Essays*. London: Faber and Faber, 1954.

Preti, G. *Retorica e logica*. Turin: Einaudi, 1968.

Raimondi, E. *Anatomie secentesche*. Pisa: Nistri Lischi, 1966.

_____. *Rinascimento inquieto*. Palermo: Manfredi, 1965.

Ransom, J. C. *Poems and Essays*. New York: Vintage, 1955.

Retorica e Barocco. Rome: Bocca, 1955.

Richards, I. A. *The Philosophy of Rhetoric*. New York: Oxford University Press, 1936.

Riffaterre, Michael. *Semiotics of Poetry*. Bloomington: Indiana University Press, 1978.

Riposati, B. *Problemi di retorica antica* in *Introduzione alla filologia classica*. Milan: Marzorati, 1951.

Rossi, P. *Clavis universalis*. Milan and Naples: Ricciardi, 1960.

———. "Ramismo, logica, retorica nei secoli XVI e XVII." In *Rivista critica di storia della filosofia* 12 (July–September 1957), pp. 357–65.

Rostagni, A. *Il "Sublime" nella storia dell' estetica antica* in *Scritti minori*. Vol. 1. Turin: Bottega d'Erasmo, 1955.

Saintsbury, G. *A History of Criticism and Literary Taste in Europe from the Earliest Texts to the Present Days*. Edinburgh, 1902.

Saussure, F. de. *Course in General Linguistics*. Translated by Wade Baskin. New York: McGraw-Hill, 1959.

Shklovsky, Victor. *O teorii prozy* (*On the theory of prose*). Moscow, 1925.

Spingarn, J. E. *A History of the Literary Criticism in the Italian Renaissance*. New York, 1899.

Starobinski, J. *Les Mots sous les mots*. Paris: Gallimard, 1971. Published in English as *Words upon Words*. Translated by Olivia Emmet. New Haven, Conn.: Yale University Press, 1979.

Studi sulla dialettica. Turin: Taylor, 1958.

Tagliacozza, G., and O. Ph. Verene, eds. *G. B. Vico's Science of Humanity*. Baltimore: Johns Hopkins University Press, 1973.

Tate, A. *On the Limits of Poetry*. New York: Swallow Press, 1948.

Testi umanistici sulla retorica. Milan and Naples: Ricciardi, 1953.

Timpanaro, S. *Classicismo e illuminismo nell' Ottocento italiano*. Pisa: Nistri Lischi, 1969.

Todorov, Tzvetan. *Littérature et signification*. Paris: Larousse, 1967.

———. *Théories du symbole*. Paris: Seuil, 1977.

Toffanin, G. *Il Cinquecento* in *Storia letteraria italiana*. Milan: Vallardi, 1965.

Toulmin, S. E. *The Uses of Argument*. Cambridge: Cambridge University Press, 1958.

Trattati di poetica e retorica del '500. 4 vols. Edited by B. Weinberg. Bari: Laterza, 1970–74.

Tuve, R. *Elizabethan and Metaphysical Imagery: Renaissance Poetry and Twentieth Century Critics*. Chicago: University of Chicago Press, 1947.

Tynianov, Yuri. *Avanguardia e tradizione*. Bari: Dedalo, 1968.

Untersteiner, M. *I Sofisti*. 4 vols. Turin: Einaudi, 1949.

Valéry, Paul. *Oeuvres complètes*. Edited by Jean Hytier. Paris: Gallimard, 1957.

Vasoli, C. *La dialettica e la retorica dell' Umanesimo*. Milan: Feltrinelli, 1968.

———. "Le Dialecticae disputationes del Valla e la critica umanistica alla logica aristotelica." In *Rivista critica di storia della filosofia* 13 (1957), pp. 412–34.

Viano, C. A. "Aristotele e la redenzione della retorica." *Revista di filosofia* 4 (1967), pp. 371–425.

"Vico and Contemporary Thought." *Social Research* 43, 3–4 (Autumn–Winter 1976).

G. B. Vico nel III centenario della nascita. Naples: ESI, 1971.

Vickers, B. *Francis Bacon and Renaissance Prose*. Cambridge: Cambridge University Press, 1968.

Weinberg, B. *A History of Literary Criticism on the Italian Renaissance*. 2 vols. Chicago: University of Chicago Press, 1967.

Wellek, René. *A History of Modern Criticism 1750– 1950*. 4 vols. New Haven, Conn.: Yale University Press, 1955–65.

Wimsatt, W. K., and Cleanth Brooks. *Literary Criticism: A Short History*. New York: Knopf, 1957.

Yates, F. *The Art of Memory*. Chicago: University of Chicago Press, 1966.

Index

Index

printing, 124; rationalization of, 78, 81; rejection of, 75; and style, 87
Empedocles, 3
Empeiría, 8, 11
Empiricism, 78–81, 84, 109; aesthetics of, 116; vs. rationalism, 78, 81
Empiriocriticism, 103
Empson, William: and New Criticism, 114
Enárgheia, 17, 73, 106, 112. *See also* Evidence
Encomion S. Thomae, 58
Encomium for Helen, 5–6
Encyclopedism, 84
Enlightenment: French, 99; Lombardic, 99
Enthymeme, 14, 17–18, 36, 48; commercials as, 14; demonstrative, 15; refutative, 15. *See also* Premise; Thesis
Epideictic rhetoric, 3; Aristotle on, 12–13
Episteme: Aristotle on, 10; vs. *Doxa*, 6; Plato on, 6–9. *See also* Truth
Epistemology, 106, 107
Epistula Mussato poetae paduano invehens contra poeticam, 55
Erasmus, Desiderius, 62
Eros, 107
Esaminazione sopra la ritorica a Caio Erennio, 66
Esprit de finesse, 76
Esprit de géométrie, 76, 85
Essay Concerning Human Understanding, 81
Estetica, 100, 101
Ethos, 21
Euclidis geometrica, 43
Euthydemus, 9
Evidence: Saint Augustine on, 40–41. *See also* *Enárgheia*
Evrard l'allemand, 48
Exempla ficta/Exemplum fictum, 6, 15

Faba, Guido, 49
Fabulae, 25, 54, 56, 59, 68
Ficino, Marsilio, 58–60
Figures, 80, 85–86, 106, 108, 111, 116, 120, 127; Bede on, 45; vs. scientific discourse, 120; in the Scriptures, 42; vs. tropes, 37. *See also* Metaphor; Tropes
Fleurs de Tarbes, Les, 115
Forensic rhetoric: Ciceronian, 125; defined by Aristotle, 12, 13; Hermagoras on, 20
Formalism, Russian, 117–18; research of, 118

Formalist poetics, 118–19
Fracastoro, Gerolamo, 60
Francesco, Giovanni, 60
Freud, Sigmund: on jokes, 18, 128; psychoanalysis of, 106–10; on unconscious, 22
Futurism: and Russian formalism, 117

Galateo, 60
Garin, Eugenio: on dialectic, 47; on grammar, 47; and historiography, 117
Garlandia, Johannes de, 48
Genealogia deorum gentilium, 54
Genette, Gérard: on rhetoric, 122
Gentile, Giovanni: on Italian education, 101
Geometrical process, 72
Georgics, 60
Gilson, Etienne: on John of Salisbury, 46; on 12th and 13th centuries, 46
Giovanni da Mantova, 55
Gondibert, 80
Gonseth, 105
Gorgias: Dante and, 50; metaphysics of, 5; on politics, 8; as Sophist, 9; on speech and words, 5
Gorgias, 8, 30
Gracián, Baltasar, 73–74
Grammar, 16, 47; Dante on, 51; and poetics, 46. *See also* Language
Greek culture: rhetoric in, 3–23
Group μ, 119, 120, 121, 127
Gutenberg, Johann, 49
Gutenberg Galaxy, 123

Halm, Carl, 44
Hamlet, 112
Hegel, Georg Wilhelm Friedrich, 96–97; diachronic model of, 89, 96; on dissociation, 91–92, 100; idealistic historicism of, 83; and Kant, 96; on poetry and rhetoric, 92, 96–97
Hermagoras of Temnos: and Aristotle, 25, 26; on thesis and hypothesis, 36; technical innovations of, 19–20, 25
Hernani, 97
Hispanus, Petrus: on dialectic, 47
Historicism: Hegelian, 83
Hjelmslev, Louis, 103, 119, 121–22
Hobbes, Thomas: on discerning, 80; on wit, 79

Holy Scriptures. *See* Scriptures
Hortensius, 40
Hugo, Victor, 97–98; on Christianity, 97; on
  sentimentality, 98
Human sciences. *See* Moral sciences
Humanism, 52–56
Hume, David: on empiricism, 84
Humor. *See* Wit
Husserl, Edmund: on phenomenology, 40, 103
Hyperides: as Atticist and follower of Brutus,
  32; elegance of, 22
Hypothesis: Cicero on, 26; John of Salisbury
  on, 46; and rhetoric, 44; vs. thesis, 20

Imagination: vs. reason, 89, 91
Induction, 14–15
Ingegno, 71–74 *passim*, 77, 79, 81, 84, 87,
  89, 90, 111
Ingenium, x
Institutio oratoria, 34–37, 116, 129
Intellect: Descartes on, 75
Interpretation of Dreams, The, 107
Intuition: Bergson's theory of, 103; Croce on,
  119; Saint Augustine on, 41
Inventio, 16, 29, 30, 48, 64, 71, 105, 117,
  119, 125
Iphicrates, 15
Isocrates, 9; critique of the Sophists, 6; as
  influence on Aristotle, 6; and *lexis*, 16; on
  the orator, 6; on physical sciences, 6; on
  speech, 6

Jakobson, Roman: on tropes, 118, 119
John of Salisbury: on rhetoric as art, 45–46
Johnson, Doctor: on Metaphysical poets, 84
Jokes, 18, 25–26, 107, 108, 109, 127, 128.
  See also Wit
Jokes and Their Relation to the Unconscious,
  107, 108
Judiciary genre: of church fathers, 39

Kant, Immanuel, 91, 113; on diachronic
  model, 89; on poetry, 90; pure reason of,
  70–71
Kinesics, 129
Knowledge: and rhetoric, 90. *See also*
  Epistemology
Koine, 81, 84, 99, 110
Kuentz, Pierre, 120, 122

Laborintus, 48
Lactantius: on religion and knowledge, 40
Landino, Cristoforo, 59
Language: analysis of, 103; and
  communication, 127; Leopardi theory of,
  88, 95; literary, 64; Manzoni on, 100;
  mediation of, 71; and object, 110;
  psychopathology, 118; scientific, 120;
  transparency vs. opacity of, 123; Vives on,
  63–64. *See also* Grammar
Latin rhetoric. *See* Rhetoric, Latin
Law: natural vs. written, 13
Lebenswelt, 11, 103
Lectures on Rhetoric, 85
Lexis, 6, 16–18; Asiatics and, 20; Isocrates
  and, 16; Theophrastus on, 19
Leibniz, Gottfried Wilhelm von, 77–78; on
  rationalism, 77, 81, 84, 109; on rhetoric,
  78
Leopardi, Giacomo, 94–96; vs. Bonghi, 99;
  vs. romantics, 98; on theory of language,
  88, 92; on urbanization, 96
Leviathan, 79
Liber annalis, 32
Liberalism: and romanticism, 97
Libido, 107, 108
Libri tres in Academicos, 40
Linguistics: and rise of rhetoric, 104; of
  Saussure, 109; stratification of, 95
Literature: isolation of, 117, 122
Literary Criticism: A Short History, 80
Locke, John: on education, 81; on primary
  ideas, 84, 85; on wit, 80–81
Logic: analytic, 82, 105; audience of, 79; vs.
  dialectic, 47, 105; vs. intuitionism, 119;
  methods of, 14–15; qualitative, 75;
  reformed, 70; and rhetoric, 13–15, 79, 82,
  116; universal of, 79
Logica nova, 44
Logica vetus, 44
Logical positivism. *See* Positivism
Logography, 4
Logopoeia, 112, 116
Logos, vii, 7, 21. *See also* Discourse
Longinus, Dionysius: as author of *Sublime*,
  20–21; and Christianity, 39; on figures, 42
Lucullus: Cicero and, 28
Lyrical Ballads, 94
Lysias: as Atticist and follower of Brutus, 32

McKeon, Richard, 115
McLuhan, Marshall: and rhetoric, 115,
123–25; on technology, 128
Macrology, 8
Magnus, Albertus, 47
Mallarmé, Stéphane, 110–11
Manzoni, Alessandro, 98–99; on language,
100
Marcuse, Herbert, 125, 132
Maternus, M. Aper: in *Dialogus de
oratoribus*, 33–34
Mathesis: vs. *techne*, x
Melopeia, 112, 116
Memoria, 105
Memory: Cicero on, 25–26; disuse of, 129
Messalla: in *Dialogus de oratoribus*, 33–34
Metalogicon, 45–46
Metalogism, 121
Metaphor, 31–32, 71, 111, 112, 116, 128; in
De oratore, 32; defined, 17, 108; and
delectare, 21–22; and Freud, 109; and
poetry, 73; types of, 17; use of, 17. *See
also* Figures; Tropes
Metaphysical poets. *See* Poets
Metaplasm, 121, 127
Metasememes, 121
Metataxis, 121
Metonymy, 31–32, 108, 109, 111, 112, 116,
128
Middle Academy, 19
Middle Ages: dialectic in, 46–48; rhetoric in,
38–51
Mill, John Stuart: on denotation, 95
Minucius Felix, 39–40, 45–46
Mittelglied, 71, 76, 89; of Coleridge, 94;
defined, 73; Kantian, 91, 92, 95
Moderns: vs. ancients, 22, 33–34
Modus vivendi, ix
Montale, Eugenio: poetry of, 116
Moral sciences, viii, 12, 13, 25, 70
Movere, ix, x, 5, 30, 37, 62, 105
Music: Dante on, 51
Mussato, Albertino, 55
Mythology: and rhetoric, 98

Narratio, 49, 54; in *Institutio oratoria*, 36; in
Praeexercitamina, 45
Naturalism: vs. art, 98
Naugerius, 60
Neoplatonists, 59

New Academy, 19, 28, 40
New Criticism, 112–13, 114, 115, 117, 118,
123
Nizolio, Marcio, 58, 61–62
Nouvelle Critique, 119, 121–22. *See also* New
Criticism
Novissimi, 116

Octavianus, 39–40
On Not Being; Or, On Nature, 5
On the Sublime, 77
Ong, Walter, 125
Operarium, 30
Opinion: defined by Aristotle, 10; and
Parmenides, 3; and Sophists, 4–5; vs.
truth, 6, 10–11. *See also Doxa*; Probability
Oraculo manual y arte de prudencia, 74
Orator: Aristotle on, 6; in *De oratore*, 30–31;
Isocrates on, 6; Quintilian on, 35, 37; vs.
rector, 57; and sublimity, 22; task of, 25;
Valla on, 57
Orator, 32–33
Oratory: in government, 125–26; in law, 125;
as past art, 33; in school, 125–26; in
unions, 125–26
Organaon, 11, 48, 57, 58, 62, 64, 74;
Boethius and, 44; vs. Cicero's *De oratore*,
27
Oxford school, 102

Paganism: defense of Christianity against, 39
Paradigm: vs. syntagm, 116
Paradixa Stoicorum, 27–28; as dedicated to
Brutus, 32
Paragrams, 109, 128
Paralinguistics, 129
Parmenides: and opinion, 3
Paronomasia, 31
Partitiones oratoriae, 33
Pascal, Blaise, 21, 38, 76–77; vs. Descartes,
76; negative rhetoric of, 77
Pascoli, Giovanni, 110
Passions of the Soul, 75
Pathos, 21, 22
Patrizi, Francesco, 67–68; absolute words of,
71; poetic furor of, 70
Paulhan, Jean, 99–100, 115, 127
*Perché la letteratura italiana non sia populare
in Italia*, 99

Theory and History of Literature

Renato Barilli is a professor of the phenomenology of styles at the University of Bologna. His fields of study include aesthetics and literary and art criticism. Barilli's numerous books include, *Poetica e retorica* (1969), *Tra presenza e assenza* (1974), *Culturologia e Fenomenologia Degli Stili* (1982), *L'Arte Contemporanea* (1984), and *Il Ciclo del Postmoderno* (1987).

Giuliana Menozzi is a doctoral candidate in comparative literature at the University of Minnesota and research assistant for the Minnesota series Theory and History of Literature. She has studied at the University of Bologna and the University of East Anglia.